WRITING WHILE RAISING YOUNG KIDS

AN AUTHOR'S GUIDE TO FINDING BALANCE

CHRISSY WISSLER

BLUE CEDAR PUBLISHING

Writing While Raising Young Kids:
An Author's Guide to Finding Balance
Copyright © 2020 Christen Wissler

All rights reserved.

Published 2020 by Blue Cedar Publishing
www.bluecedarpublishing.com
Cover art copyright © Anastasiya Subotsina/DepositPhoto
Book and cover design copyright © 2020 Blue Cedar Publishing
ISBN-13: 978-1-949056-10-5
ISBN-10: 1-949056-10-5

This book is licensed for your personal enjoyment only. All rights reserved. No part of this book may be reproduced in any form without permission.

This book is a work of fiction. All characters and events are fictitious and any resemblance to real persons, living or dead, is coincidental and not intended by the author.

Blue Cedar Publishing
P.O. Box 5275
Torrance, CA 90510

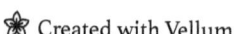 Created with Vellum

CONTENTS

Also by Chrissy Wissler — v

WRITING WHILE RAISING YOUNG KIDS

Introduction	3
My Family—Where We are Now	9
Itsy Bitsy Steps	12
Saying 'Thank You' to Dads	18
It's All About the Schedules:	21
Gut Check	25
Everyone's Got an Opinion:	31
The Keyboard Battle	36
Talking is Overrated	40
So... How's the Writing Going?	47
How Flexible are You?	53
How to Survive the Rough (Early) Years... and Keep Writing	59
Trust Yourself. Trust Your Child.	64
Taking Risks	70
To Write, or Not to Write	76
The Great Battle:	82
Workshops, Holidays, and Two Small Kids	90
Writing through Life Rolls	96
What's Your Worth?	102
A Schedule and Kids: Ha!	110
Who Are You?	116
Saying No Doesn't Mean It's Forever	122
Always on the Go:	129
Let's Get This Year Started:	136
The Reality of Little Ones	145
Surviving Taxes:	152
No Such Thing as "Perfect"	159
Restart the Writing	166
Living Dual Lives	173
Self-Care for Parents	181

Downtime	187
Needing Space	194
The Introverted Parent	202
Parenting:	209
The Hidden Toll of Parenting	216
Finding Joyful Moments	225
Am I Enough?	231
Writing with Young Kids	239
Being an Empath	245
The Right Path	253
Celebrate Our Differences	263
A Journey of Inner Growth	271
What 'Success' Really Means	281
Redefining Success	290
It Takes Time	301
Afterword	307
Author Newsletter	313
Also by Chrissy Wissler	315
About the Author	317

ALSO BY CHRISSY WISSLER

Cowboy Cat Mystery Series

Women's Justice

Mother's Justice

Romance Novels

Home Run: A Home Run Novel

Stealing Second: A Home Run Novel—Coming Soon

Second Chance: A Romance Video Game Novel

Finding Dreams: A Romance Video Game Collection

Fantasy Series

Searching for Sanctuary: Novel

Dragons in Preschool: Short Novel

The Blessings Bridge

Hidden in Time: Novel

Hidden in Lore: Collection #1

Hidden in Myth: Collection #2

Hidden in Legend: Collection #3

Young Adult Series

Swing Away: A Little League Novel

All or Nothing: Collection

For more information about Chrissy Wissler's other works, go to ChrissyWissler.com

WRITING WHILE RAISING YOUNG KIDS

AN AUTHOR'S GUIDE TO FINDING BALANCE

INTRODUCTION

Every writer is different. Every child is different.

Navigating your path as a parent-writer *will* be different than mine or anyone else's—especially when we throw in the unique demands and opinions of our littlest ones.

This book, what started as a series of blogs about how to navigate this journey of being a parent-writer and raising young kids, will not tell you what to do or dictate best practices. I will not speak in absolutes or tell you how to balance your time between parenting and writing or any of the usual stuff you'd expect from a "How-To" parenting book.

Because we are *all* different.

My life choices will be different from yours. The choices Sean and I made for our family may not resonate with you—and that's okay. The privileges in my life, of being gifted with this opportunity to stay home and raise my differently wired kids, may not be the same as yours.

In fact, for some of you, it will be the exact opposite.

The real truth is only *you* know your family and this is a truth I'd like up front and center in this book.

You know your family.

Introduction

You know the right balance between parenting and writing for your family. The right balance between schedules and school and emotional needs. The individual needs of your kids—because they will be different. They will be different from mine but also amongst their siblings and extended family.

While all this is true, there are also some themes that stay the same.

Babies still insist on waking up at all hours of the night (and very early mornings) to be fed and changed. Then there are those annoying teeth that insist on poking through in a most painful way (which these adorably cute babies *insist* their caregivers be present through every agonizing moment to sooth and comfort them). Then there are the two-year-olds who insist on having a mind and will of their own and challenge everything—

Yet don't quite have the understanding that running into a street is a *bad* idea.

Uh-huh. I've got one of those.

If you're a parent or if you know someone who is, I'm sure you're nodding your head at this.

As parents, we all go through these same stages and while these stages get physically easier as our kids get older (babies and their need to feed all night long, toddlers and their strange need to run into the street), the physical toll on us is replaced by an emotional one, an invisible one almost. Our kids must learn the rules of our society and gradually, grudgingly, accept them (such as the necessity of clothes—a concept my youngest, Eric, still doesn't much care for), and we're the ones called to teach them.

The emotional load of parenting gets heavier.

As parents we're asked more and more to sit with our kids as they work through problems with friends, how one kid was mean or a whole group refused to play with them. Maybe even called them "weird" or "different."

All these emotions which trigger our own past and childhood experiences because our kids are our mirrors, reflecting back to us *exactly* those areas in ourselves we need to work through or heal...

Introduction

And you kinda almost miss those simple, though exhausting nights and days of having a newborn.

(And the toes—those super cute baby toes.)

But through all this, through all the physical demands and the *years* of disturbed and broken sleep (I'm seriously still waiting to get back to a consistent eight hours) and the emotional weight we're asked to support our kids through, through all *that* there are some of us who dream to do what feels like impossible at times...

To be a writer.

This is the heart of what this book is about. It is acknowledging all the joys and hardships of parenting, both which exist side-by-side and often at the exact same time, and for us, for us who have a bigger, deeper calling, a yearning inside of us to create stories, to write...

To daydream.

To create.

To simply... go play and see what happens next.

This book is about how we show up for all the duties and joys of being a parent while still maintaining this spark, this need, to write.

I became a parent in 2012 when Kate was born, right as I was breaking out as a professional fiction writer (I'd done nonfiction for years but fiction stories had always been my passion). I was an independent publisher. Even back then, to sell and be financially successful, you needed a big catalog of stories—

And you needed a *lot* stories ready in the pipeline.

I knew my writing productivity would take a complete and total nosedive when Kate came along (... which... it did), but I also knew I *would* keep writing.

Somehow.

Not a lot—I'd made the conscious choice to be a parent first—but I knew without a doubt I *would* keep writing. A story here, a story there because writing was essential to my well-being and happiness and passion.

It was this passion I was determined to hold onto—somehow—and still be a parent.

I have a feeling many of you can relate.

Introduction

Writing was my happy place and my joy (and probably yours, too). I was determined to find some way to keep striving toward my dream as a professional fiction writer, but when I looked around for guidance, for all those other writers who'd clearly been writers *and* had kids, I didn't find a lot of help on *how* to do this.

Certainly not with young kids.

I heard plenty about when kids finally went to school these professional writers would get the free time to write, time when they *weren't* parenting, but... but what about when they were babies? What about when they, as parents, were literally existing on two or three hours of broken sleep? Were they writing during *those* stages of parenting?

I looked for answers...

And found nothing.

I remembered hearing about one legend in the romance community who had this rule that when she was writing she could only be interrupted if someone was bleeding (a tale which I think has grown in the retelling). I heard about caregivers, often dads, who could just turn off the sound of their baby's cry and focus on the story at hand (a feat that is still utterly beyond me). I heard about mothers who, exhausted after their endlessly long days of caring for kids, would still go and handwrite a story or idea on napkins instead of sleeping.

None of those solutions felt right to me and frankly, for me to keep showing up as a halfway decent parent, I needed *some* bare amount of sleep. These writers, while they'd found their way to be both parent and writer, none of those felt like a path *I* wanted to walk.

Which meant I had to figure it out for myself.

This idea, this path forward became a passion for me in early 2014, when Kate wasn't yet two. I'd attended my first professional writing workshop in over a year (which, although I didn't know it at the time, would be my last workshop for a good four years). I ended up selling a story at this workshop (which you can find in *Fiction River: Risk-Takers*), but I'd also connected with another fellow writer (a fantastic writer and editor in his own right): Ron Collins.

Ron had gone through the gauntlet of being a parent-writer years ago with his daughter. He listened to my struggles, my frustrations and my dreams, and shared some of his own story of how he managed to write and be the stay-at-home parent. He encouraged me to write about my journey and asked me to share it with everyone, but he also asked that I include all parents in this and not just moms.

Because he'd been the dad caregiver.

If I was struggling to find answers about how to be a present and connected mom and writer, I can't imagine what it was like for him all those years ago.

But I took his message to heart and while much of what I've written will be from a mother's perspective (because that's who I am), I also tried to hold space for anyone else, anyone who stepped into both roles as primary caregiver and writer.

This book got started back up on the Oregon Coast, eating cheesecake at the Inn at Spanish Head. It took a bit for the blog to become a reality, after Eric was born, after I'd gotten hit with one life roll after another, after adding a sibling to the family and realizing just how different Kate was from all the other kids—and how exactly perfect she was—

For Kate.

It took time, though, and my writing fully and completely fell by the wayside for several long months. There and then I was faced with a choice:

To fall down or stand back up.

I fell a lot in those early years (which you'll see reflected here) and I still fall down, but even now I'm pulling myself back up, finding my way as a parent-writer.

To be a parent first and a writer second.

Back in those early days, I felt alone. I felt lost and scared and I didn't *know* what my path forward would look like... so I decided to write about it, to write about this journey—raw and unfiltered as it was—and to possibly connect with other parents who were in the thick of it just like me. My deepest hope with this book, whatever your path, whatever children chose you as a parent, you won't feel alone.

Introduction

Because you're not alone.

There are many more of us out there, parents who are somehow balancing this tight rope of parenting and responsibility with our inner fire, our creativity, our passions. We're trying to do *so* much while at the same time we continually find ourselves coming up short in what we believe is "good enough."

Good enough parents. Good enough writers.

Except we are.

We *are*.

We have value, both in the stories we might sneak in during naptimes or scrawled in a notebook on park days, to sitting with our children as they cry over some hurt perpetrated by another child.

Because they were told they couldn't play.

Because they were told they were different or weird or mean.

And we have value as parents, allowing our kids this space, allowing them to cry and feel sad while we simply stay present and hold them—despite how we might feel on the inside.

We *are* amazing in simply showing up and trying our best to fulfill both these callings:

Being a parent. Being a writer.

I think it's time we start talking—and sharing—our stories.

Here, I'll start.

Let me tell you about my family, about Kate and Eric. About how they came into our lives and changed everything. How they changed me, both as a person and a parent, but also how they changed who I am as a *writer*...

A change I'm seeing now in almost every story I write.

— Chrissy Wissler
Torrance, California
3/11/2020

MY FAMILY—WHERE WE ARE NOW

March 11, 2020
Kate, 7 1/2 years.
Eric, 5 years.

Because the journey is never truly over. It just keeps going...

So much of what I'm sharing with you here—my journey, my shifting as a parent and a person—can't be separated or pulled apart. I can't simply label one section 'How to Develop a Schedule with a Baby' and then 'With a Toddler' because the truth is every season of parenting is different. One month your schedule will look one way and then two days later it'll be turned on its head (I'm looking at you, Daylight Savings Time).

In fact, I think the only real truth is that to be successful, to walk this path as both a parent and writer, you must be flexible.

(Well, you don't *have* to be but you might be pretty miserable—and frustrated—if you aren't.)

The other thing, which will become apparent pretty quickly as you read this book, is my children are different. They are not what our society has defined as neurotypical or 'normal.' They are not on the autism spectrum, but they are different—

In fact, they are exactly who they were meant to be.

I share this because—as I mentioned with the schedules—I simply cannot share who I am as a parent and a writer without sharing this truth about my kids and our journey.

And frankly, I want to share it.

I want to share our journey so other parents and families don't feel alone. When you discover there is no box or label for your child, a child who may dumbfound the professionals and experts and nothing those experts tell you feels right...

I want you to know it's okay.

Yes, get your medical team and those you trust, but simply know, too, that if there is no box for your child, or if you have kids sitting on top of the box (or have just kicked the damn thing to the side), know that it's okay.

Okay for your child to be exactly who they are.

You will read about my own struggles with this, how I learned to find my voice and my strength, and how fiction writing pulled me up from the dark, fearful place I'd found myself in. You will also read how it was through watching my kids and their differences that ultimately helped me find my true calling with my writing. The lessons I've learned from them, the stories I'm now meant to tell and write about, it's all coming from this courage they've asked of me, the parent they've called on me to be—I wouldn't have done any of these things, wouldn't have written the stories I'm now writing, if my kids hadn't been exactly who they are.

Different.

Both Kate and Eric had expressive language delays (meaning their ability to speak language) and receptive language delays (meaning their ability to understand and translate the words we humans speak).

Kate didn't start talking until she was four and Eric only recently started talking at five (as I write this, Kate's now seven and Eric is five). Eric also has a phonology disorder which means, from what we know and what he's shared with us, the clarity of his sounds when he pronounces words won't come in until about age six or six and a half.

We still have a ways to go.

This has been a journey for us and one we'll be on for many years to come—and one I don't regret for a minute. My kids' struggles came not just from their language differences, but also from their temperaments: being introverts, their need for control (and not having this control meant experiencing extreme anxiety and physical stress), and also how they feel the world, its energies, its emotions. Pretty much all the kinds of things most modern western doctors I've met simply can't see or define or understand.

(If you ever meet Sean or I it would make complete sense these unique kids we've created.)

So this isn't just a book about being a parent-writer with young kids, but also being a parent whose kids are different and the unique struggles—and joys—this brings.

You will very much see my attitude change as I settled into this path, as I grew as both a person and a parent. This path is uniquely ours, but I also believe much of what I share is still relevant for most families.

With each section I'll share with you the ages of my kids and my hope is you'll be able to relate if you're going through a similar stage with your kids as you try to be both parent and writer. The two-year-old stage, which I've dubbed, "The Year You Won't Sit Down." Or the rollercoaster of emotions that come when you add a second child to your family.

Take whatever insight works for you and let go of what doesn't fit for you and your family.

You, and only you, know your children best.

You, and only you, know the right path for your writing and how on earth you can balance the two—if there even is such a thing as "balance."

Let's find out... together.

ITSY BITSY STEPS

May 23, 2015
Kate, 2 years
Eric, 5 months

It's the tiny steps that really matter—in watching your babies move, grow, and roll, but also in your writing. Any forward movement, no matter how small or tiny, counts.

So, this has been on my mind lately.

Not that Eric's walking yet, or even crawling, but that everything worth doing requires small steps to get there. I don't know about you, but I tend to skip right over the small stuff... I'm often too focused on whether or not my kid is going to bolt down the beach or if baby Eric, even though he's in the middle of our giant, king-size bed is still a tad too close to the edge since double-rolling is now on the table.

We, as parents, have to be aware of *everything*. Every moment of every single day, we experience this constant sensor that can't shut off because our job is to keep our kids alive and healthy and thriving, which means we may not always be aware of the small steps... and yet at the same time, all I *can* see is the small steps.

Eric as a baby, just five months old, and there he was in those first stages of learning to roll over. How he'd lift both his hips and legs up to his ears and sort of hangout there for a moment. This slight movement of his body to his left side, but not quite all the way to his tummy...

He was learning to roll over—and that's how it started with these little, tiny movements.

I saw all those little steps as he moved through this process and I knew they'd eventually lead to a full baby-roll (it helped that this wasn't my first foray into the baby-rolling department). It took Eric time to get the roll right, to actually *roll over* from his back to his stomach (and in a safe place, mind you). This is big and important step for babies.

Eric got that first roll over, from his back to his tummy, and then he practiced, again and again, so he could consistently make this roll happen. this happen.

Little by little, his efforts led to something bigger.

Sort of like this blog post, which started as just a title. Two hours later... and that was all I'd managed.

Then—oh boy!—I got the first sentence done.

Now, I'm on Day 2 of trying to write this blog... one kid is taking off my fuzzy socks to put them on her feet, the other is trying very hard to sit upright while still playing with toys that seem to defy his wishes (and his best efforts) of going into his mouth....

Right now, all I've got are these itsy-bitsy steps when it comes to my writing. Just little steps forward, but each tiny step is a success. This

That realization hit home when later in the week (and still writing this blog post) I met with a few parenting friends at the beach (kids in tow, of course). One mom, who knew I was a writer and actually *trying* to be a writer even with the young ones around, asked if I'd gotten in my thirty minutes of writing for the day.

I told her, sadly, no.

Why not?

Mostly because I've been mentally swamped with being a parent while getting ready for an upcoming month-long road trip to Montana and Glacier National Park. But her question got me thinking. It encouraged me to take a good, hard look at my writing for each day, not just my writing this blog post but *all* my days... even the ones when I was mentally swamped.

Could I write?

Sure, I had to be ready for our housekeeper and Kate's speech therapist (and by 'ready' I mean have myself and two kids clothed, teeth cleaned, hair tangles beaten down with a heavy-duty brush), but... could I get in my writing time? Could I?

And you know something?

I totally did it—even though I didn't have the time to get in a full thirty minutes of writing. But instead of giving up and saying, "I'll try again tomorrow," I did what I could.

I wrote for fifteen minutes.

It wasn't a lot.

Heck, I didn't even do that many new words. But I got myself back into the story. My creative voice peeked out from where it was hiding —or where it was waiting—as I cleared out a moment from the parent-clutter and endless to-do lists and gave me a small glimmer of direction. I stopped when the doorbell rang and switched from writer-mode back to parent-mode.

Itsy. Bitsy. Steps.

Just like Eric as he's now learning to sit up on his own and stay there. How he's now slowly moving from be able to sit upright on the floor, his weight perfectly balanced forward, and is now playing with some manner of toy (or a not-toy but some pretty darn-cool thing, like Sean's keys), without toppling over.

He's sitting up.

Just like Kate's comfort with her therapist. How, after a quick hug from Sean, she ran right over to the blanket and was ready to play. It was a small but subtle shift from the first session we'd had with her speech therapist, and one I'm absolutely celebrating.

Just as it did with the baby-rolling process the first time around, and just as I've learned over the years with writing, everything worth doing takes steps.

And time.

And effort.

And patience.

Not to mention the path to language isn't just a simple snap of the fingers.

(Kind of like writing.)

Talking isn't as simple as the question I'm often asked, "So, is she talking yet?"

In order to get to language, there must be a thousand small steps in place. To imitate language and words, a child must first imitate sounds. To imitate sounds, she must first imitate play. To imitate play, she must first care about what you think—a child needs to look to parents and grandparents and siblings with an attitude of, "Hey! Look what I've done!"

Okay. That's an incredibly simplified process and I'm skipping over about six dozen steps there, but if there's a hiccup in any of those areas, then you can't answer that simple (and sometimes judgmental) question, "Is she talking yet?"

The answer would be, "No."

But...

She's making eye contact.

She's imitating play.

Heck, she's even imitating the voice's *inflections* for a word she might hear.

In many ways, I'm actually blessed because I GET TO SEE these tiny, tiny steps in action. I have a greater understanding and appreciation for those steps. I'm celebrating and encouraging each of those steps.

And you know what?

It *is* encouraging.

For me, too.

As a writer, sometimes people ask me, "So are you finished with your story yet?"

First off, I want to know which story you're talking about. Back in my more prolific days (you know, before I had two babies) I'd finish one project and move to the next. But right now, the answer to the question would be, "No. I haven't finished the story yet."

But...

I'm working on it.

I got in fifteen minutes one day; another thirty minutes the next.

The word count is adding up. Bit by bit. Sure, it depends on how my life and role as a parent is going (and how crazy I'm feeling that day or if my brain is going to explode), but it *is* adding up.

If anything, being part of this journey with Kate is an inspiration.

She's an inspiration, and she hasn't a clue. She's just doing her thing, playing and learning, and doing what comes naturally. But I see those steps now. I'm learning right along with her and each of those steps is an inspiration.

I have no doubt that she will talk. I have no doubt that I will one day hear her say the most beautiful word ever:

"Mommy."

Just like I have no doubt I'll finish this story. And the story after that.

Bit by tiny bit. Step by tiny step.

I'll get there, and so will Kate.

I just wanted to say thank you for all the support and encouragement I've received, especially in regard to Kate's speech delay. It was unexpected, but very, very welcome. We are moving forward as a family, while I also move forward as a writer.

I even got the warm joy in my chest from getting in those rushed fifteen minutes of fiction writing and then immediately watched Kate engage and play with her therapist, Miss A.

It's a feeling that tells me, without a doubt, we're on the right path.

Thank you, also, for more warm feelings and all your encouragement. It feels great to not be alone.

SAYING 'THANK YOU' TO DADS

June 23, 2015
Kate, almost 3 years
Eric, 6 months

A short and simple thank you to all dads on Father's Day (or however you choose to acknowledge and celebrate the partner in your life). Thank you for the love and support you give our children—and for those of us who are writers, the space and calm, where we just get... to write.

I'm just coming off our giant road trip to Montana and Glacier National Park (not quite the vacation-from-hell, but pretty close to it at times), and I'm bone-weary exhausted.

Still Sunday was Father's Day and regardless of how mushy my brain is, I need to write this. I need to tell Sean, my husband, and all those dads out there, just how awesome they are.

Because, truthfully, I could not do *this* without my husband.

I couldn't do the blog or the fiction writing or the homeschooling.

I certainly couldn't be the kind of mother I am, and the kind of mother I want to be (which means lots of learning and unlearning, trying and failing), without him.

From the writing side... I could not do this without having a supportive, patient, and *very* understanding partner.

Let's face it. Nothing about writing falls into the 'get rich quick' category (or even the 'constant, steady paycheck' category).

Being a professional writer means I'm on a very long, *slow* road to success. And just to make things a little more challenging, I'm gonna do it while also raising two small kids. So, really, I'm talking an even longer process (decades, probably). Whatever money we invest in my learning and in my publishing company goes into this never-ending black hole—at least that's how it *feels* like since these days I don't have the time to write enough to even pay for the business expenses.

I made the choice to be a full-time parent first, a parent of two different kids, and a writer second.

And through all this, Sean has been beside me, supporting me, cheering me, knowing this work I'm doing is what I was called to do.

He encourages me in his silent way. Standing in support as every day I struggle and crawl closer to my dreams. How he drove down from Seattle, Washington to the Oregon Coast when I was eight months pregnant with Kate so I could attend a writing workshop. How he now keeps our kids happy and somehow not crying so I can sneak in my thirty minutes of writing.

He understands that we're working the long tail of writing and publishing and he's not only cool with it, he's supportive.

And even more than that, he wants me to succeed.

He never questions my burning desire to fit in any workshops I can... though he does provide a soft reality check after my excitement dies down and asks, "Are you sure you can handle this? Right *now*?"

(In most cases the answer is no. But still, he lets me come to that realization on my own instead of just saying 'no' with me getting all grumpy and resentful.)

And probably, most important of all, he understands how important writing is to me. How it's a core part of my being and I'm only at my happiest when I'm writing.

It's never been a question of "the writing or me," which is why we're together and sharing this life and a family in the first place. Still, I know other writers aren't as lucky. I certainly know how difficult it is to try and parent and write and *still* somehow maintain this all-important partnership.

But in all honesty, I could not be the *mother* I am without an equally supportive husband.

Saying 'thank you' just isn't enough. I know it's something he doesn't hear enough of, especially when it's so easy to overlook the support staff role he plays in our daily lives. How he gets home (after working all day) in time to help ease the bedtime battles, finish dinner, then deal with the endless cleanup of dishes because, truly, how many dishes can a toddler and a baby dirty?? (A LOT.)

He does this all without complaint.

He'll bring me the baby at three o'clock in the morning because I'm so tired I can't move.

He'll bring me much needed chocolate on my hardest days without judgment, only understanding.

He'll be my rock and my comfort because dear Lord, I need that most of all.

And he's not the only dad making these little silent sacrifices. He's not the only dad putting his family before his own dreams and goals.

I couldn't be more fortunate to have him as a husband and a father. Someone who, I know for a fact, isn't afraid of wearing a baby in public.

Because, that's what Real Men do.

Excuse me—that's what *Real Dads*, do.

Being a mom is hard and wonderful and filled with both frustration and joy, but I know these feelings are no less true for dads as well.

I do my best to remember and tell him just how much he means to me.

I do my best to simply say, "Thank you."

IT'S ALL ABOUT THE SCHEDULES:
PART 1

July 3, 2015
Kate, almost 3 years
Eric, 7 months

I'm writing a series of blog posts about schedules, how to set one, and how the heck you make one work with kids (especially the super young variety). I'm not sure where this will take me—only that it will consistently change because parenting and change seem to go hand in hand.

It didn't take me long to realize this topic wasn't going to fit in one post —I started trying out one schedule, which then shifted and changed. That led to another attempt at a schedule and then another... and then my kids did what they always do:

They changed the game right underneath me.

So here's to a series of posts (however many demand to be written) about figuring out schedules, writing, and finding some measure of success when you've got zero control over the schedule (and demands) of your kids.

. . .

So, I want to write again. Like, seriously. The urge is there. It's got me hard and now all I need is to figure out... how.

Yep.

How?

That one word is the big million-dollar question for all us parent-writers out there, especially those with the super-tiny humans that consider schedules downright laughable. In fact, my little Eric would flat-out baby-giggle if I tried to put him on a sleep schedule. And a feeding schedule? He'd laugh in my face.

Actually, he'd cry and wouldn't stop until his needs were filled, but you get the point. Eric is his own person with very real, very *exact* demands. It's my job to follow them and damn whatever artificial schedule I impose on him.

Kids like their routine.

Their routine.

Not mine. My routine is completely bendable and flexible to their whim, at least for the next several years.

And truthfully, that's the way it should be.

I mean, I signed on for this role when I decided to be a parent. I'm cool with that (on *most* days, if I'm being honest here).

But, I still have my own needs and dreams, and if I feel the writing urge again, it's my subconscious telling me that we can make this happen—so long as I play by the rules and times and allowances my kids set. (All of this is kind of funny since I'm writing this post with one hand, rocking a baby with the other, and somehow not getting hit by falling shoes as Kate plays in the climbing structure at the playground above us.)

I'm fighting off the last bits of an annoying cold and I haven't slept in what feels like days. Kate's also finishing off this cold, since I only get sick when one of the kids are sick—I think that's the golden rule of parents everywhere.

And yet, there's that writing urge, telling me it's time to keep moving forward...

To keep telling stories.

In fact, I've got this short story I started last week, a whole 500 words (woohoo!) and I'm pretty psyched about it. But—here's the tricky part—how am I going to get into the swing of things again?

Since I'm me, I thought a checklist was in order. Checklists help me see all the simple details right and clear, and these days, right and clear is the only way my brain can process things (more *sleeep* please).

So, first step to getting back to writing: the desire.

Clearly, I want to write again. No problems there. Check that one off the list.

Second step: Sleep/energy.

Okay, well, that one's a bit tougher, but hey, if I've got the urge, I'm gonna say I've got the energy. The subconscious, my creative voice, is pretty awesome. It tells me when I've got the extra juice to tell stories, so I'll follow my gut on this one. (Note: I completely accept this step will vary by day, by hour, by minute even... but I've got to start somewhere, right??)

Third step: A schedule.

Okay. This is where I keep getting hung up, so I'll break this down even further.

Before I even started with the schedule, I needed to know a bit about myself as a writer (and you can fill in this part about yourself). I know I'm a morning person. I write better in the mornings because I have energy, and if I have energy, I can be creative.

No energy = no creative juice.

I also know I do better when I've got a schedule. Whether this schedule goes by time (8:30 a.m. my butt is in the chair) or event (after a browse of the internet and 2 cups of coffee...). So long as I have a schedule, I have an easier time being accountable, being *consistent*, and getting back into the swing of the writing.

And yet, here's the problem...

Two. Young. Kids.

With their own schedule. Each of them.

Chances are, they're on different schedules (because they simply cannot *both* sleep well the same night, right? That's another rule of parenting, I've discovered). I accept that. I'm not going to fight their nature as little kids and that acceptance, hopefully, will help my mood and attitude so I won't feel angry or frustrated when my kids change the plan as they inevitably will).

So besides knowing your self as a writer, you *also* need flexibility.

The second is forgiveness because I know darn well there's gonna be days when I can't write.

As I said, the last thing I want is to get mad at the kids for interrupting me (can you tell that's happened before?). Writing might be part of me, but so is being a parent—in a much deeper, core-reaching way that writing can never *touch*.

Still, I want to respect both while also being true to both.

And going back to my journey as I (try) to figure out this elusive beast called a 'schedule'...

Well, I'll let you know how it goes.

GUT CHECK

July 17, 2015
Kate, almost 3 years
Eric, 7 months

Who you are as a parent, who your family is, and the limits on both—because as much as we want to, we can't do everything.

There are some mornings where I just *miss* writing fiction. Miss the constant learning and growth. Miss seeing the potential of my stories and my career literally coming together, piece by piece. Miss catching a glimpse of what this means for me and my business in five years, ten years, and more.

All these feelings come on more strongly after I've finished a story, designed a book cover, or held a finished paper book in my hands. I feel all this more keenly because the work I'm doing now, all these steps toward being a professional writer, is a long and sloooow journey.

Especially right now.

Here I am, enjoying my morning coffee and reading about the writing business, as my pen is a handbreadth from the paper, Kate runs over and grabs said hand.

She's hungry and I need to supply the correct kind of food from the refrigerator (the non-correct kind results in a tragic, frustrated meltdown). I help her because that's what you do as the parent or caregiver.

Then I sit down and try again. Pick up my pen, get a whole *paragraph* down —

And now it's Eric's turn...

Eric woke up from his morning nap, which means he's hungry (and in need of a diaper change).

That's how quickly my day can veer off the writing path and into parenthood. Most days, I'm okay with that. Heck, most days that one paragraph was the last individual, Chrissy-only thought I'm graced with before the epic to-do list wraps around me...

Or before Eric starts crying because he bonked his nose while attempting to crawl, which coincides precisely with the exact same time Kate spills her glass of cream all over the table, the floor, herself, and...

You get the idea.

But on *some* days, the urge and desire to write holds on. Strong. Some days I'll glance over my work, the stories and novels and publishing bits practically frozen over in a glacier-created time capsule, waiting so patiently for me to return to it, and, well... I miss it.

I miss feeding my writing. Miss the learning. Miss the storytelling.

I miss my writing.

And the feelings that come are real and I shouldn't try to deny them.

And—just as importantly—having those feelings doesn't make me a bad parent.

I'm allowed to feel this way and I think it's important to step back, see and evaluate these feelings, then continue on with all the daily and emotional demands of parenthood—and all the extra bits that come with having a late-talking child.

Maybe it's because of the world we live in, our particular American culture (and I'm sure my own upbringing too), but I've needed to constantly remind myself that it's okay to feel this way. Okay to want more for my writing and myself while at the same time acknowledging that the time for my writing, for my success and my business, isn't now.

It's this really weird inner struggle.

To be a successful, long-term writer, I need to write a lot. I need to publish and sell what I write. I also need to keep learning.

But...

I can't do that now.

Heck, I can barely switch my brain over to read a book for simple enjoyment, to get lost in a story and its characters.

The parent side is just as conflicted... feeling that wanting this —*my* writing—means I'm being selfish. That I'm not enjoying every moment I have with my kids. It feels like every time I go outside, go to parks and playgrounds or the grocery store, strangers smile joyfully at my kids and then remind me (as if I could possibly forget), how precious time is and how kids grow up so fast...

Because watching Eric already in the first phase of figuring out crawling isn't a cold enough bucket of water in my face.

All this judgment—in myself, but also in the messages surrounding me—keeps swinging around me like a vortex and I'm doing my best to push through, to figure out how *I* feel and not what everyone claims I *should* feel.

I *am* catching some moments of clarity and they still leave me feeling conflicted!

Accepting and sad.

Joyful and sorrowful.

All at the same stickin' time, too.

Just this week I received an email about a two-day workshop put on by Writers of the Future, including amazing instructors Kevin J. Anderson and Rebecca Moesta (who I attempted to sell stories to at the WMG Anthology Workshop last year). And this workshop? Yeah, it's right here in Los Angeles.

That's pretty darn cool. Exciting too.

And I can't go.

I can't go, because I'm a breastfeeding mom.

Sure, there's a way around that like pumping and teaching Eric the bottle, but that's extra work and stress (for us, as a family—I hold no judgment on anyone else and the choices they've made for their family). And maybe I could have brought Eric, though who knows how the workshop moderators or other attendees would feel about *that*.

But I simply knew this wasn't an option.

I'd learned firsthand at the California Homeschool Network Conference as I walked around with Eric strapped to me, just how difficult learning with a baby is. My focus, my intention... it's still mostly on him. At least when he gives me pause and breath so I can learn (meaning he's content and quiet) I can actually turn off the parenting-brain and just be me.

Meaning: The baby's asleep and I'm on my feet rocking back and forth regardless of how my poor back feels.

Actually, it's a pretty smart quirk of our evolution. When the baby is up and making noise, *any* noise, a parent's aware. Any baby. Any noise. Coo or cry, laugh or the distinct warning of 'I'm-going-to-lose-it-if-you-don't-help-me-out-here' sounds.

Either way, I'm tuned into the baby.

So the learning I do is piece-meal at best. And you know? I accept it.

Sure, I miss this learning, I'm sad that I have to delete the email about the workshop, but I can't do this right now; not at this time in my life.

The same was true for one of my favorite anthology magazines when a notice went out that a bunch of invited authors didn't turn in their stories, providing an opening for those of us in the know. I read the call for submissions, and then, deleted the email.

I knew I couldn't do it.

Not then.

Not with all the stress and pressure and just plain ol' being a parent of two young kids.

I call this process my 'gut check.'

I take a look at my life and my sleep (or lack of), my calendar and the upcoming commitments and outings, and most importantly, how I feel.

Overwhelmed.

Exhausted to where I can't exercise.

The dialed-up craving for chocolate needed just to survive the day.

(Eric's in the middle of a teething episode, and no exaggeration, we haven't had a half-decent night's sleep in a month.)

All this makes up my gut check, and lately, I finish with this check, shake my head and say, "No."

No.

I can't sign up for the newest, oh-so-needed WMG Online Workshop regardless of how much I want to or how it'd speed my writing light-years ahead...

No.

Not right now.

Not today. Not this week.

But maybe next month.

That's where my fiction writing stands for this whole week. Every morning I check in with myself, do my gut check, and every morning the answer has been no.

(See my reference to the 'not sleeping in a month.')

This saddens me, to say no, and honestly, it's frustrating too... but I know it's the right call.

What is *your* right call?

You need to work with the opportunities your children give you, because really, you can't control them. You can't control the natural ups and downs in your family life, your children's feelings or yours or your partner's. If your children are different and late-talking like Kate

—all the emotional stress and fears that come with this extra challenge.

You also need to be accountable for your writing. Not just be lazy and say, "Well, I'm busy today. I'll give it a go tomorrow."

You need to give your writing, and your role as a parent, an honest assessment.

Hence, the gut check.

But part of it (which, I'm still clearly learning), is accepting what you find. Yes, you can write. Or, no, life's got you by the balls and it's best just to get through it, day by day.

There's only so much my brain, body, and heart can handle and I think part of this process, part of being a successful parent-writer, is understanding this... my limits, my family.

Accepting *this* instead of fighting against it and resisting.

As much as I can, anyway. And I guess that, too, is part of being a parent.

EVERYONE'S GOT AN OPINION:
SCHEDULES PART 2

July 26, 2015
Kate, almost 3 years
Eric, 7 months

Yes, I'm still trying to figure out this schedule thing...

So, schedules are important.

They're powerful motivators to help you hit deadlines, help push through moments where writing is the last thing you truly want to do, and also, schedules just help get your butt in the chair. (Once in the chair, the writing part is a heck of a lot easier. Forcing yourself to sit for a set amount of time, even if only fifteen minutes, means you're going to start typing just so you're *allowed* to get up again... and it's amazing what can happen in those fifteen minutes!)

But... fitting a schedule into my day, even if I'm only shooting for fifteen minutes, isn't exactly a cakewalk. Not with my busy life. Not when I've got kids needing attention and turning the switch on high when it comes to my parenting-brain.

So, I need a plan. And because I'm a list person, well, I made a list.

I started out with stuff I want to happen:

Write fiction.

Play!! (with Kate and with Eric).

Working out (getting rid of this last bit of baby fat is gonna do wonders for my overall calm and happiness).

Then, I looked at each item on the list and asked myself how I could make these happen... and of course problems I might run into.

I worked out reasonable ways to reach these goals (at least, they *seem* reasonable so far) and brainstormed around the potential problems.

The process sort of went a bit like this....

I'm a morning person and my creative energy is best in the morning, but I can't write when my kids (or at least Eric) are awake and demanding attention. Okay...

How about waking up before them? Is that possible?

Hey, maybe 5 a.m. is possible. But to wake up that early means I need to be in bed by 9 p.m.

I won't get much time for myself or time with Sean. Hmm. That's definitely a problem area. A happy marriage is key to surviving our children's baby/toddlerhood. Maybe we can have easy dinners with less dishes to clean up? That's possible.

Also, early bedtimes mean no evening movies or TV shows, at least very few and not all the time.

But I like those shows and while I can cut back, I don't want to fully give them up.

So... why not incorporate this downtime into my afternoon siesta before the usual bedtime battles and frayed nerves and overtired eyes take control of my two munchkins?

Hmm... maybe that would work.

Of course, afternoon TV shows means Kate and I will be battling for the remote since she's under the impression that the giant TV is her personal viewing screen for all things Tinker Bell and My Little

Pony. (Then again, she's three. She thinks this way about everything.)

I fiddled with the list. And the problems I might (read: WOULD) run into.

I can't say I came up with solutions for everything, but I didn't think I would either. Part of being a parent is being flexible (perfection leads to madness... the kids don't give a damn about 'perfect').

Step one is giving something, *anything*, a try.

Step two is just as important: getting Sean on board.

Actually, that's not so much a problem. He respects my writing, the work I put into it, and—almost as important—he understands my writing business still exists even though my main job is currently raising our children (while the writing gathers its fair share of dust).

Still, talking things out is important. Really important (see again my above note about a happy marriage). I needed to communicate to him just how important this was, how I needed to get some kind of schedule going to make this happen, and find out if he had any thoughts or concerns.

We got the talking part down, no problem.

The real problem?

Yeah, that's relying on him to get up early in the morning to watch the kids so I can work on the above writing goals.

Sean's not a morning guy and doesn't move well or fast or have much coherent thought really before a certain time... let's say around ten in the morning (which is the complete opposite to the kids and I). I respect that. I respect his need to sleep, so I decided to give this a go, at first, without resorting to bugging and shoving him out of bed. Hence my decision to wake up at 5 a.m.

But we also needed to be on the same page—which was getting me an hour of quiet writing time before he left for work.

And that's when it dawned on me that this schedule, this goal for my writing and self-care, wasn't just about me.

I mean, to make this work, to have a *chance* at working, I couldn't go at it alone. I couldn't shoulder everything, all the responsibility, all by myself.

I needed everyone on board.

That included Sean.

And Kate.

And little baby Eric.

Which is where I ran face-first into that wall of parenting and realized just how damn difficult this was going to be.

Trust me, my kids have an opinion when it comes to my writing. Or reading a book. Or talking on the phone.

Even as I write this, Kate's having a meltdown in what Sean has lovingly called her 'crying castle' (one of those fold-up *Frozen* fort-type castles). Seriously. The second I try and 'work,' Kate suddenly decides she is absolutely starving and any delay, any mention of 'waiting,' means the world will end. Whether it's food, attention, or just... I don't know what... just *something*.

Hence my soon-to-be-first-attempt at fiction writing while everyone is still sleeping.

But I also realize that Kate's giving me her opinion. She's telling me loud-and-clear what she thinks of Mommy's schedule and attempt at writing and being a professional writer again—

She's also doing it without using words. And Eric's right there with her. He has his own opinions and his own thoughts and there are times when Daddy holding him will *simply not do* and he *must* have Momma.

To be honest, I only have the vaguest idea how to make my schedule, and the opinions of my kids, work.

A lot has to do with my awareness of them.

A lot has to do with flexibility and this season of life we're working our way through.

I have a feeling I will need a ton of forgiveness and letting go on my part when I can't get that writing time in, at least on a regular routine basis. Meaning, I can't get upset with myself (or the kids) when the schedule to write (or just take a breather) doesn't happen.

I know each day will be like a new start.

There will be writing streaks in there, days where I'll be plugging in the writing, word-by-word, just like I know I'll have long chunks of stops when I need to deal with this parental roller-coaster. But to make this work, to make the writing and the parenting part work together, I need to listen to my family, my body (because getting a handful of hours of sleep—*thanks, Eric*—won't cut it).

I also need to listen to my writing voice, the storyteller inside me. Right now, that voice is working hard to come out. All I can do is set the stage as best I can, write a sentence. Then, write another...

And stopping when the kids need me.

Because that's how I'm going to make this parent-writing thing work. I think, anyway. All I can do is try, adjust, and then try again.

(And maybe catch up a little bit on my sleep. Maybe.)

THE KEYBOARD BATTLE

August 2, 2015
Kate, 3 years.
Eric, 8 months.

Learning when to put our needs, as parents, first... and when to let go, to laugh and join our kids on the floor and simply... play.

This morning Kate and I battled; it was a full-on tug-of-war over the keyboard. Okay, maybe not *literally*, but pretty damn close.

It was, in fact, a battle for my attention.

I sat down to get in my thirty minutes of writing. Thirty minutes. That's right, you heard correctly. I asked to be left alone for *thirty minutes*.

To which Kate said, "Oh, Hell No."

The battle then began. Every five minutes, she was there. Pulling at my hands. Bringing me her empty water cup (never mind there was another cup with plenty of water on the counter). Oh, and my favorite... tossing her special Lady pillow, her blanket, and her Bunny on my chair, behind me, so she could climb and cuddle right *there*.

Meanwhile, I'm trying to write.

Every time I said, "No," (or, shit, said *anything* at all) she'd go into meltdown mode.

Which made me angry.

I mean, this is my time, my *thirty minutes* of parent-writer self-care time. Not to mention I'm dealing with this kid for twenty-four hours, pretty much nonstop. Caring for her, comforting her even when she wakes me up an hour after I finally fall asleep because she's thirsty, and she now can't leave me alone for *thirty minutes??*

I get it, okay?

I get that she wants Mommy. But you know, Mommy wants Mommy, too, and this is the *only* time during the day I'll get me time. After the kids go to bed doesn't really count since I'm falling over from exhaustion and that simply is not the time for me to write.

And so you know, what I'm writing about here doesn't just relate to me being the mommy. If you're the primary caregiver, if you're the dad trying to find some much-needed, daddy-care-time, feel free to switch the word to 'daddy' or whatever works best for you.

Now, Kate's still young.

She's turning three years old next week (which is crazy and scary and awesome all in itself), and I know this is part of the learning process. In fact, it's going to be a *looong* learning process because she is so young. But I want to help guide her and teach her this, about me needing this time to write.

Because it's important.

For me.

I am still Mommy, but Mommy is also a writer. And when Mommy is writing, Mommy *should* be left alone... unless hurt or bleeding or something equally dire. I picked up this tidbit from a legend in the writing world and instantly added it to my own ideas of being a parent-writer... and how I could balance them being both a writer and a parent.

(Now, I could be an awesome journalist and do a bit of Google searching and digging to find out exactly where I heard and read this, but seriously, I'm a parent and I'm typing as fast as I can cause Eric's making his grumbling, fussy noises letting me know that he needs to be picked up... very, very soon.)

But I liked the goal, liked the idea behind what this writer was talking about.

When it's time to write, it's my time.

It's *my* keyboard.

Not Kate's. Not Eric's.

Mine.

Especially when I've already taken the time to get Kate her morning snacks and water and movie ready. And yes there are many out there, parents and professionals alike, who are fearful of screen time. But seriously, movies are great at keeping young kids occupied so I can sneak in these minutes of writing and self-care, so I can take this time for myself for a whole thirty minutes...

Thirty minutes that became 316 new words in my story. And you know, that was an incredibly hard-fought 316 words. Actually, when I look back at my usual progress (you know, before I had kids), when I reflect back on how much writing I used to do... that low number feels frustrating. I used to write twice that amount.

But still... I wrote.

I got the writing in when I was tired, when my brain was still fuzzy from needing sleep, and when I simply *knew*, right from the moment Kate got up, the writing was going to be a battle.

But... I got my words in.

I even had a few moments when my creative voice took off and enjoyed herself, and I got a deeper glimpse of the story I was trying so hard to tell. I got a glimpse of fun and *why* I was trying and working so hard to write again.

And then it was time to be a parent again. Because Kate needs my attention, needs a long hug while curled up on my lap. I'll give it to her... while doing my best to let go of the lingering anger and frustration from that keyboard battle.

I'm not perfect. I'm certainly not a perfect parent, but I'm trying.

So I'll see if I can pull a page from Kate's book at how easy it is to forgive, to move on, and still love unconditionally and without pause.

Wow.

Just thinking about her and her smile. About how she sees the world, even when she doesn't have words and, in many ways, honestly doesn't need them.... and already it's made me feel better.

Kids are something else.

Even if we battle from time to time. I think that's okay too.

Now, though, I'm give some hugs, sit on the floor, and play. Get in a little mother-daughter time before Eric wakes up and just enjoy what this is all really about... seeing Kate's smile, seeing that bright, light shining through her when I sit down to play.

Because that, too, is part of my own self-care.

TALKING IS OVERRATED

August 11, 2015
Kate, 3 years
Eric, 8 months

When life calls us on an unexpected journey; a twist and turn we hadn't seen coming yet have to navigate anyway. Changing your mindset, accepting your path, and how this slowly—and unknowingly—seeps into your writing.

It's only been five months since we took Kate to see her pediatrician and officially learned that her speech was delayed. Except that moment felt like we'd opened a door and everything tumbled out—more than we wanted, more than we felt Kate *needed*. An appointment with the audiologist, an appointment with the neurologist, a request for speech therapy. Occupational therapy? Why not!

It's been five months since we went to our regional early intervention center whose evaluation of Kate left me in tears and Sean pissed off as all hell. Why? Because they looked at Kate and, within that short evaluation, decided she fit into a particular box.

One box.

One clear and simple answer.

Because Kate wasn't talking, because she didn't want to engage with the evaluator (a woman who did *not* radiate kindness and warmth for children, and instead the exact opposite). Because Kate scored poorly on the evaluation and was so miserable she tried to open the door and leave, they were ready to push for an autism spectrum diagnosis and all the services that came with it.

First, I have the utmost respect for parents whose children are autistic and who *do* need these services.

For us, in our hearts and gut, we *knew* they were wrong.

We knew our daughter and we knew this diagnosis did not fit her.

And as we continued this journey and fought for answers, we learned the evaluation that Kate was given at the regional center (the Bailey's) was one she *would* score poorly at.

Because she had a receptive language delay.

Here they were, giving her a test and expecting her to understand what was being asked, and she couldn't. It's not that she couldn't perform what they were asking of her, it's that she didn't even *understand* the question.

None of this questioning about her language, about looking deeper into the many language disorders that exist, came up with our pediatrician or neurologist or evaluator.

Not once.

Instead they'd all fixated on this one diagnosis, this one area, and for them that was the only answer they needed.

But all this realization of Kate, of who she is and what *she* needed support with, came later.

First was my realization, in a cold, numbing kind of way, that the professionals we'd met so far didn't care about helping Kate for *her* sake, in a way that was right for *her*.

No one did, but us.

It's been a journey, that's for sure, and it's a long, long way from being over.

And you know what?

I'm okay with that.

Even though there were tears, even though there were more curse words than I've probably said in my entire life, there's also been acceptance for me. And probably just as important, peace.

Because finally I've settled in.

Settled in with who my daughter is, with the choices we've made and the path we've chosen—and damn what anyone else thinks or what society and the world around us defines as "normal."

This 'settling in' wasn't easy and it took time... but I found a way to get through it. Lots of questions about how my gut said there was nothing wrong, but all the experts were pushing and beating against our doors with hints that there 'was' something wrong.

And when I say 'nothing wrong' what I mean is nothing wrong—for *her*. That Kate felt exactly as she was meant to feel, that this was *her* and *not* something that needed fixing. Supporting, absolutely, but fixing? What all the professionals saw in her... I can't begin to tell you how wrong this felt on so many levels.

So, I tackled the problem head on... which means—I read books. As many as I could get my hands on and found something all those experts hadn't mentioned before... *language disorders*. Not something grander with all the nuances you could imagine, but a developmental focus simply on language.

It started with a book I discovered at a homeschool conference, "*Late-Talking Children*" by Thomas Sowell. He described a type of child that felt exactly like Kate, someone who was incredibly aware, puzzle-focused—Kate could even give directions to my parents' house—but who just *didn't want to talk*.

And then I found another book, this one called, "*Late-Talking Children: A Symptom or a Stage?*" by Stephen Camarata. This led to a Google search where I found something truly invaluable....

Other parents.

And I realized I wasn't alone. Not alone in fighting against the professionals and their expert opinions who (in my experience), had wanted to push for a diagnosis and slap a label on Kate (doing so = more funding—again, in my experience). And those other parents often felt just as lost and fearful and alone as I did. Parents who constantly struggled between worry for their own late-talker, making sure their child got the help *they* needed, while letting that child be who she or he was.

Parents who forcefully push society's beliefs and expectations away to let their child be who they are. To trust their child.

Trust your child.

That's an incredibly easy thing to say, and a damn hard one to actually do.

Trust that you're *listening* to your child's wants, interests, feelings. Trust that *you're* making the right choices—for *your* child (because everyone's child is different with their own wants and needs and ways of showing up in this world).

Oh—and you totally get to do all this while your kid's not saying a word.

What I love about this late-talking group is there are parents who are like me, who are right in the thick of it, deep in the trenches and we're damn lucky to catch a glimpse of sunlight and insight into our children. And there are other parents who've been down this road, some for just a few years, others who've come out the other side. Kids who are growing past their language differences. Who are healthy and 'normal' in their own unique way.

One message I continually hear from those parents is to love your child.

Love the child you have... *right now*.

I have a very dear family friend whose daughter was diagnosed with autism who told me once that when she looked back at everything she went through, "I wish I could go back in time and just tell myself that she was going to be fine."

We're parents.

We worry about our kids. That's just part of the deal when we become parents. The difference is choosing to live in that worry, or somehow, find love and joy in your life *right now*.

Which again, is a very easy thing to say and an incredibly hard thing to do.

In a way, this is exactly what I tell myself when I see friends and their kids—and it's also the exact thing I tell myself when I see other professional writers who release book after book.

Enjoy the life that I have—right now.

I could *be* writing more, but I'm choosing not to. I'm choosing this time with my children, to be with them during these very young years, because I'll never ever get those years back.

Eric, who's now figuring out the logistics of crawling, reminds me of that daily.

I mean, it feels like I blinked and he's already moving out of babyhood. I have No-Idea-How-that-Happened.

Just like I'll never get this time back with Kate. If I live in the worry, let myself be consumed by that worry, it's the same as blinking.

I'll miss this time with my kids, with Kate, and it will be gone. Forever.

This understanding, this acceptance about Kate and who she is, where she is at developmentally and with her language (and not caring what the world has to say about it), has come about slowly. Bit-by-bit. A huge part my understanding, of this shift inside me is because the *joy* I feel watching her play with her speech therapist. Seeing how happy she is. Witnessing her accomplish these giant, yet very miniscule, leaps towards language.

If I blink, I will miss this time with her.

I would miss seeing, and feeling, this *joy*.

That's right. I said, "Joy."

That's my heart telling me I'm on the right path. For me. For Kate. For our family.

Now, don't get me wrong. There are times when I feel the worry, when I feel the grief like a sharp-cutting knife despite all this talk of joy. It can happen during an innocent conversation with a friend or at a party when I hear another child, younger than Kate, is speaking in such clear, full sentences. Or, it can even be at Kate's third birthday party with her not understanding what the other kids are saying, how she's being mean by running off with the puzzle box while others are playing with it (she sees this My Little Pony puzzle as special and hers—which is completely *normal* in any child's development).

The difference is I choose to live in that grief, or not.

I choose not to (most of the time!), but I also don't deny the grief. I let myself feel it. I let myself cry, and then I pick myself up and focus on the joy. Focusing on playing with her. Seeing through her eyes.

To be honest, a huge part of this comes from watching Kate in her therapy because *every* session I get a deeper glimpse into her and just how much she knows. Not just therapy but during our normal day-to-day lives, where out of *nowhere*, Kate goes up and hugs Eric. Just wants a hug from her brother. She's never done that before, and let me tell you, my heart melted.

Again and again.

Kate just turned three.

Three years old and according to every checklist given and taught to pediatricians and professionals, there's something wrong with her. And you know what? *They're* wrong.

All of them.

Kate is who she is. She's going at her own pace and I'm providing what I can to encourage it.

She's fine; she's who she was meant to be.

This is what my family and I have always known, in our hearts, but the world around us said no. That we were wrong. That she needed to be labeled and diagnosed and put into special programs that wanted to force her to sit around a table for an hour and learn to attend, learn to talk.

And I want to be clear here as well: this is for us, for our family. So many of you will have your own experiences, your own children who are in those programs and therapies and are thriving and I'm thrilled for you. I'm thrilled you found the right path for your child. For us, it was knowing in our gut which options that were presented to us were wrong—for *Kate*.

For my part, I want Kate to smile. To be happy. To play.
To just be herself.
Like Sean says every time I feel the grief, "Talking is overrated."
And he's right.
For our family, for our little girl, he's absolutely right.
Kate will talk—when she's good and ready. In the meantime, with the resilience and happiness only a child can have, she's getting along just fine without it. And you know what?
So am I.

This particular post was much more focused on my journey with Kate, with her being a late-talker, and me finding my peace and acceptance of our path forward. This was not a heavily parent-writer focused entry, but it is about parenting. It's about how my mindset needed to change, to move from this place of fear that kept me paralyzed for four months, time during which I have little memory of what happened in my kids' lives. Four whole months just... gone.

There was nothing but fear and darkness.

Little did I know how powerful this experience would be in my writing, how it would open doors to deeper emotions, to places I couldn't touch until I was down in that darkness and eventually climbed back out.

Curious about what those stories are? I have two scheduled to come out in 2020 for Pulphouse Magazine.

SO... HOW'S THE WRITING GOING?

August 20, 2015
Kate, 3 years
Eric, 8 months

You're not alone—even when it feels like you are. And no matter how productive you are during this season of life, no matter how small and tiny your successes are right now, you are amazing.

It's been a year and a half since I was surrounded by other professional writers and boy do I miss it.

I mean really, really miss it. Because, at the end of the day, writers some of the only people who *get* what I'm trying to do.

I mean, some may not get the parenting thing and many others have put those days of small kids, naptimes, and middle-of-the-night feedings long, long behind them... But still, when I hold out a book, one I wrote, designed, and published, they get it.

They get all the work and time that went into such a simple-looking thing, this paperback book.

Before there was Eric, when Kate was eighteen months old, I went to my last (for now) Oregon Coast Workshop. It was the big one. Six editors buying for Fiction River anthology magazines. Six chances to sell a story. (And even if the editors passed on your story, that was still *six* people with their different opinions talking about *your* story.)

Oh, and about fifty professional writers talking business and craft morning, noon, and way, way into the night.

For a whole week.

It was amazing. Energy was coming out everyone's ears... and honestly, it was a bit much being both writer and mom at that point, especially with Kate in tow and missing her momma (Kate came with me while my mom did the babysitting).

But I remember that time, being around all those writers, and I'm holding it very, very close to my heart right now.

These days as a parent, I feel lucky to have enough time (and energy) to plop myself on the couch and watch an episode of *Agents of Shield*, or when I *really* have no energy and just need fluffy bunnies, I'll watch *Once Upon a Time*. These days, I'm barely making it upstairs before collapsing in bed.

A few weeks ago, I mentioned how I missed feeding my writing—missed the practicing, studying other writers, taking workshops. But what I really miss is just being around other people who *get it*.

People who get that progress moves at a snail's pace.

People who get that it takes time, focus, and practice to write a novel—and even more practice to write one that, you know, readers actually want to *buy*.

I miss the other writers, the other professionals, who understand that publishing a book takes effort. I miss those writers who get that making my book look like it came straight out of New York is a whole new level of learning (because cool-looking covers don't happen with a snap of your fingers).

Instead of asking me, "So how's the writing going?"

These writers instead say, "*Wow.* I can't believe how much you're getting done!"

And those words of encouragement warm me in ways those writers can never understand. They have no idea how much that distinction means to me.

And, yes, it's a distinction.

I say all this because I'm still in the middle of a life roll—the birth of Eric—and I'm still working at a snail's pace. And that's totally fine. I knew it would happen when I decided to be a parent not once, but twice. I also knew, without a doubt, that I'd be writing.

Somehow.

Maybe not a lot, but some.

And you know what? I am.

Other professional writers who know me, who know my work ethic and goals, have no doubt I'll get back on the writing career horse when I can. They understand what life rolls do to the writing process so they cheer me on when I hit these little successes (or big, depending how you look at it), like turning in six stories for this anthology workshop in six weeks.

All that writer support is awesome, but it's unfortunately not the kind I'm surrounded with in my day-to-day life.

Instead I get asked the question, "So how's the writing coming?"

Which sounds pretty innocent. And sometimes, it is.

Sometimes that person truly just wants to hear what I've gotten done, even those days where no writing happened. Those same people are often amazed I found any time in front of the computer to begin with (they're also generally parents of young kids). And for those people, I do like to share. I like to tell them what I've accomplished—or oftentimes—what I haven't.

But there's the group. When they ask, "How's the writing?" they're not actually being sincere.

I mean, they might think they are, but they're not. Not really.

Not when I can *feel* the judgment dripping off them when I say, "Well, not much writing this week. I've barely gotten a solid four hours of sleep and my creative-brain is shot."

Their 'innocent' question makes me feel like I'm *not* a professional, like what I'm doing is this so-so thing that's unimportant.

And this judgment?

Yeah, I almost always get this from hobby-writers who want to make a ton of money off their one book—or even someone who knows just enough about writing and books to have an opinion—but don't actually *care* to know about all the hard work I've put in over the years. These people make me feel less, that—because I'm both a parent and a writer, because I'm writing so little—clearly, I'm not a *professional* writer.

At least, not to them.

And okay, maybe they don't *actually* mean that, but it feels that way to me. When they compare their little side project to all the hard work, patience, practice, and money I've put into my writing for over a decade now, how can it not feel like anything but them belittling my work? That this small amount they've done equals all I've done and put into my writing?

Those conversations infuriate me because they *can* make me feel this this way, but also because there's nothing I can physically do to change my situation, to write more, to make more money.

I mean, I've got a pretty close eye on my critical voice these days and on when/if I can even write. And, I'm not saying that critical voice hasn't taken advantage of my exhausted, crazy-tired state and convinced me to not write at times... but you know, I'm doing my best.

My best to write. To write and still have fun. I do what I can, when I can and I'm proud of it. Proud of what I've accomplished.

But my life now, my goal to be an amazing and supportive parent, but also to somehow pursue being a professional writer... means I *can't* produce more stories.

Not now, anyway.

Honestly, what I should do is stop being so damn polite to those people and tell them exactly how I feel and where they can go stuff themselves and their opinions...

Or at least let them know how much their words, even innocent ones, hurt.

But I am polite person and being assertive is one of my own personal works-in-progress. And truly, I have enough dealing with family and haven't the time or energy to take on these hobby-writers and friends with opinions.

Which takes me back to the beginning of this blog post... I truly *love* to talk about writing. And publishing. And learning. I mean, I get tons of energy just from sharing this writing thing I love so much, and wow, having a conversation and connecting with someone above the age of three??

Seriously, I'm all in.

But this is also not a conversation I can have with just anyone because so few people understand this professional, independent writing field (as I learned a few weeks ago and which spurred this whole topic).

I now know I must protect my writing, especially the sloooow progress I make these days. Protect it—and defend it.

Somehow.

I'm still working out the logistics of that one, but I will. Through trial and error, most likely. (Huh... kinda like being a parent.)

For now though, while I figure this out, I'm going to save the writing talks and trials of being a parent-writer for people who get it or even just people who are supportive and cheer me on.

Writing isn't hard work. Actually, making stories up and seeing characters literally jump out your fingertips is pretty amazing. And *fun*.

What's hard is the dedication, patience, and practice.

What's even harder is when you've got kids who, not kidding, have a sixth sense for when I'm trying to write. Who don't care that it's my half hour of writing time and Daddy's on kid-duty.

So, really, the last thing I need is someone else's opinion or judgment mucking things up.

I've got a hard enough job figuring this out.

And when those people dismiss me, dismiss my writing, dismiss the effort *my whole family* has made to provide me with this small amount of time to write, I'm going to remember what all those professional writers told me...

"I can't believe how much you've done."

And they're right.

Because, seriously, I think I'm doing a fine-ass job of it. Four hours of broken sleep, a teething baby, a three-year-old who's a late-talker, and somehow I finished a short story I started three months ago (it's also nowhere near being called "short").

I call that success; maybe not by others' standards, but by mine. I might not be producing a novel a month, but I'm writing.

And honestly, that's all that matters.

That, and seeing how quickly my kids are growing up... and enjoying every moment of it.

(Well, enjoying it *most* of the time... I'm still in desperate need of a good, good night's sleep. Not to mention Eric's crawling phase has *Begun* which is its own whirl wind of fun with him constantly on the move.)

HOW FLEXIBLE ARE YOU?

August 28, 2015
Kate, 3 years
Eric, 8 months

Parenting means constant change. Going with the flow. Doing the best you can in each moment. Oh... and not having a brain-melting, panic-induced sweat because the Plans Changed.
  (As a parent-writer, you'll need flexibility... a lot of it.)

When I'm talking about flexibility, I'm not talking about whether or not you can touch your toes or do a good upward dog pose in yoga. I'm talking about how well you can (or can't) go with the flow. How you change plans, how you adjust.

Oh—and not have a complete brain-melt or a stressed-out, panic-induced sweat because The Plans Changed.

In many ways, that about sums up parenting.

(The constantly changing part, not the stress part—though there are definitely days when we get our fair share... or not so fair share... of stress.)

The first time I came across this idea was when I used to train for Kung Fu. (Most people don't know this, but polite, quiet, understanding me is also a black belt.) The first philosophy I was taught (and about the only one I remember) back when I was a baby white-belt was about being flexible, to be strong, but bendable. To not be brittle and dead. Sure, this concept relates to the physical function of Kung Fu and body movement and all that jazz, but I've continued to see the direct correlation to other aspects of my life throughout my life, especially in both writing and parenting.

Certainly to parenting.

Honestly, I think flexibility should be labeled one of the Virtues of Parenting.

So much of my life revolves around being flexible and it's the days where I can't be flexible—when I'm crazy exhausted with no sleep and appointments that actually require me to be at a certain place *AND* on time—when I feel the most stress.

Those are days when I end up calling my super-important support network and ask, "Is it to early for wine?"

Or chocolate.

Or ice cream.

When I'm not flexible, I become more controlling and the more I try to control my kids, especially Kate... well, let's just say the crazier my life becomes... and just as important, the unhappier Kate is.

Me, too, quite frankly.

That control aspect is huge and the longer I'm a parent, the more I'm around other parents, the clearer this becomes. From a friend who tried to control her baby's nap and feeding schedule to the parents at the park. I mean, seriously. Kids climb up slides, parents. Let them. That's what kids do. Leave 'em be and let them figure it out. You'll be surprised just how careful the ones going down actually are —and the kids going up? Yeah, they think it's GREAT fun to have someone 'crash' into them.

Even when those accidents happen, when kids get bumped and the tears come, there's so much learning in that moment, learning that goes beyond the need to 'always' be 'safe.'

What I find too in those moments, when kids are being kids and climbing up the slide backwards or purposefully bumping into each other on the slide, like they're one giant dog-pile of toes and pigtails... those same kids are also laughing. They're happy. Even this tall, 8-year-old boy who's holding Kate carefully as they reach the bottom (and after he's 'crashed' into her, too) because he innately understands she's smaller and needs protecting.

This is part of their children's play, their world. Not mine.

And I'm sitting back and just observing. Enjoying. Watching. Seeing if I'm needed by Kate... or not. I watch as one angry, older dad is clearly looking around for me to reprimand Kate for again ignoring his demands that she not climb up the slide and go around like she's 'supposed to.' This dad finally gives up trying to find me, trying to control Kate, and stomps away while at the same time he's completely missed the complexity and the joy of that moment, of these kids being kids.

His need for control and the anger that came when he wasn't listened to —why was any of that needed?

I'm going to leave this park whole and happy and full of joy and he won't.

I think it's this idea, to live my life as a more flexible person, that's making me a better parent. I'm not perfect (see the above list that could and *does* require chocolate), but I'm trying. I'm learning. It's something Kate taught me. I can either listen to her cues, her moods, or I can fight her. Every. Inch. Of. The. Way.

That's not to say Kate runs the show or we never do things she doesn't like, but we usually find a middle ground. If I see how tired she is—and since I know her I also know the 'tired' will turn into massive misbehaving—I'll change the plans; we'll go to a park instead of errand shopping.

Let's face it, as parents we genuinely *want* our kids to be happy. Oftentimes happy means reading our kids and their moods, assessing the situation, and setting up a situation that leads to happiness. (On the flipside though, if you wait for a 'perfect' situation, you may never get out of the house.)

But truly, nothing warms my heart more than my kids and their giant, whole-face smiles.

You know the kind... the *smile* that's all joy, all love, all happy... well... smile.

I naturally want to change and adjust our circumstances and lives to make those smiles a bit easier to shine.

And, no surprise, this same idea holds true for me and my writing. Having rigid, difficult-to-meet goals means stress. Telling myself to write every day without fail at this point in my life will lead to massive failure. And unhappiness. And stress. Telling myself to write even one short story a month will do that as well.

I'll feel stress because I won't/can't hit the goals, because I'll fail, by choosing not to write at my special allocated, carved-out time means I'm not serious about being a professional writer.

It's a real slippery slope.

The more stress I feel, the more negativity I put on my writing, the more I'm ensuring I *will* fail.

But if I change that mindset, just shift it, even a little bit...

I can find success. Even if it's small.

Just the other day, while crazy-tired and looking at my writing time, I *knew* I couldn't write for an hour. Instead of giving up, tossing in the towel for that day, I stopped and asked myself, "Can you write for fifteen minutes?"

The answer was yes.

I could do that.

And I did.

Getting in that writing, that very small snippet which didn't even reach 200 words, made all the difference. Instead of being cranky all day, I was recharged and happier. I was a more whole person (though still tired) and a better parent. I allowed myself to be flexible with what life was throwing me and because I was flexible, I found success.

It was a teensy, tiny success, but that's how I finally finished a story I'd been writing for months. It was only the second one I'd written since Eric was born, but I did it. I wrote this story thirty minutes here and there, sometimes with a one- or two-week break in between sessions. But, I did it. It's no longer a short story either as it's coming in at 12,000 words.

But because I was flexible, *mentally* flexible, and allowed myself to say, "No, today's not a good day to write," it took away all the extra stress. It allowed my writing to be my fun, enjoyable time. It allowed me to finish one story, and like today, to start on another.

As parents, we definitely need to roll with life's punches and surprises because our kids throw them at us daily (or, on a really bad day, hourly). Just the other day I knew I couldn't even squeeze in my fifteen minutes because the kids wouldn't let me. It was one of those 'every time you sit down they're going to cry or whine or need help,' and if I'd tried to write, I'd have end up frustrated and mad.

Instead I just said, "Okay. Not writing today."

And that's okay too.

If you stay rigid against all the surprises kids like to hand out, it's just going to wear you down. It's going to make you unhappy and frustrated and angry, and once you're down that road it's hard to pick yourself up and do an about-face (trust me, I'm very much speaking from experience here).

But you know, it's okay to have those days too.

No one's perfect, especially us parents.

We need to forgive ourselves for the short tempers or when our minds are on the never-ending lists and we forget to take a moment to simply be with our kids. If I look back at my weekly writing logs and see dozens of blank pages.

It's okay.

That's another part of being flexible. Just accepting and moving forward. Try to do better tomorrow. To do the best that you can in each moment. Little bit by little bit.

The same is true about touching your toes and stretching. You need to practice pushing those muscles to stretch a little bit further, to get a little bit more flexible. The more you practice, the better you get. And the better you get, the happier you'll find yourself.

And everyone likes a happier parent.

Especially our kids.

HOW TO SURVIVE THE ROUGH (EARLY) YEARS... AND KEEP WRITING

September 20, 2015
Kate, 3 years
Eric, 9 months

Some hard-learned tips to hold your perspective, stay sane, and keep your writing going. And oh, having fun.

This idea—of being a parent-writer—is pretty much the core of why I'm even doing this blog. In a way, you're all seeing my trial-and-error process as I figure this thing out—and it's definitely been a hit-or-miss process. But at the end of the day (so far, anyway) I'm proud of where I'm at and what I've done (most days).

The truth is this is where my life is Right Now—and I'm totally in survival mode.

So much of what I do, day to day, is still being handled on autopilot. And you know what? That's okay.

Of course, there are times when I need to step back and look at what I've had (or still have) on my plate. I need perspective and a reminder for all the things I *want to do* and all the reasons *I can't*.

At least for right now.

And you know, it *has* been a crazy year. From a rough end to an otherwise normal pregnancy, with my needing a C-section and the oh-joys of recovering from that—not to mention the normal transition of going from one kid to two and how the oldest didn't exactly have a say-so in gaining a brother. Then there was learning that Kate was a late-talker and how the medical community freaked out with their doom-and-gloom evaluations. To the here and now where I'm in a better, happier place...

I just haven't slept in four months (thanks, baby Eric and your stupid, nonstop teething—but hey we're *almost* there—I think. I hope.).

Survival mode means doing what I can, when I can.

Survival mode means that I don't often take those moments to breathe, to reset, to really get down on the floor and connect with my kids... at least, not often enough.

Survival mode means this last bit of baby weight is hanging on because days are rough and sometimes *I Just Need Chocolate*.

I recently listened to a podcast, *In the Boat with Ben* (thank you to Irette Patterson for the heads-up!) and their first episode talked about surviving as a creative and being parents—a family which knows something about surviving because they've got six kids and they're both musicians and writers.

What really struck a chord with me was when the wife defined surviving as that time when she was so busy she couldn't take the time to connect with her kids. To be with them physically, to emotionally have her *whole* focus on them.

I love that definition because this emotional presence is one of the first things I drop in my parenting (right after patience) when things get hard and busy. When I'm in this survival mode I'm not present with my kids. I might be meeting their physical needs, but my mind and focus is elsewhere.

And hearing another parent talk about this, talk about this reality 'm so often living, eased my guilt. I'm not alone in this struggle—and neither are you. I'm not the only who, when I'm so busy, can't take a moment to reconnect and simply be with my kids. It's nice to know that right now, especially *right now*, I don't have to be a perfect parent.

(See my last post about trying to be perfect and always in control... how that perfection leads to madness, my parenting friends. Best to not go down that road as much as possible.)

This emotional presence is also extra challenging because I'm striving to be a different kind of parent than how my parents raised me. Not that I don't love my parents, not that I don't believe they did their best—they did. They did their best with what they knew. For me as a parent, I'm shifting my idea of what parenting is—and what I believe it should look like. I'm moving from a reward-and-punishment type of parenting to one of support and understanding. To setting boundaries, yes, but at the same time giving my kids the freedom to learn how they want to learn, to trust in them and that they know exactly what they need. I'm teaching my kids principles to live life rather than to live by a never-ending list of rules.

All of that takes patience and energy, especially when it comes to rewiring my own childhood experiences, experiences I didn't know were hiding in my memory until certain words came out of my mouth or were reflected in how I reacted (which was how I decided I didn't like this way of being and *I* was the one who needed to change).

Survival mode means writing when I can.

Just this week I looked at my fifteen-minute slot and saw that Kate was limit-testing and bouncing off walls and I knew trying to write would just lead to anger and frustration and tears. Probably from both of us. At that moment, on that day, my life situation wouldn't let me write.

And that's okay too.

I tried, I evaluated, and then I moved on.

But the next day I did write and in fact, got in thirty minutes.

It's not much, but it was something. Those little bite-sized bits of success will lead to one story, then another. Right now, in survival mode, that's all I can manage.

It's important to mention here that my life situation really dictates the *kinds* of stories I can write.

I have a big epic fantasy series that's (sort of) patiently waiting in limbo, but my brain can't handle the complexities, the over-arching plot and twists, the depth of world-building going on in there. Heck, I'm not willing to tackle a novel of any kind right now simply because the brain is running on empty.

It helps knowing this time, the hard physical and emotional demands, isn't forever. That when I look back over this five- or ten-year time period and the slow rate I'm producing new words, this time here, when my kids are young and require so much from me, is only going to be a tiny blip in my writing journey.

These years aren't going to matter for my writing and my productivity, not really. Not when I plan on writing until the day I physically and mentally can't.

It can be hard when I look at all the unfinished projects and barely started series. There's so much I want to do, to write (I won't even talk about the publishing side of this!). And it's hard to keep positive sometimes, to keep my life and what I *am* accomplishing in perspective.

But for the most part, I am.

Thanks to my own trial and error, and also to the help and advice I've gotten from other professional writers and parents. Here are four tips I've gathered and I'm sure they barely scratch the surface...

1. Look at each day, not at the big, giant picture.

Focus on the small successes, the tiny steps forward. It's a heck of a lot easier to stay positive that way.

2. Recognize you are in a different place from other writers.

You know those types, the ones who are writing and putting out book after book, making one short story sale after another. Right now, your primary job is getting through the parenthood trenches. That means your focus is on patience, understanding, love, and oh, more patience. (Your friends are also probably sleeping a heck of a lot more than you, so cut yourself and your creative brain some slack. Brain needs rest to do its thing.)

3. Read for pleasure.

If you can read, if you can switch off the parenting-brain and lose yourself in a good book, chances are you're ready to start writing. Another good sign is if you're dreaming up stories when you do snag some sleep. Do the smart thing and jump on that energy. Who knows how long it's going to last?

(Translation: How long before your kids shake things up again. Which they will. Soon.)

4. Have fun.

This is my favorite. Whenever I look at my writing and it feels like work, like it's this thing I needed to do back when I had a regular day job, I immediately hit the brakes. I'm not writing because it's work. I'm writing because I love it. It's fun. I get to go and make up these cool worlds and cool characters who, when my subconscious is going strong, do things that surprise even me!

It's those surprises, it's that *fun,* which keeps me coming back. Keeps me writing through these early parenting years. Even now with two small kids, too much coffee, and not nearly enough sleep.

But here I am, somehow, still going strong.

TRUST YOURSELF. TRUST YOUR CHILD.

September 21, 2015
Kate, 3 years
Eric, 9 months

Trust in yourself as a parent, even when experts or friends might tell you otherwise. Trust that you know your child best, especially when they can't speak for themselves.

This is another of my posts of my shifting mindset as a parent, of slowly coming into my own place... and frankly into my own power.

No one knows your child better than you.

Not your friend with kids similar ages to yours. Not relatives who see your child a handful of times per year (and usually in giant-sized group settings). Certainly not all those medical experts with fancy degrees and titles that spend anywhere from ten minutes to an hour and think they 'know' your child. Oh, and let's not forget those fancy checklists of symptoms where at one point you could say 'yes' to almost everything (because all toddlers do them *at some point).*

You are the expert on your child.

No one but you.

You see your child in the morning when she throws opens your bedroom door, worn and loved stuffed bunny in hand, to drag you downstairs for the start of another day. You see the smile and the greeting. You see her figuring out a puzzle she's never seen before, one piece at a time. You see her gentle touch as she strokes her baby brother's head, and again, smiles at you as if to say, "This is my brother."

There's love there. And understanding.

Without saying a single word.

As a parent, you know *your* child. You know it in your gut when they're acting a bit 'off' and then the next morning they wake up with a runny nose. You know when they're uncomfortable and unsure because they tell you in a hundred different ways—ways that you can't write out on a checklist to give to the babysitter.

You just *know.* You've been around them for so long, are so attuned to them, listening and helping them.

And because you know your child so well, as much as a person can without actually *being* that other person, you know when something's 'wrong.'

You get that sense, that little niggly warning bell in your tummy because you're a parent, a damned good and loving parent.

When you *don't* get that sense, when the warning light doesn't go off but everyone else might say differently?

Trust yourself.

Trust yourself as a parent; trust what you feel.

Trust in your child.

My warning bells and intuition never went off with Kate, especially with her not talking. Sure there was a speech delay, but in our quiet, mellow home containing three introverts, we were okay with that. We preferred it. It was always Kate's nature to be quieter than most kids. We were okay with letting her speech come at her own time and pace.

We trusted her then. We trust her now.

We also trusted our intuition as parents that said, "Don't push."

Our intuition is still saying the same thing, probably even louder since we started the at-home speech therapy. I can literally see Kate putting the pieces of language together, bit-by-bit. Working and trusting the words. It's a slow process, but it's there.

It was there for Kate. It'll be there for your child, too, but you have to look for it...

And when you do see it—when you see all the little successes, all the inching forward she's doing—you know that this *is* happening, but at *her* pace.

It can't be pushed or rushed or forced.

Trust in the process and in your child.

Which makes life all the more challenging when other people burst in on your lives—on your happiness, on your sense of peace and trust in your child—with their own opinions. I want to tell them all, from friends to our pediatrician with her checklist and stack of referrals, to mind their own damn business.

I know my kid. Mine.

If it was your kid or heck, even if it was Eric, we'd be doing things differently. We'd be on a different path because Each. Child. Is. Different. They require a different touch and a different approach and a different understanding.

Some people will say, or hint, that we're blind because we're parents.

I say bullshit.

As parents, we *know*. We know because we are so attuned to to our children. We know because we love them.

It's taken me a good two weeks to process my emotions and thoughts after seeing Kate's pediatrician for her three-year checkup. The visit wasn't terrible, not as bad as it could have gone, but I left with a sense of frustration. Frustration with how the doctor kept pushing for a follow-up appointment with the neurologist. How the doctor repeatedly commented on how social Kate was acting, the eye contact, the 'showing' me the tuning fork the doctor let her play with (all of which are *good* signs). And then the doctor saying, "Well, she's severely speech delayed."

No shit, Doc.

It was later I realized her response was because *she* didn't know what was going on. She didn't know what was 'wrong' with Kate because Kate didn't (and does *not*) fit the checklist for autism—

Except for not talking.

Except for her not being attentive or responsive if she doesn't care for who you are as a human being because—guess what?—she can sense insincerity, she can sense kindness. Can I really blame her for not wanting to interact with someone like that? As an adult, *I* do this same thing.

(We won't even mention how there are in fact a whole bunch of kids like Kate, kids who are late-talkers, who can have different language disorders that are in no way linked with autism, but this particular doctor wasn't impressed or interested when I shared this with her.)

The doctor repeatedly ignored what I had to say about Kate, about the progress she was making with speech therapy and how we wanted to go at her pace.

She ignored me, the mother and expert on *this* child.

Instead she wanted me to see some other medical expert that, as a family, we had already decided wasn't right for Kate.

This isn't to say that seeing a neurologist is bad or not a good choice for you or your family, but it's not right for *us* at this *time* (and frankly we'd already done it once and received no satisfactory answers).

For one, Kate is making progress, but it's slow and at her own pace. We trust in that.

Also, we are not going to do any testing, which is about all the neurologist could do at this point with Kate. So, no. I'm not okay getting an MRI for my 3-year-old, not when I feel in my gut and heart there's nothing serious to warrant such a test. My Kate, who wouldn't understand what was going on, or why, and how she shouldn't be scared as they stick her in the metal tube and ask her to sit there, nice and calm...

No.

For us there's no rush to get Kate 'school ready' because we've chosen a different path for this as well.

As parents, we looked at our family, our values, and made decisions.

Those decisions made it even more upsetting to hear the opinions of a close friend in regards to Kate and our choices... and fighting me on those choices. While my friend's opinions were mostly supportive and encouraging, that didn't make it hurt any less. She argued with me about how helpful a diagnosis could be, even though we're not going through our health insurance or the school system where special education services could be helpful (not to mention how a mental illness, misdiagnosis or not, can stay with the child for the rest of their life). My friend kept pushing and telling me how a neurologist could see if/where in the brain the motor issues might be occurring... even though I told her, repeatedly, no testing (she finally shut up when I mentioned the MRI).

My point with all this is simple—we didn't come to any of our decisions lightly. We evaluated, we researched, we talked it over, and most importantly, we decided to trust in our parent-sense and in Kate.

These are our decisions, for our Kate.

Your decisions can, and will, be different... and they *should* be.

We've chosen not to follow up with our neurologist, who may or may not be supportive of what we want as parents. Instead, we've found her a phenomenal speech therapist, are paying quite a few pennies out-of-pocket, because Kate means that much to us.

And, we're reaching out to known experts in late-talking children (I *highly* recommend Stephen Camarata's, "*Late-Talking Children: A Stage or Symptom?*" or even speaking with his wife, Mary Camarata who has her own private practice, latetalkersconsulting.com). These are people we've found we can trust and help guide as further.

People who are on our side, as parents.

As parents, we're not powerless. I can choose to find another pediatrician (an option that is definitely on the table). I can choose to see this 'friend' less or not at all.

Right now, I need people who are 100% on my team. People who trust me, as a parent, to know my child best.

Frankly, I've worked too hard to get to this place. I'm happy. I have a sense of peace and hope for the future. I'm not living in worry and missing Kate growing up or even Eric. Because that's what happens if you let the worry and fear control you. You miss it. And these are times you will never get back.

Those first couple of months—when I was fighting through the system of early intervention and insurance, trying to come to grips with what the 'experts' were telling me versus what I knew of my child—those months are gone. The memories wiped clean, like I have this big gaping hole. And it isn't just memories of Kate that are missing, but of Eric, too.

I'll never get that time back.

So now, I'm choosing to live in trust. In myself. In Kate.

She will talk.

I have no doubt of this. I know this with my entire being. Because I'm a parent. Because I'm *her* mother.

And I'm going to trust in that.

Always.

TAKING RISKS

September 28, 2015
Kate, 3 years
Eric, 9 months

Taking risks as a parent and as a writer... and what you gain when you find your way through all that fear and uncertainty.

Are you afraid to take chances? Are you afraid to step outside the normal, well-trodden path that's been declared 'safe' by parents, friends, and pretty much all of society? Afraid to take a risk on a career or a life choice that makes you happy... but one you might possibly fail at?

Risks are everywhere.

Everywhere.

When I take a step back and look at my own life, I'm amazed at all the risks I'm taking. In my choice as a professional fiction writer, in our decision to homeschool our children in a child-led learning approach instead of the traditional school system, even in our choice to follow Kate's lead and trust in her own, very unique, language development.

Each of those decisions, in one way or another, pose risks.

They're risks because we don't know how they'll turn out. We can't look at the people who've gone before us and know the outcome (truth be told, even when you stay on the 'safe' path there's no guarantee it'll all work out... especially as you expected). But when you try something different, when you do something outside the norm, it feels like there's this extra pressure on you.

Fear that's ready to hold you down, to keep you from taking a chance... or keep you from taking that chance in the first place and seeing what happens.

It's so easy to give into that fear.

Easy because there are no assurances. There's not even the *illusion* of assurances.

I mean, sure, we have our feelings, our gut sense that all choices we're making as parents will work out. And even if they don't work out in the way we expect, we have the ability to adjust and change to suit the new situation.

But we don't *know* if this journey will be okay; we don't *know* how everything will look when we come out the other side.

Not for sure, anyway.

And all those risks I mentioned earlier? My fiction career, homeschooling, Kate's language path? Those are all Big Deal Risks. Risks that are tied not only to my happiness as a person, but to my children and their happiness and long-term well-being. But—and this is important—the risks are actually mitigated. No, I can't break out some percentage or average of success versus failure (Sean's the numbers guy in the family), but I can say with certainty the risks are minor.

Why?

Because I took the initiative and educated myself. I've researched, met with others who *are* on these different paths, thought and discussed the choices as a family, tried to see what our future might look like.

And then we came to our decisions, chose those 'risks.'

In terms of our alternative to traditional schooling, I found books from experts of all walks of life, one was from a psychologist, Peter Gray. Another a tribal elder teaching hardcore survivalists out in Wisconsin. Yet another were the dozens of homeschooling families I met and connected with at a local conference, many who are now supporting me and guiding me and showing me there *is* another way of doing things.

Another way our kids can learn.

All this is coming from different experts and from different walks of life, yet each are talking about the same thing:

Trust in your children, trust in how they learn and how they love to learn.

And that's encouraging to me enough to give this alternative to traditional schooling and learning a shot, to take this risk and see what happens. If I mention our homeschool choice to friends or even passing strangers, they have their own opinions and they (often) see what we're doing as a huge risk, that we're taking a gamble on my kids' future.

I don't agree with that assessment.

I've gone and done a butt-load of learning (in fact, I still am), but I especially don't agree when I'm seeing the growth and learning already taking place in Kate. Just watching her playing and being a little kid, doing stuff that comes naturally to three-year-olds, late-talking or not, all the learning and the curiosity... it's right there. Her desire to play with other kids and learn from them, kids of all ages, and even much older adults.

But to get this far, I had to take a risk. I had to build a new awareness of Kate, and then I had to trust in her.

Trust.

In my three-year-old who doesn't even talk.

Most people would call me crazy. You might even think that as you're reading this, and that's okay. I mean, everyone has a right to their opinion and their beliefs. Just know that this choice we made, as a family, didn't come lightly. And even though I trust in Kate (am still learning in many cases) doesn't mean she gets to run wild and rush off into traffic (here comes that awareness I was talking about). Instead I'm giving her the lead and—as needed—teaching and guiding her from there (don't run into the street even if it looks chill).

I've seen this idea, of taking risks and trusting in the outcome, from the other side... not just as a parent, but as an entrepreneur and even a fiction writer.

First off, being an entrepreneur, of any size, shape, or color, means *Risk*. I mean, serious risk. If you think you want to start your own company, be your own boss in whatever field you choose, you better have the chops to take risks... and be okay with the bumps along the way. Or straight-up, nose-dive failures.

Being an entrepreneur means stepping off the beaten path.

You might fail.

You probably will.

The difference is in how you pick yourself up, dust yourself off, learn from those mistakes, and keep going. One day Sean might want to start his own game company, be his own boss and make the kinds of games he likes, but he understands that it's a risk. Hence the 'one day' part... when our kids are grown and we're ready to handle an extra dose of uncertainty and constant change. He also knows that anyone he partners with has to be prepared for those risks, partners that need to be okay with the idea of trying and failing and trying again.

Not everyone is cut out for that kind of life, and that's okay too.

For others, it's a gradual process, sort of like how I'm learning to trust in my kids and their own learning.

Heck, all I need to do is look at my life to see the risks I've taken and the moments I've let slip by (whether on purpose or not). It was many years before I was ready to take the plunge and quit my day job to be a full-time writer. Even though we had Sean's income supporting us, it was still the scariest thing I've ever done in my life. When we decided to move to Seattle and then back down again to

Los Angeles, that was scary as well. In some ways we were ready to make this happen and in others, there was still a great deal of fear and uncertainly.

Well, there's *always* uncertainty and then there's that little, fearful voice asking, "Am I making the right choice?"

The cool thing about taking risks is even if it doesn't work out, you're already on a different path with a different set of choices than if you hadn't taken that risk. Choices that you wouldn't now have if you hadn't jumped into the deep end.

You have new opportunities *because* you stepped off the beaten path.

I think that's one reason why risks don't scare me as much as they do other people (at least, so I've found). First off, I'm really not a leap-first kinda gal. I really do take my time to reach a decision, and once I'm done, I'm all-in. I might still be scared and nervous, like when I decided to quit the day job, but there was no hesitation when that scared voice in me asked, "Is this the right choice?"

The answer was a definite "Yes."

Life really is about risks. And if you want to be a fiction writer?

Oh, yeah. Risks. Everywhere.

A risk in trusting yourself, trusting that you will continue to improve with each story, that you will one day make a living if you just keep at it, keep striving, keep learning. Even in your stories themselves there must be risk....

Your stories need to be different and unique. They need to be stories that come from you and ones that *no one else can write*.

Trying something new, something different?

You betcha, that's a risk.

Whenever I attend an Oregon Coast workshop, especially the Anthology one, I see this firsthand. Every time. A room of fifty professional, *amazing* writers, but it's the stories that are different, that connect, that try something outside the box, that sell.

Those are always the stories that weren't the 'low-hanging fruit' ideas (the first idea or two that come to mind while ten other writers had the exact same idea). The stories that sold were the ones that didn't fit in a box, that were unique and could only come from that writer and their own unique voice.

Heck, this is the exact same message being said by the superstar coaches on the TV show, *The Voice*. And these coaches continually say it, again and again, season after season.

Be different.

Be unique.

Take risks.

I'm doing my best to incorporate this into my life, into my writing, and into the choices I'm making as a parent. Even choosing to write despite having my very young kids (and still zero sleep) is a risk of sorts because I probably won't succeed. And yet... I also know it's the right choice.

There will be mistakes and failures along the way. There will be stories that didn't work because my brain was too distracted with being a parent (the jury's still out on the online writing workshop I'm taking right now), but still, it feels right.

For me, 'feeling right' means happiness. It means my personal compass is pointing in the right direction.

Even if I don't know where I will end up.

Even if I don't know where we'll be in five years or even next month.

That's all okay because we're continuing to learn, continuing to find our path as a family, and as a family, continuing to take risks.

And that's just part of life isn't it?

Honestly, I think it's a good path to be on. It's mine, and no one else's.

TO WRITE, OR NOT TO WRITE

October 19, 2015
Kate, 3 years
Eric, 10 months

The reality of parenting young kids and the need to write... Or just giving it a shot and seeing what happens.

When you have very small, very young kids, your waking hours are focused on them (and to be very honest, even the hours when you're supposed to be asleep). That's really the name of the game; it's a stage in parenthood that just *IS*.

Babies are born. They're these helpless, mewing, beautiful little creatures that need constant help, constant love and bonding, and thank God, constantly napping. (Though there are some of you gifted with babies who defy sleep as much as humanly possible and I hope for your sakes they're still beautiful mewing little creatures!)

As our kids slowly move out of babyhood, what you thought was hard and a ton of work, becomes laughable in hindsight. Because man, those toddlers. Sure there might be no diapers to change, but now there's cleaning up potty accidents on the couch, being constantly alert around cars, traffic, turtles crossing the road because you *know* your kid is gonna bolt the second your attention shifts. Not to mention parents have the epic responsibility of guiding our kids to be kind, caring, and independent little thinkers.

And through all this you still want to keep writing. You know, doing that special thing that gets your whole being to light up in joy like a Christmas tree because *you love telling stories.*

So... what do you do?

Do you give writing a try? Or do you toss your hands up and say, "I'll try again in five years when I'm sleeping again?"

This was a question I'd asked myself long before I was pregnant with Kate and I struggled with it long after she was born (and especially during the stage when she realized that she didn't need to listen to everything I told her).

It's an even harder question now that I have two kids. I mean, since I'm a stay-at-home mom (formerly a full-time writer), the hours of quiet time, when it's just me and my stories...

Yeah. They don't exist anymore. And I know, beyond a doubt, that I do my best work as a writer when I'm *not* the one currently watching the kids.

No kids around me means that my constant, hyper-aware parenting brain can *actually* switch off and I can lose myself in the story. I can actually *hear* my characters peek their heads out from under the rock or bridge they've been hiding under, waiting for the Small-Children-All-Clear sign.

Now I can get writing done with Kate around. I'm usually in an adjacent room and she's quietly engaged in some Pixar movie or playing on the iPad or with her toys.

And seriously... no judging, please. Yes, I let my kid watch movies or play with screens. Me having this quiet time in the mornings with my coffee and my writing makes me a better person. I'm a better *parent* when I write. I'm happier, I'm calmer, I'm more patient. (Not to mention that I'm constantly around screens and using screens, especially with the writing, and I'm very aware of that double-standard of that 'she can't be on screens' but 'I can.')

So, Kate and I had this little routine in the morning with just us and it was going along fine...

Until Eric was born.

Now, there's this strange quirk concerning me and my babies (or, maybe not so strange; perhaps it's a really smart evolutionary coding by Mother Nature). See, when the baby is awake and near me, I cannot write.

I just... Can't Do It.

It's like my parenting senses are on super-charge power and I can't get anywhere near my creative voice to tell a story. Heck, I can't even escape into a book and lose myself in someone else's story.

And yet... I still need to write. Somehow. In some way.

Writing is a part of me. It makes me happy, makes me a better and more loving person. Too bad my kids can't time their naps so I can get the snippet of quiet that I need.

While I've been questioning the "how" of writing around young kids (always knowing that I would write, but never how much or when or where), this very topic was brought up on a podcast produced by two parents, both creative entrepreneurs, with six kids.

Their answer to this question was simply this: don't try.

My takeaway from that podcast was they do their best work when they're not caring for their kids, that writing will take longer if the kids are around and they, as parents, are more prone to losing their patience. They're also not focused on being with the kids and enjoying them in the moment. Instead their mind is on the unfinished, interrupted project.

I've been going back and forth about their answer because honestly, they're not *wrong*.

I mean, it's all true.

But here's my dilemma: I *need* to write.

And ironically, as I try and write this blog, I've got Kate climbing all over me like I'm her personal jungle gym. Apparently, she missed me during the two hours Sean and I were gone on a few-and-far-between lunch date.

Even though I've got my three-year-old climbing over me, distracting me, I still *need* to do this. This is a blog post about a question I need to answer. Or think through more...

Yet again.

But I'm not angry with Kate for the distraction. She missed me. Now she wants to play with me while I sit on the couch. I'm keeping her needs in mind—my needs, too. At this stage in my learning and growing as both a parent and a writer, I'm doing it without the anger and frustration.

Because *not* writing isn't an answer. Believe me when I say I'm aware of any free time or in-between time during our days. I've worked on assignments on a laptop in the car while both kids were napping. Taken my notebook to the park where I jot down a few sentences in between glances to see where Kate's gotten herself to. The time I have to myself is incredibly limited. Sure, I can wake up early and get in some writing, and I do—when I can. But sleep is even more precious than writing and these days cutting down on sleep isn't an option either.

So... do I write? Do I not write?

The ultimate answer, I think, is yes, I write. But it's more than just making up my mind to write. It's attitude. The attitude I have towards my writing. Do I see this as a job, one that I have to push myself and all those negative feelings aside to get to? If I do, then the answer is to not write that day. But if I'm able to see the writing as fun, as an enjoyable escape that I can go and play with... then that's the day to write. Because it's so important to keep the love and freedom and fun of writing prominent.

Sure I need to push myself to get in those fifteen minutes, but I know if and when I can, I always feel so, so much better.

And some days the answer is that I can't write. I honestly might be too tired or the kids are a handful or we've had a busy week and all I can do is just sit and breathe.

I think acknowledging this part of parenting is huge. I mean, all that I just mentioned isn't anything new to parents. All of that is part of the job (and the fun) of being a parent.

You've got to know yourself. Know how much life and parenting *you* can handle. It's going to be different than what I can handle—and that's okay too.

You've got to know, too, that writing around kids *is* distracting. If you choose to give it a go, be sure to breathe through the frustration when it builds (because it will), when the kids decide they suddenly need milk or food or water every thirty seconds (because they will).

While it's easier to write when the kids aren't around, I truly believe that my dedication to my writing is important. My kids are learning what my writing means. They're learning that I'm busy and that it is important to me. Yes, I can help them... but in a few minutes. I mean, yeah, Kate's still too young for this (asking her to wait while I'm nursing Eric usually ends in some form of crying and her believing I've utterly rejected her), but they are slowly building this awareness of my writing and what it means to me.

Another point is I'm going to homeschool them, so I'm certainly not going to put the writing on hold until some date long into the future just because I'm their primary caregiver and now education facilitator.

Which all comes back to me saying, "Yes, I am going to write."

I think this will be a different choice for different writers and the different seasons of parenthood. But more important than the question *if* you should write is *how*. How will you go about your writing life and with what kind of attitude? Are you aware of what's going on in your life each day, each moment? Are you okay when there are those moments when writing simply isn't an option?

As parents of young kids, unless we've got a babysitter or parent-helper or spouse who can squeeze in an extra hour during their regular work day... we don't have good writing "days" (and what I mean here is hours of uninterrupted writing). We might have good writing hours... or we might only have a good fifteen minutes of writing.

That's just part of it, I think. Get in what writing we can, do the best that we can, and at some point this novel or story we're tinkering with will be done. We'll have a novel or a short story finished. Or we'll have more practice in our craft because we've just finished another online workshop.

Or... you could have no writing done at all for years at a time.

That works for some writers. They just go away and focus on their family until the craziness of parenting and life settles and when they can, they come back to writing.

There's truthfully no right answer; there's only what works for you.

I'm not a big fan of waiting, either. Waiting means I'm not in control, that I'm letting some arbitrary time or life event decide when I get to start writing again. Honestly, that feels like the too-many years I wasted at an office job before finally following my passion as a full-time writer.

So, I'm not going to wait on the writing.

And instead of focusing on all the projects I want to do but can't, or all the time I want to be writing but am too busy caring for the kids, I'm going to focus on how much I love telling stories. How much I love seeing characters take shape and what adventures those characters are taking me on. I'm going to focus on sharing my writing with my children (along with the *act* of writing) instead of waiting until they're older or we have more help.

I'm going to write right now—when I can—and see where this journey as a writer, and a parent, takes me. Because really, it's already been a pretty cool journey so far and there were some stories I'd never have written if I hadn't been a parent.

I'd call that a win—even if the word counts are low these days—because every little glimmer of success counts when you're a parent-writer.

THE GREAT BATTLE:
UNCERTAINTY VS. JOY

November 2, 2015
Kate, 3 years
Eric, 11 months

Don't let fear and uncertainty stop the joy (and the journey) of parenting.

Fear—and especially uncertainty—can be a sneaky thing.

There's the grip-your-stomach-so-hard kind of fear. You know, the kind where you can barely breathe because your heart and soul are terrified for your child. That kind of fear, well, it's pretty obvious. But it's the *uncertainty* that can be tricky to identify.

Uncertainty can wiggle its way deep into you like a tree's big, long tap root. You might not even notice it at first. Maybe it's only a slight hesitation or a teeny, tiny voice that whispers, "Everything will be fine... Right??"

If you're not careful, this uncertainty can be even more dangerous than the obvious, terrifying fear I mentioned above.

Fear can be pretty darn obvious. Uncertainty on the other hand... not so much. And I'm sure—as many of you know—it doesn't take much for that wiggling, nagging voice to turn itself into fear. And when you're working with your child, especially when it comes to developmental delays or any challenge that requires us parents to have a peaceful, hopeful, kind mindset, *nothing* stops you faster than your fears.

Our kids aren't dumb. They *know* how we feel... which is why when you specifically tell them not to do something they straight-up look at you, smile, and do it anyway.

Right now, I'm battling a bunch of my own uncertainties. Why? Lots of reasons, but one is because it's November. No, it's not the big, giant holiday month that is December, but it's big enough for me... especially because it feels like a giant, ticking clock is over my head, striking its long tones as it gongs closer to midnight.

Why all this uncertainty?

Time and fear.

Time that I'm running out of (at least it feels like it is) and fear constantly asking and badgering. Am I doing enough? Am I a good enough parent?

Eric is nearly 11 months old. One more month and he officially won't be a baby anymore. That terrifies me. Terrifies me because it feels like all of his babyhood was a blur. Moments and smiles and laughter that I didn't take enough time for and I'll never get back. Entire moments when I was so down in my own dark fear, in my worries for Kate and her future and what our path forward would like, giant chunks of time are missing. Time I have no memory of. We've decided there won't be any more babies for our family, a decision Sean and I both feel is right for us. We're happy with the family we have now... but boy it's not making this moment, this loss of Eric being a baby, hurt any less. This grief that I'm feeling, any less real.

I know this whole year I've done the absolute best I could with the life I was given.

I have no regrets about decisions I've made or how, after an outing at the zoo or aquarium or several hours at Disneyland, I propped my kids up with toys and entertainment while I checked out to recharge my own, very depleted, introverted batteries. Every time I do this, take a needed moment for myself (especially lately as we move into the busy, busy holiday season, I've got that little voice asking, "Are you sure about this? Are you *sure* you want to check out and rest? Because, you know, you'll *never* get this time back."

I usually shut the voice up with a definitive, "Hell yes."

You see, while it's *so* important to play with my kids, to connect with them, I desperately need to watch my own energy levels. I've learned what I need to keep functioning, to be a somewhat patient and kind parent (and trust me, this was a trial and error process... mostly error). If my battery hits zero, it's not like I can call my mom or Sean and say, "Drop what you're doing. I need a break. Can you come over and make dinner? Put the kids to bed? Give 'em a bath to get the playground sand out of their hair because Kate thought it'd be super fun to go swimming in it?"

I *don't* have the option to call in the cavalry when I'm in need of a recharge.

Even though my reasons for tuning out, for choosing to sit quietly or check email instead of connecting with my kids is not only valid, it's *needed*, there's still that stupid, nagging voice of uncertainty trying to derail everything I've carefully built.

That fear that I'm not doing enough.

That I'm not good enough.

That I'm still missing *this*.

And it really, really hurts thinking that way. Thinking that I could have been giving them even more, thinking if I hadn't chosen to write a blog post or a short story or taken that online workshop, I would have been more *there* for them.

See how that uncertainty turned itself into fear?

Sly and tricky, that's what it is, and this whole month I've been second-guessing my choices.

Should I take this other workshop I signed up for? After all, I'm better prepared with scheduling and have babysitting set up. Should I bother writing?

And... here's a big change... should I drop Kate's speech therapy to once a week or—heaven forbid—simply trust in myself and the work she and I are doing together? Because while Kate enjoys *playing* with the speech therapist we're not actually seeing any progress with her and talking—certainly not for the unbelievable amount of money we're paying out of pocket. I'm seeing more success when *I* work with her, when *I'm* being coached on how best to be her speech partner.

(And my goodness is this one terrifying; I can feel that uncertainty hitting high, *high* into the parenting red zone for me.)

Then there's my little Eric, who's slowly morphed into my own crawling, climbing clock that follows me (and big sister) everywhere. A reminder of the time I've lost, time to stop, to stare into his eyes, time to just make him laugh. I don't want to lose any more time or joy. Except...

It's so easy to just pick up Eric and cart him around while I do shopping, errands, or laundry. Just pick him up and off we go, my mind always focused on the next task, the next item on my too-long list, constantly in the future or in the past and never where I am in each moment.

Part of why I feel this way, this constant questioning if I'm doing enough, if I'm a good enough mom is the product of our society where two people do the work of an entire tribe and somehow try to raise well-balanced, independent, kind children—which is our family situation (and that of many others). I can't change that and I'm totally doing my best, but boy, am I feeling the loss of that connection with both of my kids.

It's not helping that Eric's made my sleep these days a living nightmare. Not sleeping *really* makes everything *so* much more challenging.

Which is why I keep telling myself it's okay.

I'm trying to forgive myself for not being as patient or as 'there' as I want to be. I really am doing the best I can, and I'm making changes that are best for me and our family.

Each day I'm looking at where we are in terms of physical and mental abilities. Did Eric not sleep last night? Kate, too? Is everything inside me exhausted and ready to unravel at a moment's notice?

If yes...

Okay, then. Time to adjust. Let's nix that trip to the museum. Or Disneyland. I even made the difficult decision to rehome my blue-and-gold macaw, Timothy. It broke my heart, but it was the right decision for everyone—including him—and I have no regrets.

One of the reasons I needed to write this post was to get my own uncertainty out there. Sort of putting a big, fat label on that uncertainty—in neon, with blinking blights and a fog horn bellowing, "Hey! I see you."

I've found that when I talk about my fears, because that's what this uncertainty really is, it's almost like I have the power to get hold of it and wrestle it to the ground. Talking about my fears takes away their power, like I can finally open that locked door to find solutions or a better way of coping. Or shift my mind to see the positive in each moment and not just the scary, negative part.

Talking helps... at least, it does for me.

That's one of the big reasons I'm building a new support network around me. People who are supportive and understanding. People I can talk to who don't bring negative and toxic vibes into my life. They have a positive influence on me and help ground me when I've got all those uncertainties declaring war on my inner peace.

For you, dear parents, your support group will be different than mine—and it should be.

You've got a different life, a different family, a different path than mine, which is as it should be (and I do hope you're going out and building that right-kind-of-group-for-you because it makes a huge difference in getting through these parenting years).

I'm building support with other stay-at-home moms through the Moms Club. I've recently joined a local homeschool group, and I've got my writer network from the days of before-kids. I'm also taking the time to build a closer bond with my family and in-laws.

Granted, some of those relationships will bring the uncertainty roaring back in, but life can't all be perfect, and most of the time, I've had the opposite experience. I'm finding people who can support me and this different journey I'm on with my kids. I joined a Facebook group for parents of late-talking kids and that has helped me find, and really believe in, the sense of peace I have now with Kate and who *she* is. I have little fear about her future because I'm so confident in the choices we made and the path we're on together.

I'm more afraid of that ticking clock.

I'm afraid that if I take this next workshop, I won't have the energy to work with Kate, that I'll be too stressed about hitting my deadline instead of working one-on-one with her or just smiling and playing the roll ball game with Eric.

I'm afraid that I won't have the energy to be present and connect when my kids need me... when they *want* me. That I will continue to miss this joy that I should be feeling *right now*.

Just like I was completely missing the joy over Kate having her first true words. And that statement, right there, comes from that sneaky uncertainty worming its way in. I didn't even realize that's what it was, fear in disguise, until I talked with another mom who's had her own experience with delays.

I told this mom about Kate's saying, "Uh no!"

How Kate will then say those two words over and over again, dozens of times per day, and in context. Kate had never done this before. Never used words consistently and continuously.

My friend, upon hearing this story, exclaimed with the utmost joy, showing how excited and thrilled she was... for Kate, but also for me.

This friend had been there before, in a different way and a different circumstance with her daughter, but she *had* been there. She understood. She knew what I was going through.

This being *seen*... it took me by surprise.

Mostly, because she was right.

That moment *was* exciting. It *was* something that should break my heart with joy, bring me to the point of crying and laughing all at once... and though I enjoyed every time Kate said those words—I would smile and love and treasure her voice and how those words carried so many meanings—

I never felt that excitement my friend mentioned because I was too scared. I was scared, and I didn't even realize it.

It took some reflection to recognize that everything I was feeling was fear.

Fear.

Fear that Kate would say these words and then she'd tuck them away again. Fear that I wouldn't hear her voice and the many inflections and meanings she gave to those two small words.

Fear and uncertainty are crazy powerful and even me, who was pretty darn at peace with my life and where we were at, felt those moments, that uncertainty pretty hard.

I still do. Even now.

All I can do is try my best, change my mindset to not look at the fear, to look at the joy instead. That's what I wasn't fully embracing with Kate and her true words, the joy and trust that those words *were* there...

And that they wouldn't be going away.

The joy I felt when Eric crawled toward me, determined and smiling, because all he wants is his mommy. Joy when we play together and he laughs. Oh, his laugh.

Joy because I'm a parent, but I'm also me.

A new-to-homeschooling parent, a writer, and a woman who just went shopping and spent a ton of money on clothes because the baby weight was *gone* (and that was truly something worth celebrating over).

I know the struggle between fear and joy isn't going away.

I just lived it all over again right after writing this, when I began doubting myself and my ability to be Kate's partner on her language journey. I mean, I'm only a parent. I'm not an expert on language. I can't help her enough. I'm not good enough.

See? There's that doubt. That uncertainty. All that negative self-talk just desperately waiting to find any crack in my beliefs and my joy.

I might not be a speech pathologist, but I'm an expert on my kid.

No one knows her better than me and I need to trust in myself.

Trust in what my intuition is saying... which is that I can get more work done, more progress forward if I make a concentrated effort in our daily lives rather than trusting to Kate's private speech therapist. To move forward on our path, a path that looks different than anyone else's.

It's going to be a battle to keep myself looking forward, trusting, and believing... but I'm aware now. Aware of the uncertainty and fear.

And now that I'm aware I can do something about it, I can (hopefully) move closer to that joy I want so badly in my life. There will be days where I'll miss because I'm not perfect, and that's okay too. So long as I keep coming back to this place, this feeling, this trust.

Trust in the joy, in myself, and really, in my kids.

After all, if one thing doesn't work, I can reevaluate and try again. And again, and again, until I find something that works in every area of my life, in how I show up as a parent for Kate and Eric, but also how I show up as a writer and still remain true to *me*.

At least for the moment. Because everyone knows when it comes to kids nothing stays the same forever. Life always changes, and I'll find a way, somehow, to change with it. And keep smiling. At least, I'll try to and that's what matters most.

To simply try. And see what happens next.

WORKSHOPS, HOLIDAYS, AND TWO SMALL KIDS

December 1, 2015
Kate, 3 years
Eric, 1 year

Some tips on how to 'fit' it all in and still enjoy your writing, your kids, and yourself this holiday season.

I'm right smack-dab in the middle of a pretty darn advanced writing workshop and while I've had a few moments of panic—the usual oh-crap-I'm-never-gonna-get-this-done kinda feeling—for the most part the experience has been the opposite of what I'd expected. I haven't been stressed. I haven't squeezed in an assignment at the last hour, haven't eeked out that email right before midnight. And yes, I've still got the two kids and the never-ending house chores and required family feedings.

Somehow, I'm doing okay.

In fact, I'm doing pretty darn good.

Actually, I've mostly felt this tremendous excitement to be getting down into the depths of writing, to study books from absolute masters of storytelling like Stephen King and Lee Child (who so eloquently demonstrate how very much I have to learn... which I haven't a clue how I'm gonna make that happen any time this century... or at least until Kate starts driving... at which point that's a whole other stage of worry).

Somehow, though, I've carved out this time for myself. Somehow, the whole family's on board, giving me this chance to just lose myself and my thoughts to my craft.

Which translates to Sean graciously taking the kids while I lock myself in the office for two hours as I try to figure out the different assignments and afterwards he tells me, "If I was the stay-at-home dad, we'd only have had the one kid."

But you know, it feels *good* to take care of myself again.

And this might sound silly, but for me writing is just as important to my health and happiness as exercising or nutrition or even laughing. That's what writing is. It's a core piece of my own mental happiness and boy do I feel it when parenthood has forced me to shelve my writing for these long dry spells. Which is also okay, because this is what needs to happen. My main responsibility isn't being a writer, it's caring for and raising my two kids (who then give me fodder and a shitload of ideas whenever I get the quiet time to squeeze in some writing).

But... when I give the writing, the learning, a whole six weeks of intense focus?

Hot damn, I feel like I could climb a mountain.

Okay, not really, but it feels like just about anything is possible. And I've managed on only a couple hours of broken sleep and a stupid cold that's running its course through the whole family. And we've got that Thanksgiving thing, too. At our house no less.

Which I suppose brings up the question: how the heck am I doing all this?

I mean, I just found out that a bunch of people in my workshop didn't turn in the last assignment, and it was only a *study* assignment, not an actual writing one.

I think I only got three hours of sleep—*total* (being sick is so fun). Yet here I am, writing this blog post while simultaneously keeping an ear out for Eric, who's desperately trying to find a way to hot-wire the baby gate so he can open and climb up the tantalizing stairs while Kate works out her *My Little Pony* puzzle for the 100th time.

I haven't missed turning in a single assignment. Not for this workshop and not for the one I took in September either (also six weeks).

So... how did I do it? How can you do it?

This is definitely going to be different for each parent-writer out there, and it's definitely dependent on how old your kids are, but awareness is what you're striving for.

Awareness of your schedule, your kids and their temperament, and *your* temperament.

This is something I learned from an online workshop I took in September. Scheduling matters. It really, really does. And that's not to say I've gone and blocked out X-amount of hours for Wednesday or Friday, but taking a step back and really looking at my life, my family, it helped me to realize what was possible...

And what would send me over the edge into crazy-town.

And when you've got kids, you also need to be constantly aware when *they've* had too much because no one likes a crying, screaming, tantrum-throwing kid in the middle of a mile-long Costco line.

You see, before even *signing up* for this workshop, there were a couple of days when I looked at my schedule and knew I'd need help (Thanksgiving, anyone?), so I arranged for babysitting.

Also... I told a lot of people, "No."

I cancelled a Disneyland trip with Grandma, which was fine since Kate ended up with a fever and wicked cough that day. I also prioritized my outings with friends—should I go to our regular park date in the afternoon or on the morning outing instead, because that pumpkin pie ain't gonna bake itself. Not to mention I've decided to completely drop Kate's private speech therapist and am doing the brunt of the work myself (while being coached and trained by a speech pathologist I trust) because I didn't have enough going on, right?

So far, though, it's all working. The choices I've made are working. For now.

It helps too that I'm constantly learning—and I'm not just talking about writing here, but parenting.

I'm learning what's working and what isn't (like that beast called a 'schedule'). And my being flexible is huge. *HUGE*. If I wasn't flexible, yeah, if this wasn't my mindset, I could straight-up forget the workshop and any sort of writing altogether.

But I'm also asking for help from our family, and believe me, that's not something that comes naturally.

But I am—asking for help, that is. And I'm learning just how human I am (you know, *not* super mom). I've got my amazing 95-year-old grandma staying with us to help with Eric (boy, does she *love* playing with the baby!), washing dishes, and chopping vegetables (a huge lifesaver).

Heck, I've had people come over just so I could *nap*.

But the other thing I'm doing, the most important this, is being persistent.

And patient.

And willing to learn... which I guess is three things.

But persistence is key. Not kidding. I *am* going to keep at this. I *am* going to keep finding ways in my schedule to watch these instruction videos, to take notes, and I *am* going to ask (or beg) a family member to help.

Me and my writing aren't going anywhere.

Sure, there's that dusty time on the shelf while we adjusted to having Kid #2, and then the scare and worry over Kate not talking, but I've always found my way back to the writing and now... finally... I've found my way back to learning.

And like I said earlier, there is so *much* I have to learn and I can't wait to keep moving forward. Even if my forward is so much slower than everyone else's, but... I'll get there. And while it (often) feels like I'm barely getting the work done and there's another five (or ten) things left to do on my list, I'm forgetting the most important piece:

I'm awesome.

What I'm doing, caring for these kids, helping them learn and grow, spending three to five hours a week on this workshop while just getting back into something resembling sleep... that's impressive. So is finding the time to build new friendships for both me and the kids with our local homeschool group. And now being Kate's main partner on her speech journey.

I bring this up because I don't always see that. I don't always see the *accomplishments*.

Okay... I never do—unless someone points it out first because that's not how I was taught to see myself.

My writing mentor, Dean Wesley Smith, once told me how impressed he was that I'd stuck with the writing these past three years *and* that I'd kept it fun. Then, last Sunday, Sean told me the same thing.

He was impressed.

It's so easy to see all the things I can't do or can't get to and I've finally realized how important it is to see what I *can*. And I'm impressed, too. Really, really impressed. The fact that I'm giving myself the time and opportunity to study my craft and then to realize that... Wow! I guess I'm still a writer even with these two cuties and no sleep. In fact, I'm still growing, still improving my craft from when I got serious back in 2010... and that realization is so uplifting.

You see, right now, my job is to be a parent and a facilitator for my kids' learning and growth.

I'm not going toe-to-toe with other writers I'd started with (nor should I compare myself to them—which, to be honest, can be hard when the writing only comes in short bursts these days). Even though I'm a parent first, that doesn't mean I'm not a writer.

I am a writer even with the little bit I can do... and I'm getting better.

I'm still learning.

It might only be little bits like these blog posts, especially with family birthdays and Christmas right around the corner, but I'll take whatever I can get.

Or should I say, whatever I can make happen because it's only gonna come from me. The writing will only come from my initiative, my passion, my willingness to go and try and do my best... and then pick myself up when I fall down again.

And perhaps even more important—remembering to enjoy the time I have right now with my little family. The writing will always be there, but these moments, of Eric stuffing his face with his first Thanksgiving sweet potato or Kate practicing her newest word, "Hi..."

These moments are only going to happen once and I don't want to miss them.

And that makes all of this journey of parenting, of writing, feel so worthwhile.

Worth trying and seeing what I can do. I'm glad to give myself this patience and dedication instead of just putting the writing in a drawer until 'the time is right.'

Because the only time we *really* have is now.

WRITING THROUGH LIFE ROLLS

January 12, 2016
Kate, 3 years
Eric, 1 year.

Shift your focus from missed opportunities to what you can get done—right in this moment—especially as you look towards the New Year and everything (hopefully) you can accomplish.

If you want to be a parent and if you want to be a writer, a successful one (insert your own definition of success here), I think it's really important to acknowledge and accept where we each are in our lives —*and* in our children's lives.

There's only so much writing that can be done when our primary focus is our family. There's only so much sleep we can skip before, you know, we actually *need* sleep.

And as we all sadly know, there's certainly only so many hours in the day.

But sometimes (okay, often) it's not so easy to have this perspective. You need to actively look back on the road you've walked to see just how far you've come. I find this especially important at the end of the year, to look back and *really* see what I've accomplished, not just in terms of financial success but everything—including what was going on in my life. To be honest about the whole spectrum and colors of what my life looked like for the year, for me, for Sean and the kids, to see exactly what we managed to do —together.

Because I'm no longer 'just a writer.' I'm a parent and I need to be real and honest about those days when my brain was utter mush and I did my best to get the kids fed, bathed (mostly bathed), and off to bed. All the times of keeping calm and patient when boundaries were being tested. Or when my oldest was so excited at the aquarium she totally bolted and I needed to follow (read: *run*) because there were a few shark exhibits and touch-tanks within range.

You've got your own stories about your family and it's time to be honest (real honest) about what the year looked like... and if we could possibly, maybe, have done more writing. Or if, at the end of the day (or year in this case) we'd done the best we could in each and every moment.

Go ahead and take a hard look at your life last year. See what you had to face, what opportunities in parenting you might have missed, and challenges that you overcame.

Got it? Got a strong picture of what Your Life was like?

Great.

Now don't let yourself dwell on all the stories you didn't write, how maybe you only wrote one or two novels (or none) for the whole year. Don't focus on how you weren't present enough with the kids, how you didn't play with them enough or, or, or—

Focus instead on what you *did* do.

You wrote. With kids. With all the house crap and a to-do list that was (and still is) *never* done.

Now celebrate.

I'm not kidding. Celebrate however you want, either internally with a hard, good pat on the back or do a little dance with your kids (all kids seem to love when parents let loose and do a little dancing).

As parent-writers we *need* to do this.

We need to see where we are in the lives of our families, to see beyond that list of stories and novels we wanted to write and couldn't get to, the list of book blurbs and covers and interior designs still waiting in limbo.

This hit me the other day after I read some year-end blogs from other writers, about how all these writers were putting their main focus for the new year on writing (as opposed to publishing), and it made me pause. Made me think over what I wanted for next year moving forward as a writer. I couldn't help but be discouraged because it felt like I had so much to do, so much catching up in terms of writing because there was so much I *didn't* get done this past year.

That was my first thought and it pulled me down.

Hard.

I mean, what was the point? Why should I even keep trying with what is going on in our lives? Even though I'm in a secure and comfortable place with Kate and her speech delay, even though I'm at peace, sometimes it still feels like I'm battling dragons to keep everyone's negativity and judgment away.

I'm now taking long, hard looks at so-called friends who choose instead not to celebrate when Kate said 'Mommy' for the first time, but questioned Eric's speech instead.

(Eric, who is quite vocal, is only thirteen months old, but yeah, thanks for that, so-called friends. Thanks for putting a whole new line of fears into my life when what I was looking for was for you to celebrate and share in this joy with me.)

All this made me wonder, made me question...

Why *should* I put in the time and effort to write when at the end of the day I only finished four or five new short stories this past year?

That's nothing special; nothing to sing praises about.

But I paused at that thought, right as I was folding Kate's *Frozen* pants, nice and stained at the knees and butt (my little girl, a climber she is), and actually thought back over this past year as a whole, in its entirety. Everything we'd gone through and shifted through...

We welcomed baby Eric, which is a huge dynamic shift all its own, but throw in my needed surgery (a C-section) and you've suddenly put a whole new twist on adding a new family member. We had all those all-encompassing fears brought on by so-called professionals and 'experts' when we learned that Kate had a speech delay. Then I wrestled my way out of those fears (mostly) and decided to trust in myself, as a parent, and trust in Kate. There were many more life rolls, smaller rolls along with the big ones that made each day difficult at best (ahem, Eric, not sleeping for six freakin' months!).

And I was shocked, *shocked,* at how much I'd actually gotten *done.*

I didn't *just* write those stories.

I started a novel.

I started this blog and am writing regular posts.

I've taken two intense online writing workshops. I had a story published in the amazing anthology series, *Fiction River.* I'm building new friendships with other homeschoolers and learning more about parenting and trying a different path than the one I'd been raised on.

I've also taken on the role as Kate's speech partner, which feels like a giant responsibility, especially with all those doubters and judgers shedding a floodlight on me, waiting to see me screw up or to see my baby Eric start following Kate's speech path because then they can 'definitely' point and say, "It's the parent's fault; she's clearly not reading enough or talking enough or getting her kids around other kids enough..."

(Because, yeah, the research *completely* backs up their judgmental claims. My personal goal for this year: find new friends, happy friends. Haters can take a flying leap.)

And on top of all that, I survived another Christmas, which is no small feat when Sean and I (and Kate) are super-introverts!

So you see, it would have been easy to simply look at those handful of short stories and say, "The hell with it. Clearly, writing with super young kids is a no-go."

I *could* have focused only on the negative. I *could* have only looked at what I *didn't* do, in terms of writing.

But that would have been a lie for 2015.

Because it's not about the result. It's not about the 'completed' status of those stories, but the actual journey. Funny enough, this is one of the first philosophies I learned in Kung Fu all those years ago.

It's about the process.

And the process of writing is pretty darn good. In fact, every time I sat down to write I had fun. I let myself play a little, let myself get lost in my made-up worlds, and came out the other side a happier person. A happier parent.

And everyone loves a happier parent (certainly my kids). I even have more patience (or a longer fuse) for putting up with other people's uninformed judgments and 'expert' opinions... although I'm still finding myself new friends.

When I started looking back over the last year, I immediately felt a depressing weight pulling me down, but now that I've changed my mindset I can see this past year, this journey, for the success it is— which is helping me see that next year will be an even bigger success.

I'm committed to waking up early before the kids so I can give my subconscious a chance to peek out and tell some stories. I've got some online workshops planned in the next couple months to keep on learning and pushing myself. And, now here's the big one: I signed up for a workshop on the Oregon coast for 2017.

The reason it's a big deal is because I'll have to write a *ton* before I go. Like, a story a week. Seven weeks in a row. That's normally fine, no worries. I could totally hit that, no problem... before kids. Now though, there's some maneuvering required. Some very early mornings and begging family for babysitting while I squeeze in one hour (or even fifteen minutes) at a time to get those stories done.

I did it once before, when I had only Kate. Not Kate *plus* Eric.

The kids will need to come with me to the workshop (they're just too young to be apart from me for a week). So I needed to talk *my* mom into coming with me and babysitting (she said yes, by the way).

But I'm committed.

I'm committed to my writing and to myself. And you know, I think my family is too even if they're too young to understand. I think they know.

So, here's to the next year and to my writing, *your* writing—the dreams, the goals, whatever it is for you—and to what we *can* get done, right at this moment, even though we're parents.

Because really, this is the only moment that matters, the one happening right now.

WHAT'S YOUR WORTH?
THE STAY-AT-HOME PARENT

February 27, 2016
Kate, 3 years
Eric, 1 year

To stay loving and connected with our children is not always easy. And yet we do it, time and time again, and we don't get paid a dime. But it's worth so very, very much.

It's been a couple of weeks since my last post, mostly because life started hitting the top of my tea kettle. Mostly because I over scheduled. The speech work I'm doing with Kate, my expectations, but also just not enough down-time (which is perfect fodder for another blog post).

But I what I really wanted to talk about today was another idea that's been on my mind lately:

Money.

Why am I wanting to writing about this now? Why do I have this sudden fret and worry, this need to tear napkins into little bitty shreds?

It's tax season in the United States and while I've been on top of all that stuff—business records and filing and spreadsheets with numbers to keep the IRS happy (and off my butt) —the numbers are still... *Right There.*

In red.

A lovely little reminder of how very little my writing and publishing business is actually making.

It's depressing.

I can't help but *see* those numbers, see the income and expenses, and feel like I'm worth less. Here I am, spending our family's money and my free time (Ha! As if I *had* free time), waking up God-early sometimes just to write, and oh look, it's not doing a damn thing. It feels like I'm a failure. Like this dream I'm pursuing will never actually become a reality no matter how hard I try.

And yes, seeing the numbers and feeling like a failure has been happening ever since—like clockwork—about four years ago when I was pregnant with Kate.

When I became a stay-at-home parent.

Granted, I *knew* this would happen. In fact, while I was pregnant I was asking my writing mentors what I should do to keep the writing alive even though my focus during the early years would be on keeping my children alive (which, they are, and doing marvelously to boot... go me!). My point is I knew this would happen. I knew my writing and my productively, my ability to publish (anything), would take a hit.

It did.

I thought I was mentally prepared for it. Ready for it, even.

That's hogwash.

You can never be ready (or maybe you were, in which case you're lucky). I *thought* I was ready, that I could handle the negative self-talk that came with those consistent low numbers. It doesn't help that in our American culture so much of our *worth* is tied into money.

I'll be clear here: I've never, *ever* gotten this feeling from Sean.

He's the one who supports me and pushes me through these humps and has never given up on my writing and is the first one to advocate and protect my writing time (there are many reasons I married him—this is one and it's a *big* one). Even though I have his absolute, loving support... I can't help but *feel* the judgment from the world around me. And no, people don't actually say anything about this, about my worth, but it's still this living, breathing, nasty little thing in the back of my mind—since I'm not bringing in money, I'm worth less than others.

What I'm doing, raising these two children, taking care of pesky house chores and feeding the family, is somehow worth less.

And that's where this free-fall depression and failure hit me hard. You see this year, *this year*, I'm close to writing on a regular basis. So close... and then Eric started walking (ahem... RUNNING!) and now I'm in supermom-mode to keep that boy alive. And sleep is sporadic again from teething and the endless slew of winter colds.

I looked at our family's bottom-line income (and my writing business and continued learning takes a bite into that) and I couldn't help but think: if I just made a couple hundred dollars a month, it would be enough. It would.

I would feel better *about myself* if I could provide a little income for our family.

Even a little.

Well, my writing and publishing is a long-term process. It's the kind of business where even if you're on top of your game, putting out professional-looking books with the right covers and blurbs... it'll *still* be a couple months before you see any income. And I'm so far behind on the publishing side, with *several dozen* stories that need covers rebranded and somewhat related to the genre they're in (a task I'm woefully behind in... wait for it... because I'm a stay-at-home parent).

So, there I was, not feeling great about my writing, not believing in it. So I started looking at different options.

I had two that seemed pretty good, other ways of earning income.

But... I kept hitting a wall whenever I tried to go forward, when I tried thinking about that 'other' way of earning income. It's mostly a feeling kind of wall, because that's how I work—something didn't feel right, didn't feel comfortable. So I kept probing and digging until I finally understood what my subconscious was trying to tell me. It took a little bit, but the realization was huge.

And that realization is the whole point of this blog post.

You see, to help me figure out this possible new venture, I started re-reading a bit of Kristine Kathryn Rusch's, *The Freelancer's Survival Guide* (a fabulous read for anyone thinking of freelancing or who already is). In it, Kris suggests writing out a list of your priorities with things like family, health, work, writing, etc., and putting them in order of importance.

For example: for me, my number one priority is my family.

Even if I do start another business, I'm still the primary caregiver of our children. I need to care for them and teach them and guide them. On my list, I included other important pieces, such as being Kate's primary speech partner.

As I started writing this list, I also started writing out questions for what a new venture might look like and how it would take shape. The question that stopped me cold was this:

How many hours of *work* would I need to make this money?

Work.

I hate that word. Hate it.

Work is what I did for years, *years*, at the full-time office job so that one day I could pursue my true calling, my passion, which was writing. I swore to myself that I wouldn't *work* again. Unless our family was in dire straits and money was needed, I wouldn't do *work*.

You see, for me, writing isn't *work*. It's fun, it's uplifting... it brightens my whole being and I simply love it. I love it. I don't associate the word 'work' with my writing. And yet... here I was, ready to plunge back into *work* instead of my writing and for what? A couple hundred bucks?

I asked myself another question: would I be okay spending those hours every week (because they *would* be hours) on *not* writing? On not publishing?

Why should I start a new business, with its slow start-up, when I already had a business ready, patient and willing, if I would just invest time back into it?

I had one single, definitive answer:

I didn't *want* to do else but write.

I was not willing to spend those hours at *work* (we are fortunate—no, *blessed*—to be in a situation where I don't need to work). I wasn't willing to take away those hours that could be writing or publishing so I could *work*. So I could make money that would justify my writing expenses for me to keep learning, to keep getting better and better at my craft of writing.

And that's when I realized something, something very important.

All these feelings I had—the lack of self-worth, feeling like I was a burden on our family because I wasn't bringing in money—they weren't my feelings at all. They were what the culture around me had been pounding into my head since I was a child. Those feelings have only gained in intensity since I became a mother, and more specifically, a stay-at-home parent.

The idea that even though my day is filled with children and chores and errands—a 24-hour *job*—I should still be bringing in money. Because what I do doesn't have the same worth or value in our culture as what Sean does. That this 'work' I do, this caring for our children, isn't worth the same as his *job*. That, even though my 'day' doesn't end when the lights go out—I'm the one who gets up to handle wet beds and midnight feedings because Sean has to go to work and function the next day—what I *do* is worth less.

After that realization, I looked at my list of priorities.

I looked at my week and the hours I had in my week and where, if any, I could add in this new job. And I realized this whole feeling I had, this feeling of being worth less because I didn't bring in any money, was a bunch of bullshit.

My hours were filled. *Filled*.

I could *not* take on another job without taking away from ones I already had.

My family.

My writing.

My own self-care.

And this 'problem,' this feeling I had of my time being worth less wasn't going away any time soon. We had decided to homeschool our little family almost two years ago, so no shipping them off to school to free up a couple of hours. Which meant I needed to deal with how I looked at myself and the jobs I do (and don't get paid for). To stamp these old, outdated beliefs into the ground and (hopefully) out of existence (though doubtful—at least completely).

This continues to be a constant struggle for me, mostly because so much of the world around me places emphasis on money and status and success. Because my books aren't bringing in hundreds of extra dollars, I'm already less inclined to believe in myself, less inclined to share and tell others that I am a professional writer because I can't justify or prove that I *am* a professional writer with money alone. And somehow the work I do as a parent means less because I'm not bringing in money.

This is how our culture functions. It's the culture I was raised in and it'll be a struggle and take time to break away from this mindset. Sometimes I'm successful, and then there are times, like tax season, when I can't help but look at those numbers and feel like I'm less.

Less of a person.

Less of a writer.

And yet... when I look at what I *do* during my weeks, I realize how false that is. I'm *not* less of a person.

In fact, it's the opposite.

Sean jokingly calls me "super mom" when I try to do everything (and, especially when I admit that I *can't* doing everything). And he's right. What I can accomplish is amazing.

My house is straightened (note, I did not stay *cleaned*) at the end of the day. My kids are happy. They're growing, they're smiling, they're playing. Kate's words are coming in, slowly and bit-by-bit. There's good, homemade, healthy food on the table for breakfast, lunch, and dinner, and those really annoying dirty dishes are (mostly) done by the end of the day.

All this is what I do as the stay-at-home parent, but my real job, the most important part of my job is this:

To stay loving and open and connected... a task that isn't always easy. Sometimes it's not even possible. And yet those of us who stay home, we do this work, time and time again, and we'll continue to do it, even when the money we bring into the home is less than what our spouse or partner contributes.

Or maybe, there's no money at all.

The truth is this will take me time to wrap my head around and work through, this new way of thinking. To rewire all those beliefs society has shoved into me. But it's a start. And I realize, too, that if I want my dreams to happen, if I want to bring in extra money, I'm going to have to start doing the work. I need to make the writing and publishing a priority—even with all the demands and exhaustion that come with parenting small kids.

This *is* a long road, but I've got to start somewhere... even if it's small.

Your story, your situation is going to be different from mine. Whether you're a new parent with your first little bundle of (sleepless) joy, whether you're homeschooling, whether your child is developing normally or is a late-talker and you're navigating the waters of special needs and therapy... each story is different. Regardless of your life story, it can be so easy to see the work we do as less.

But we've got to start somewhere in order to change not only the way *we* see our own value, but how those around us see our value (I'm not going to say the wider world because really, those guys don't matter).

Start small. Start with seeing value in yourself and the work you *can* do and the work you *already* do.

See where it takes you.

For me, what I can do is write a little each day. Some days it might only be ten minutes, others maybe an hour, but all this tiny progress, these tiny steps forward... they mean something. That's how novels and stories are written.

One day at a time.

The same is true for my publishing and being the stay-at-home parent.

One day at a time. One smile at a time.

And for Kate especially, one spoken or even understood, word at time.

Let me tell you, it's a damn good feeling. Worth a whole lot more than any dollar figure or any number on a spreadsheet... *especially* when my kids smile.

And that, right there, is why I'm doing this. Every day, every night (and sometimes a couple of times during the night). This is the best job I've ever had, one that doesn't pay much (or anything), but it's one I would never, *ever*, in a million years, give up:

Being a parent.

A SCHEDULE AND KIDS: HA!

SCHEDULES PART 3

March 7, 2016
Kate, 3 years
Eric, 1 year

The secret to kids, writing, and a schedule... be flexible. Try and try again and expect a whole lot of trial and error—our kids certainly don't make this easy on us.

That's right. The title of this blog is one about straight-up laughter because if you're a parent with kids, whether one kid or two, whether they're fifteen months or fifteen years, you know darn well that there *is* no schedule when it comes to kids.

I mean, if you send your kids to school or daycare or some other similar type of structure, sure those places put a schedule on the kids, but when it comes to you, the parent, I'm getting this sense that kids pretty much laugh in our faces about this whole schedule thing...

And after laughing they give you a mischievous grin right before your fifteen-month-old boy dives his hand into the trashcan and you're sweeping up coffee grounds and potato peels with one hand and with the other trying to keep the kid from eating said grounds.

And that's pretty much what kids can do to our schedules.

It's like you're *finally* ready to head out the door and someone decides *at that moment* they need to use the bathroom.

Or, they already did and you just got a whiff of the diaper.

This is my life circumstance right now. Yours will be different (especially if you have a fifteen-year-old). But within all this chaos (because it sometimes feels that way), I'm still pursuing my writing...

And trying to figure out this illusive idea called a schedule.

You see, I know having a schedule is powerful. Powerful when it comes to being productive. It gets you to the chair or easel or whatever it is that you're pursuing. It's like that extra push when the creative endeavor you want to do is *actually* the last thing in the world you feel like doing, but you have a schedule and it's easy to follow that schedule. Having a schedule takes a huge piece of the distraction away and following the routine doesn't require the same amount of dedication and willpower that flying-off-the-cuff can require.

Schedule.

It sounds great. I want one...

Except, again, see above about my life circumstances.

For the past year I've been struggling with The Schedule.

Struggling because life keeps throwing one curveball after another.

Struggling because even though my writing makes me *a better mother*, there were times when I couldn't write. When I was worried and fearful of Kate and her speech delay and journey. When Eric decided that letting me sleep was a silly idea and proceeded to wake up *six times*.

Every night.

For six months.

But I kept going and kept taking a crack at this schedule thing and I finally, *finally* feel that I'm on the right track. The really funny (ironic?) thing is my *schedule* doesn't look like much of a schedule at all. In fact, the 'schedule' is this flexible, moving, living thing that follows one goal, *one goal*:

To write.

Every day. For at least fifteen minutes. (If you couldn't tell by now, breaking my writing into these bite-sized little chunks is the only way I've found to consistently work and I keep coming back to it.)

It doesn't matter how tired I feel. It doesn't matter how much I *don't* want to do it. I write.

Sean knows this, too. He knows how important the writing is. He knows how much better I feel and—this is important here—he knows he *needs* to help when life circumstances (AKA kids) don't allow the writing to fit snuggly into my schedule.

My goal is to wake up at 4:30 in the morning—just enough time to drag myself out of bed, make some coffee, and get in an hour of writing before the house starts waking up.

That's the ideal, perfect world.

Some days this happens and I'm seriously ready to run a marathon. That writing time absolutely recharges my batteries. My energy is clear and shining. I've gotten in the alone time I personally need to function.

Of course, there isn't such a thing as a perfect world when you have kids.

There are days (like today) when I get up at 4:30 a.m., and the kids follow me downstairs. Or if we're having a hard morning and even with Sean watching them, maybe I only write thirty minutes... or maybe just ten.

But the very, very important part is that I write.

I write.

That is the only piece of The Schedule that *must* happen. I write. With no kids around. Which is critical (for me) and I'll explain.

I've been slowly reading through a book by Jerry Mundis, "*Break Writer's Block Now!*" and something he wrote really struck me. It had to do with affirmations and changing your focus from the negative to the positive, that it was safe to write.

This right here was my issue. This is what I'd been struggling with for a year.

Safe for me to write.

It felt like every time I'd sit down to write or even *read* stories I'd get interrupted. I'd have to turn off the story in my brain and be a parent. It never mattered what I wanted; I needed to be Mom. The more this happened, the harder and harder it was for me to let go and dive into a story. It became harder and harder to see my characters and where they wanted to take me next.

My subconscious just... shut down that part of my brain. Shut off the part that was trying to tell a story. It was no longer safe.

That's when I realized so much of my struggle with writing and telling a story had to do with my subconscious and this constant focus on my kids and our home. I still felt the urge and need to tell stories. It was there... but I couldn't (wouldn't?) give my subconscious the time it needed to tell those stories. I'd start writing again and putting aside that time, then life would get in the way and the writing, the safety to tell a story, went away again.

And the story stalled.

Even if I kept typing new words the story wasn't right because I couldn't go deep enough into myself. Into the place where those stories lived.

But I keep at it.

I keep putting in the time, keep making even those *fifteen minutes* a priority... and you know what? The stories are coming back. Even more than that... my schedule, while fluid, really does exist.

I spent several hours this week thinking about productivity, thinking about my goals, and The Schedule. I listened to podcasts about using the calendar or following David Allen's, "*Getting Things Done*" (which I'm ordering as soon as I write this blog) and I realized I can do this. But only if I work at it, only if I prioritize the time that I have, when I have it (because that part there isn't always in my control).

I'm reorganizing my morning routines. I'm saying no to play dates or events that are in the morning, when I'm most productive and focused (unless they're what I call 'field trips' and require an early morning/most of day outing... and I've got one or two days set aside for that).

I've realized that even I, with my two kids, can have a schedule.

And if I wake up early to get the writing in, and Kate (and Eric) wake up before any child or other human should... that's okay. I have another 'work block' I can use to get the writing in (when Sean's watching the kids). Or when Eric's napping (electronic devices can be real lifesavers when entertaining 3-year-olds). And worst case? I muster up that fifteen minutes when the kids are in bed and I've kissed Sean on the cheek as he walks in the door and I hit the computer.

But... all the opportunities are there. In a schedule of sorts.

I can hardly believe it.

It's a schedule that works for me and my life, for this 'season' that our family's in.

It's a flexible schedule because that's what I need—and frankly the only one that will work.

I'm already feeling lighter and more in control. I have time to fit in projects from redesigning my poor, outdated website and doing publishing research, to paying bills or making the weekly run to our farmers market. I even know the best time to make phone calls to friends I've been neglecting because it just wasn't 'the right time to call.'

And the really, really cool part?

The story I've been writing away at, redrafting and restarting since the start of the new year, is finally nearing the end. It's taken way, way longer than it should have... but I'm recognizing this might be my process for the particular world I'm playing in. But hey, I can see the light at the end of the tunnel and it's only, *only* because I gave my subconscious this time, time to help the writing feel safe again...

Safe enough to tell a story.

And it's this schedule, as flexible and fluid as it is, that's giving me the chance—and opportunities—to make the writing happen. Not all days will be perfect. I just spent a two nights camping in a trailer with my little ones, two grandparents, and a dog. Let's just say the kids and I were lucky, *lucky*, to get 4 hours of good, solid sleep.

But, I got the writing in.

It wasn't much that first day, only eleven minutes of new words, but I felt that little dip as my subconscious went down and touched the story-part of me.

And the next day?

Well, I'd gotten better sleep and stayed up after Eric woke me at 3:46 in the morning. But it worked. We even drove three hours to get home and I managed to get the writing in... a full hour, too!!

Hot damn, does that feel good.

It's a wonderful, wonderful feeling and that feeling is carrying over to the other, very important part of my life:

Parenthood.

Finding a schedule that fits you, that fits your family and the season that you're in—if you've got young ones that require a lot of attention and care, or older ones who need less of you, or heck, even if they've moved out of the house—finding a schedule really is key. It's going to take adjustment and trial and error—a lot of trial and error—but every time you adjust, you get closer. You'll start pinging on what works and what doesn't, and somehow, if you keep at it and keep moving forward, you'll find what works.

Because even us parent-writers, even with young kids, even *we* can have a schedule. A fluid, constantly moving one, but that counts.

Who knew, right?

WHO ARE YOU?
LESSONS LEARNED FROM MY LATE-TALKER

June 16, 2016
Kate, 3 years
Eric, 1 year

Let go of fear. Embrace your differences. Find what makes you (and your kids) unique. Then, go with it.

There's a running theme that keeps popping up throughout my life right now. I've seen it with my writing, with my parenting, and now with my journey for Kate and her late talking. Part of me is amazed at the correlation, and part of me is like, "Well... duh."

It's simple, and yet at the same time is such a struggle to understand, especially in this American culture, but here it is.

You ready? Are you sure?

In so many areas in our lives, our culture is pushing us to be the same. To be like everyone else. To be 'normal.' To stand in line and patiently wait for our name to be called. To clock in and follow the directions we're given. To be, for all intents and purposes, a cog in a factory line.

But that's not who we are, certainly not as individuals. It's not what gets us up in the morning and puts a spring in our step. It's not what makes our life feel fulfilled. It's not what makes us happy.

Being original? Being ourselves?

That does.

Truthfully, it was being a parent... being *Kate's* parent, that really caused this idea, this realization to hit home. Because I get to see this every day, this embracing of being different, simply by living our lives. It's something I can see when I look back at this past year, from the moment we realized there was a concern with Kate's language and talking through the past six months when we dropped our private speech therapist so I could work with Kate myself (having been coached by an absolute expert with these kids). I learned a lot during that time; heck, I'm still learning.

But I am starting to get the message, especially when I'm seeing this same message repeated, again and again, over so many different areas of my life...

Maybe that same message will help you shed some of your own critical voices. The voices that say you must to do write this way or parent that way, how you must listen to this person because *they* are an expert and know more than you.

Are you ready for the message?

Okay, here goes: *It's okay to be different.*

In fact, you *should* be different because that's what makes you, *you*. That's what makes you unique and special. From a writing standpoint, as a storyteller, it's the reason readers pick up your books and no one else's. They're yours. Your story. Your voice. If you are you, an inherently different person than anyone else, your stories will stand out.

They won't be boring or feel like everyone else's. Think all those Hunger Games and Harry Potter clones that came after those monster book releases and successes. Most of those knock-offs? They didn't do so well. Can't remember them? That's because they weren't memorable.

I'm currently taking two workshops with WMG Publishing, one on Author Voice and the other on Originality. In both of those workshops I'm constantly hearing, again and again, the same thing:

Be different.

Be *you*.

It's a message I'm not just hearing in these workshops either. Every season of *The Voice* that I watch (and take notes on), I routinely hear these superstar coaches say time after time: you're unique, you're different, you don't sound like anybody else. The singers who go far into the competition are the ones who've embraced who they are. They're putting their own spin on songs, tapping into their own emotions and their own journeys. When you hear them sing, especially those who get into the finals, you hear people who don't sound like anybody else.

And one of the best quotes by Pharrell Williams one season (which I'm very much paraphrasing here):

Same is boring.

That's all great and good, you might think. We should be ourselves. Not afraid to be different, in parenting, in raising a child who doesn't talk. No problem. Easy, right?

Ha.

As if.

I often find myself with my local homeschoolers at our weekly park day where I hear story and after story about their kids being different. How each of the kids' learning styles is different, how these kids respond to different situations, and how the parents had to find a new way, a new path for their kids to succeed.

I've even heard about a type of therapy that's all about riding horses and how some kids who can't talk will actually say their first words while on a horse. I was amazed. Fascinated. Never once during my journey to understand Kate and her language disorder was this ever mentioned to me. Not by her pediatrician. Not by the early intervention unhappy lady at our regional center. Not by the neurologist. And yet...

Here was a story and a path that has helped some kids.

That's not to say it would have helped Kate. I honestly have no idea if it would, but the point is that the choice is there. It's an option. And it's a different one. It may not be right for *Kate* but it was right for someone else.

Differences.

But it's more than that; it's courage too.

It's having the courage to write a story from your heart and not what everyone else is writing or what the latest bestseller clone was. It's about discovering your child's learning style and going outside the traditional education system when everyone around you might say otherwise. It's about all those medical professionals and experts who've refuse to listen to you and your concerns, and you finally telling them to screw off. Because guess what, you and only you, are the expert on your child.

Not them.

Not their expensive degrees gathering dust in those fancy wall frames.

Our children are different... even the 'normal' ones.

So much of my journey with Kate is asking the question: who is she? How can I help her best?

It's not the way *I* think is best—she is very quick to correct me when I try this. Of course, I have goals for her. I'd really like her to talk, and there are steps we can take to help her get to that point. But she's still in the driver's seat and for Kate that control is very, very important.

Not all kids are like this.

Kate will flinch and pull away and close up tight if a stranger touches her... even from her grandfather if she hasn't seen him in a while.

Meanwhile, there's my little guy Eric who will go up to a random person and asked to be picked up so he can see the empty cup he threw into the trash and then marvel at his accomplishment.

See? Different.

And that's okay.

And that's all this post is about, telling you it's okay to be different. More than that, being different is something we should embrace. It's the part that makes us unique and exciting.

If your child's interests lead you on a different path, trust in them. Trust that they know their own wants and desires. Trust that they know what they're doing.

Have the courage to go with it.

Kate's early assessors insisted that her problems were more than just speech related. They felt her fine motor controls were behind and we should sign her up for occupational therapy.

We said no.

So what if she didn't draw a circle for them—or, for us—on demand?

We let her be.

We loved her.

We followed her interests at home.

And she likes video games. Can you blame her? She sees Daddy (who is a video game designer) playing all the time and wanted a part of that action. And you know what came before Kate ever started drawing circles (which she does do now)?

She played *Yoshi's Wooly World*.

That's right. Kate was three and a half years old and already learning and mastering the controls, which she did, in just a few short weeks. That includes those hard-to-reach buttons on the 'bumpers,' a place that is *not* natural for kids to use.

And now? Now she's playing *Mario's Super 3D World*. Seriously. And she's seriously good at it. She'll even play in matches of *Splatoon* against other people and win some battles. Not kidding.

But she wouldn't draw a circle on demand, so the *experts* decided she needed therapy.

Screw that.

Kate's fine motor controls were just that—fine—but they came about in a different way. They came about in her way, when *she* was ready and doing what *she* wanted to do (which was apparently not coloring, but using Yoshi's long and sticky tongue to eat all the minions that tried to eat him).

Kate and I have our special play time sessions, where I get on the floor and play with her and help her become comfortable with words using play. Sometimes she talks (usually when I forget that I'm supposed to be 'working' with 'her' and lose myself in the actual play) and sometimes she doesn't talk. But... I'll hear the words she *does* use in other places and at other moments. Like when Mario walks through a door and she waves and says, "Bye-bye."

Or when she played *Super Smash Brothers* and the screen said, "Ready, set... GO!" And I hear her saying, "Go!" right along with it.

Or like just yesterday at the pool while I was telling Eric to kick or to step down onto the concrete steps, I hear Kate mimic me.

Because the words sound fun. They sound like play. And so, Kate decides to say them.

All on her own.

All at her pace.

Always... different.

So again, my question is—who are you? Deep down? What makes you happy? What makes you shine bright?

Go with it. Go for it.

Don't be afraid to be different. Don't be afraid to step out of line and be unlike anybody else. Don't be afraid to let your kids be different. All of us, our kids included, will be happier if we do. And I've a feeling if you do this, the results will surprise you.

SAYING NO DOESN'T MEAN IT'S FOREVER

June 27, 2016
Kate, 3 years
Eric, 1 year

Still searching for the balance between parenting and writing (and everything else in between).

I'm right now in the midst of battling my way back to fiction writing and I say battle because that's what it feels like.

Writing is fun, or at least, it's supposed to be fun, but tearing my conscious thoughts, my constant conscious awareness away from parenting and back into storytelling... *that* is my battle. It's like there's this switch in my brain that has to go to 'off' before I can start saying hello to my characters, before my creative voice can poke its head out and say, "Oh, hey, the story's over this way. Boy, wouldn't it be fun if we did *that*?"

And then, like a dog, I run after and chase that squirrel.

But here's the problem: the only way I can get to my creative voice, the only way I can get to all the stories that are bubbling inside me, stories that really, really want to come out... is when I feel safe.

Or, I should say, my children need to be safe.

Wait... what??

I know. That sounded confusing but hear me out.

Right here, I'm going to say I am truly envious of all the dad writers. Truly. I usually try to write these blog posts as mother-father neutral, because parenthood is just hard and wonderful on both parents and you never get a break until your tiny bundle of joy turns six (and even then it changes into a different kind of 'hard'). However, I've come to this understanding (a completely non-scientific one, mind you) that there's this difference between our brains, between mothers and fathers, when it comes to our children. Or maybe not mothers and fathers exactly, but those who were born more maternal compared to those who aren't.

My experience (so far) has been watching dads easily turn off the parenting-brain while us moms are left with the work and focus and keeping kiddos alive while the dads go off and chat with each other. I've watched how easy it is for them to tune out the noise and cries (and if tune out isn't the right word, they can definitely tune *down*). I'm not at all saying this is a bad thing; in fact, I'm positive it was an evolutionary necessity for a mother to become hyperaware and hyper-focused when their baby cried.

It's important to keep our little ones alive, after all.

What is not so helpful is when I'm trying to get down deep into a story, to lose myself in the story and hear the voices of my characters...

And I straight-up *can't do that* when my children need me.

Or when I hear Kate opening the fridge door from two rooms away.

Or when Eric gives this frustrated whine-cry as he attempts to climb onto a chair (which he can do just fine, just not as *fast* as he wants).

You better believe my brain considers all this as:

Emergency!!

Lately it's like there's this wall between me and my stories—the part of me that's the mother. If I'm being really honest here, it's hard *not* to feel frustrated at times.

Sometimes I am frustrated. Sometimes I'm okay and I can shrug off those feelings.

But I want to write; I *need* to write. When I do I'm a better person. I'm a better mother (more patient, understanding, kinder... all because I'm taking the time to fill up my own cup, all because I'm taking care of myself). It's harder, too, because I've been pursuing this pseudo-writing state for nearly five years (including my pregnancy with Kate). I haven't gotten a decent night's sleep (or at least a week's worth) in over five years.

All that takes its toll, especially on the storyteller part of me.

There are times when I get back into the writing, when I've battled my way back to the stories, have convinced my creative voice, "Hey! It's okay. It's safe, you can come out and play..."

Only to have another life event disrupt the process and I feel like I'm smack-dab at square one again.

It's hard not to feel frustrated. It's hard to remember that yes, this is such a short time in my life, that my writing is forever and these young years of our kids are not (and please, truly, stop reminding me, random people at Lowes or Costco or farmers market, to treasure these years. I *know* these years are short. I also know I haven't slept four hours in a row in at least two years and I'm doing my best here).

And that's why I mean it's a battle.

One day, it's all good and I'm accepting and okay with where we're at. Other days I have this deep, deep ache in me to do more, to tell bigger and deeper stories, stories I had to stop mid-series because my brain and all my focus were on my two children.

I always come back to the same feeling though: acceptance.

Even if that acceptance isn't always easy.

I just sent off an email to Dean Wesley Smith to pull my reservation for the amazing Anthology Workshop they host every year on the Oregon Coast. I'd known it was a gamble for me to attend when I signed up. I knew it would be hard to write seven stories in seven weeks. I knew that, even taking my children with me, my being in the workshop all day for seven days straight, would be brutal on them. But... I missed it. The writing. Being in the company of other professional writers (although it's a double-edged sword because I would love to put all my effort and focus into writing as many of them can). But most of all, I wanted to try. I wanted to see that maybe this year, I could go back.

And, ultimately, I couldn't.

Believe it or not, the writing deadlines weren't the issue. I knew I could make the hour I needed to write every day happen. I might have needed my mother's help more, I might have needed to call in favors of grandparents and dear friends, but I could do it. I had control over that after all, just like I have control of when I go to bed and when I wake up (sneaking in the writing before my little ones wake up and need to be fed and loved and changed). But what I couldn't control was the actual quality of my sleep.

Or when Eric decided his second set of molars should start.

(Yeah... the timing of the workshop timed perfectly with Eric getting his molars in. And teething, especially molars, usually means that I don't sleep. Like... at all.)

So, sleep was a huge concern.

Also, Eric being away from me all day and being *okay* with it was a huge, huge concern. I took Kate to this workshop when she was seventeen months old and she was totally fine hanging out with Grandma. Totally fine. Eric is a different kid. He would *not* be fine. So, I needed to ask myself—would Eric be okay? He would be only be two. Just barely two years.

I realized that no, he wouldn't.

So I could either battle my way through the workshop, fighting this pull of wanting to connect and help my children through a week-long workshop, with my coming and going and Grandma watching them... or I could give next year a try.

I decided to wait.

It was a decision I'd been thinking about for a few months and it took going to a local homeschool conference to realize how difficult it would be with both kids. I needed to wait. Wait until Eric was a little bit older, maybe three, maybe four, before I could go back to the coast and all the other professional writers there. I needed to be able to separate myself, at least partly, from the needs of motherhood, to say, "It's okay. They're safe."

And to have this actually be true.

That will come with time. I know it, though it's not always easy to accept. Saying no now doesn't mean I won't go to a writing workshop again. It's not forever. It just means until Eric has been potty trained, until he's comfortable and safe enough with himself, independent and *ready* to be away from me. And Kate, too. The older she gets, the more language she understands, the more words she has and the more trust she has with the people watching her (which isn't something to be taken lightly, especially for my little girl).

And it doesn't mean I can't do my own learning; it just means that I need to focus on online workshops right now. Ones that can go with the flow of parenting, where if I don't sleep one night and can't do the assignment or the reading the next day, it's okay.

I can adjust. Because I have the leeway, I have the time, to do that.

So maybe it's not really a battle.

Maybe what this is, is actually a river. Sometimes the river moves fast, sometimes the river moves slow. Sometimes there are rapids and everything feels like it's going wrong or crashing all around me, and other times it's calm and tranquil and it feels like I can take on the world. But there's definitely a flow. There's a flow to our energy, mine and the kids, and what we can each handle in our lives. That flow is a bit off right now because the kids are hitting developmental milestones.

Kate and Eric are at the stage where one wants to play with the other, and the other doesn't so resorts to shoving. Then there's crying. Then there's trying to take the toy away from the other.

I need to figure out this new flow, this new stage in our lives as a family, including the outings we go on and identifying when those outings and activities have become too much (homeschooling for us means there are so *many* choices and friends, from spending the day at Disneyland to going to the tide pools where I slipped off a wobbly rock and somehow managed to save the phone and Eric but not my poor knees).

But through all this learning, figuring out the flow of our life, through my speech play with Kate, my writing is still there. My stories *are* coming back, even if really, really slowly.

But I'll get there; I know it will.

My writing, my storytelling, will keep getting easier. My creative voice will learn that when I sit down to write it means that I'm safe, that the children are safe, that I can turn off this part in my brain long enough to go deep, to find the characters and see where they take me.

Because it's time.

Time to write.

(As I've taken the two minutes from writing this blog to throw another load of laundry in, I heard the distinct squeak as Eric climbed (successfully) onto my chair and reached for the laptop. Apparently, the time to write is not at *this exact moment*. But thankfully, he takes huge naps and Kate likes playing video games. I'll get my quiet and my writing in; I'm getting to be a master at finding all these stolen bits of time.)

So, for me, it's time to write again.

It may not always be easy, and I may have to keep working and trying to write these different stories until finally my creative voice gives up and says, "Okay, fine. *Here's* the story. This is where you want to go."

Also as I'm writing and trying to find my way back to my creative voice, I tend to write a lot of extra words. A lot of words. I need to be *okay* with tossing out those extra words—and the hours I put in to write them. It's not easy, but I do it. All those extra words were not wasted —*never* wasted. They convinced my creative voice it was safe.

They brought me to the real story and when I feel it, I *feel* it. And the almost-pulsing excitement, feels really, really good.

So, it's time. Time to have fun. Time to see where these stories take me —as both a writer and a parent—and I really, really can't wait to get started.

ALWAYS ON THE GO:

TODDLERS AND WRITING

August 2, 2016
Kate, 4 years
Eric, 1 1/2 years

So you've got yourself a toddler. Always on the go, always exploring, always doing their best to push every limit and button known to man... and you want to keep writing.

Every person who's ever been a parent (or has seen one on TV) has a comment (or two or three) about two-year-olds. Heck, we've got a flashy code name for this developmental stage: Terrible Twos. Our culture has since added another for three and four... or more.

    For me though, or I should say for Eric, he moved into that transition early. Like between 18 and 20 months he went from sweet baby bundle of joy to realizing he's got an opinion of his own... and not only can he express it, he *wants* to.

Loudly.

With determination.

With the absolute conviction that The World Is Ending... *right now*.

(This, of course, translates to "the minute I don't get what I want, you're going to be sorry.")

This has been a really difficult, really challenging time for us. It's why I haven't written any parent-writing blog posts in about six months.

Well, this is why.

It's been a crazy-tough transition for everyone. It's even more challenging than what we went through with Kate. Yes, I'm still rewiring my parenting brain and philosophy, but even with all these new tools and mindset shifts, even though I'm practicing a more peaceful, cooperation-approach style of parenting, it's hard.

Like really, really hard.

Parenting Eric, right now, is a full-time job. It's no longer about feeding or nursing or diaper changing or walking outside while he slowly toddles around and has the most interesting observations over a handful of rocks or dirt or leaves.

Man, babies are easy. They're constant, in the physical sense, and you're *always* dead tired, but whoa are babies easy compared to this.

Now Eric runs.

Now he throws rocks.

Now he limit-tests because... guess what... that's what they *do* at this stage; that's their *job*.

However, now I've got two kids who are veering in different directions with different opinions of what that should be. And all the while I'm trying my best to not always say, "No," and instead, figure out what the real need is.

Oh, and I'm *still* not sleeping.

And all that I described above? That's constant. That's my daily life. I am constantly on the go, constantly moving, constantly being aware of Eric so I can step in and gently redirect (which usually fails as he's *way* too perceptive for those tactics) and try to teach that throwing rock and sand could hurt someone else and that this is not okay.

Eric usually just smiles and grabs another two fistfuls and throws again.

This makes for some very loooong days.

And... I'm still writing.

I know, right? People look at me and what I'm doing and think I'm crazy. Or superwoman. It's not like my output is huge... believe me, there are days when getting in five minutes of quiet playtime for my subconscious is a huge, huge, *huge* success.

I've been working at this parenting and writing thing for five years now (including pregnancy because oh man does that count) and while I haven't found the 'answer' I was always looking for, I've somehow managed to write and produce. But writing with a toddler has its own unique set of challenges.

Like, never really getting peace and quiet—unless you do the dreaded 'screen time.' (I can't tell you how many people give me the evil eye when I so much as *hint* at this.)

Well... I do it. The screen time, that is.

I do it because I'm an introvert. I *need* quiet time to recharge my batteries. I *need* this downtime where it's just *me* so I can step in and be a patient parent, a kind and empathetic parent.

After we've gone swimming and shopping and I've been up since 4 a.m. because neither kid could sleep... you better believe I'll use movie time (and all-things-Disney) to give me that desperately needed quiet-and-recharge time. It's a much better alternative than me losing it and yelling when Eric's goes to our small bird cage (which strategically blocks the window by the couch... and the three-story drop beyond). Eric will stand there and purposefully shake that cage and my poor bird.

But I also use this time to sneak in the writing.

Sure, my goal is to wake up before the kids and write before they're up, but when my average is four hours of *broken* sleep, you better believe I'm doing my best to sleep as much and as long as I can.

Also, I try to write after Sean gets up. He spends time with the kids and then is off to work, but that's hard, too, because he hasn't gotten much sleep either. So, it's this trade off... letting him sleep so he can go and make the money to pay the bills and buy all our food... or me getting that quiet and alone time to write.

Somehow, every day for the past three months, I've gotten the writing in. Sometimes my progress has been so small that no one who wasn't a parent of young kids would count it as progress. Sometimes I've literally tried *three times* to write and every time I sit down, I've got a kid hanging off me like I'm their own personal climbing gym.

And yet... those little dribbles do add up.

Even more important, they keep my creative voice open and willing to come out and play. I think that's been the hardest shift as a parent-writer, *especially* when kids are under a certain age. I'm just hard-wired to hear *everything* so my little creative voice shuts down if something else is going on with my kids, always being on the listen for the certain sounds that means Eric's climbing into the toilet or there goes Kate in the cupboard looking for a hidden stash of chocolate (because she's got a crazy good memory).

It's taken a lot to get my creative voice to come out and play; it's taken a lot of patience and time to tell myself, "It's safe now. It's safe to write again."

Each of those days, when the writing is a dribble, plays a huge role in keeping my stories open, in keeping me connected to my need and ability as a storyteller.

I am always on the go. Always on the ball to step in and teach. And with Eric, he's more aggressive than Kate was so I really need to step in and slowly, painfully slowly, teach him what to do and what not to do. He's got all that energy, all that testosterone flowing through him and, wow, is it a challenge.

So, how have I done it? How have I managed to write and parent an opinionated toddler? (So far, anyway?)

Little dribbles, every day.

As a parent-writer you *should* celebrate every word, especially when you touch down into your creative place. Man, that's a huge reason to celebrate and cheer right there!

Another tactic, especially when starting a new story, is to have an idea raring to go. Whether a character or place or problem... just *something* so then when I *do* sit down, I can focus and just write. When you write, one sentence, then another, it's like this little wake-up to your subconscious. The act of writing gets that part of you to wake up and come out and play.

And speaking of play, keep the writing fun. Keep it a place where *you* go to play.

Whenever I find myself getting frustrated (ahem... yesterday) as I try to write but Kate or Eric decides, at that very moment, that they *must* literally be attached and will not leave me alone long enough to get to my creative voice... I tell myself to stop.

To let go.

I've learned that trying to plow through and keep writing is miserable for everyone (and usually ends with me getting frustrated and yelling).

So I stop and try to come at the writing again when my kids are in a better place for me to write. That means I need to be okay with writing for only five minutes, or in one case, two minutes. But... it *was* writing and therefore it counts (certainly when that was my third attempt).

With kids it's all about being flexible. The more I stop thinking about what I want and focus on what *they* want and what *they* need (especially on those days when they won't leave me alone), the more I'm in a better place to handle what happens next. My ability to let go of my writing and give them my attention, to attend to their needs which my kids are very clearly, telling me—all without words.

When I do this, when I let go and accept the situation for what it is, I'm happier. They're happier.

Some days I write for a full hour or forty minutes. Some days it's barely enough to plug into my creative voice. But you know what? Every little, tiny bit really does help. For me that recently added up to a 17,000-word short novel. I just kept plugging away at it, bit by bit.

Every time I sat down, I was already tuned into that world and those characters. That made it easier for me to dive back into the story, to pick up where I left off and see where I went next.

All those broken moments of writing added up to a finished short novel.

The more I work and try and keep the writing fun, the easier it comes to me... even if I have a toddler who doesn't stop moving, who cries and stomps and turns around in circles when he's mad because I wouldn't let him take a bath in the toilet.

And this toddler-time isn't forever.

I remember, when Kate was two and I had just discovered the new (for me) world of homeschooling, and I asked another mother if it was possible to write and be a homeschooling mom.

This was huge for me. *Huge*.

I'd already (happily) put so much of my writing on hold to be a mother, but writing is a core part of who I am. I couldn't just shrug it off for *years*; I would be miserable! I told this mother that if I couldn't write, there was no way I could commit to something like homeschooling. She asked how old my child was and I told her.

She laughed.

She told me that two was the year you never sit down, and... she was right.

Totally and completely right.

But I know too that this time, this year of Eric being two years old, isn't forever. That at some point Eric will settle down into his own person. That one day the teething will end and I will one day, gloriously, sleep again.

It will happen.

(I really, really have faith in the sleep part.)

In the meantime, I'll do what I can, keep being flexible with the writing, keep having fun, both with the writing and my little twenty-month-old because this is only a small blip in his life. It'll be over before I know it.

I don't want to miss a second of this time with Eric, but I also want to stay sane and keep writing.

So, here's to our approaching two years and all the great fun as Eric does his very, very best to explore the world and my limits... wish me luck! (I've a feeling I'll need it.)

LET'S GET THIS YEAR STARTED:
MY GOALS AS A PARENT-WRITER

January 22, 2017
Kate, 4 years
Eric, 2 years

Kids and writing and how to make it work for the coming year (even when you've got zero sleep happening).

Well, January's over and I'm crazy happy because the urge to write has bit into me hard and good. I'm sure you'll have noticed the last time I wrote one of these parent-writer blogs was in August... because life got busy and crazy and I just had to hold on tight. But now I'm ready to write, to get back to my stories—

At least I will... once I actually start writing. Which means... when I start sleeping again.

(I'm sure you'll notice that *not* sleeping has pretty much been a running theme since I had kids; certainly since Eric was born).

I'll back up a minute here and explain about this strange thing of me wanting to write (really, *really* wanting to) while at the same time not being able to. To survive the holidays and our crazy mess of birthdays and events (which, pretty much, makes up all of December plus a bit of November and January thrown in as well), I had to walk away from the writing.

There really wasn't a choice.

Not with my just-turned two-year-old son... who's still not sleeping. And teething.

Again.

Seriously, this month there were too many days that started at 4:00 a.m. and I had to somehow get through the day with my two kids and not completely lose my shit. Because running around like a raving, angry banshee was *not* the kind of parent I wanted to be. And some days, that's exactly what it felt like.

So for December, I put everything on hold except for the kids and surviving the holidays.

This meant I hung up my writing streak of 160 days. Yeah, you heard that right... 160 days of writing—*straight*—even with my two young kids.

Now, however, I'm raring to get going.

Mostly.

Because... I still have a two-year-old. My cute little angel, Eric, who even as I write this is attempting to single-handedly take down the gate surrounding all of our electronics and game consoles.

We're also a month into potty training, and while it's going well, it's also pretty crazy (yep... had a couple of those banshee moments, trust me). The diaper is gone completely and I'm watching Eric like a hawk to catch all the pee and poo until he learns where it belongs. Okay. He *knows* where it belongs but actually using the potty like he's supposed to... well... he's two.

And stubborn. Very stubborn.

He's also a late-talker like his sister, which means I get no nice verbal warnings like "Pee!" or "Poo!"

Fun times, let me tell you.

Yet here I am at the start of a new year (okay... sorta starting) and am thinking about getting the writing going again. Part of me is like, "You're freakin' crazy."

The other part acknowledges that I *need* to do this. This is one of those core, self-care pieces that I need to keep going.

Yet... still. Goals? For this year? Stuff that might even slightly be in my control. Slightly?

It's almost laughable, but heck, I've done this before. The writing and having a two-year-old part. I've got a little mantra that pretty aptly defines the year I'm facing:

The year I won't sit down.

Considering Eric is now capable of climbing up the barstools to get to our kitchen counter and is even more capable of pushing said chairs to the counter to get the stuff he's not supposed to get (after we, smart that we are, moved those stools *away* from the counter)... yeah. It's gonna be an interesting year.

Somehow though, somehow, I'm still going to get words written. Specifically, fiction words.

How do I know this? Well, I actually looked back at 2016 and added up my word counts the year, for both my fiction writing and nonfiction, and I was pretty darn amazed—especially considering the hurdles I faced. We had a house move in there, Kate still not trusting in her voice, and then there was me, a mom, and it felt like I was beating the world back with my mighty stick.

And what were my word count total?

Last year, for nine actual months of writing, I wrote 29,121 words of nonfiction and 89,449 words of fiction!

Also, I completed seven online workshops (they were six weeks each) with Dean Wesley Smith and WMG Publishing. (I did not count all the fiction words from those assignments, which would also add to my word count total.)

And when I step back and look at the actual totals, look at what I accomplished in a year.

Wow.

Crazy, right? I had no idea. Frankly, I'm shocked... but there it is. Those numbers are telling a truth I couldn't see when I was down in the muck and the baby wipes. All this writing happened because I just sat down and did what I could. Little bit by little bit. Some days I got in an hour, most others anywhere between fifteen to thirty minutes.

Some days it was only five minutes.

I saw 2016 as the Year of Learning. It was also the Year to Restart My Writing. I certainly hit on both accounts.

I'd also really wanted to amp up the publishing front, deal with some of those god-awful covers and blurbs created back when I started this venture in 2012. Yeah... that didn't happen. But boy, *boy* did I learn a ton about being a writer with two small kids, especially having one with language delays and the other just learning to how crazy-fun it is to get into *everything*.

And really, if you're a parent, you know darn well that a baby's first year is *way* easier than toddlerhood. Light-years easier.

So, I had a lot of false starts throughout the year as I tried something new (or even the same thing again and again until I caught a clue), and slowly... eventually... I figured out how to write with my kids around.

This is a question I *needed* to figure out since we decided to homeschool. Yes, it'll get easier as my kids get older (and way, way easier when Eric actually puts his poop in the potty instead of running to me first), but I still need to figure out this balance, this time for myself and my writing while at the same time caring for my family.

And I am figuring it out...

Piece by piece.

If you're a parent of littles and you have this crazy-ass dream of being a writer (or anything creative, really) and regardless of how little you've slept in, I don't know... *five years*... you *still* want to write—here are a few tips and lessons I've learned along the way.

(And I'm sure these will only continue to be refined and tried again and adjusted and thrown out as the month, or heck, as *weeks* progress in this new year.)

Here's the thing: when it comes to fiction, I truly, truly need to be away from my kids. That's when my subconscious comes out, when it feels safe enough to dive into a story, to lose itself with the characters.

I will also say that this isn't forever.

With Kate I managed to write in the next room while she was watching her all-time favorite movie *Frozen* or when she was playing the WiiU and jumping on those little mushroom-like dudes in *Yoshi's Woolley World*. My point—if she was sufficiently occupied and happy and independently playing (and not strategically climbing into the cupboard to get the (no longer) hidden chocolate), then I could write.

But with Eric, especially as young as he is... forget it. What worked with Kate will *not* work with Eric (because there my kids are, totally different from each other).

I needed to be alone and *away* from Eric to keep from triggering all manner of my parent spidey-senses or I couldn't write.

Now, when it comes to nonfiction and learning, I've got a lot more leeway. I can keep going with this blog even though I've already been interrupted *seven* times since I started writing this thing. Which is great because it means my precious alone time is reserved only for fiction writing.

So in 2016, I learned I needed to be away from the kids. I also learned that I'm a morning person (or I refortified this knowledge) and if I have any dream of writing these days, it needs to be in the morning (by the end of the day my mind is zombie-*mush*).

How about you? What are your writing parameters? What do you need to escape into your fiction, to let your creative voice come alive and simply *shine*?

Once you've got your baseline, the little pieces that simply *need* to be in place for you to make writing happen, you come up with the next part: The Plan.

Easier said than done, I know.

I talked this plan out with Sean (... make that eight Eric-led interruptions in the writing of this blog... sigh). Sean will watch the kids for an hour—and *I will leave the house.*

That's right. I grab my laptop and head outside to sit by the pool (or on rare days when it actually rains down here in sunny California, the common area of our complex). I've got my headphones to drown out any annoying sounds and I've got the clock.

This change, this slight adjustment, has been huge for me, a real piece of the puzzle I was missing. It's allowed my subconscious to feel safe again with the storytelling. And it worked, because I kept getting the writing in, even on days where the last thing I felt like doing was writing.

It wasn't always easy, but words were written.

I've also come to understand there's another critical piece still missing: time to just *think*.

Time when my mind is free to come out and just have fun with ideas, to live with the characters. What might happen next? What kind of world would that be?

This part, feeling that it's safe enough for my creative voice to come out and play, is still a struggle. There's so much clamoring for my daily attention. Any downtime I have, any ounce of quiet time, I have this need to fill with something... from listening to podcasts about publishing or health or board games to watching a TV show while doing dishes because it's one of those rare moments where I can do something just for me.

The idea of just thinking and letting my subconscious have some fun is not nearly as powerful as those other distractions. I'm still working on this and it's one of my big goal areas for the coming year —giving myself time to think, and really, to daydream.

This is also a matter of recognizing myself and putting a finger on my own creative pulse.

When I'm feeling overwhelmed and stressed and my resources are low, it is not the time to expect myself to easily slip into this creative-thought stage. But if I can't do that, maybe I can grab one of my research books on the west and Butte, Montana (which I just *love*) and read. Maybe in the reading of that book, new ideas will spark, new characters or situations or stories, maybe this small act will take some pressure off the need to create and... oh look, there's a story idea peeking it's head out.

That's how I'm going to handle this coming year.

For myself to get a goal in place, a plan, and like all things in parenting... be flexible.

(And more often than not, prepare for everything to go sideways, too, because *that's* certainly a theme in my parenting world).

I need to focus on what I *can* do (rather than what I can't).

What I can do: write every day. Even for five minutes.

This daily goal became *so so so* powerful for me. On days where I was sick and just plain exhausted and wanted to melt into a pile of mush... it pushed me through and got me to the keyboard. I'd always heard of the power of streaks, but I'd never thought streaks could conquer the utter exhaustion that (often) comes with parenting.

Certainly parenting a toddler.

In addition to writing every day, I actually have a goal of writing for one hour, five days a week. I say five days and not *every* day because that would be totally unrealistic for me and this season I'm in, and I don't want to get discouraged. In fact, when I schedule this hour of writing in my calendar, this will be a flexible hour, especially if we've got a Disneyland trip planned or are driving up to visit the grandparents or friends. This is *not* a hard and fast goal because the last thing I want is to feel shame or guilt when I can't hit that goal. In fact, the *only* reason I'm committing to an hour is because, darn it, I'd like to write some projects this year!

Like a novel.

I really, really want to write another novel. That's been a challenging goal for me, mostly because my subconscious is so wrapped up in my kids and supporting them and keeping them safe and alive. I've had to stand up for them, to allow them to develop and grow at their own pace and not worry about what society has deemed 'normal' and 'appropriate'.

In fact, the last novel I wrote was when I was pregnant with Eric. Granted, I've written some long-ass short stories in that last year that are more novella length, but a multi-character novel? Haven't done that in two years, and novels are more my natural length.

I want to get to writing those novels again.

So, I sat down and did some math, figured out how I can actually, physically, make this happen.

I estimated 100,000 words is a good novel length for me. I also want to write a couple of short stories and do these blogs, of course, which considering how long I write will be another 100,000 words. I know that my usual pace is 1,000 words an hour, so I did the math for the year, for each month (and because I'm expecting life to be what it is, I'm scheduling only for 10 months), and then broke the numbers down further until I got to days... which came out to 500 words a day.

And you know what? I can totally hit this.

I see that number and I *know* it's doable. Some days will only be five minutes of writing, but it will hit my *daily* writing goal. Other days I'll pound out 2,000 words because the story's gripped me and I can't type fast enough.

I've also got plans to do more online workshops, to keep the learning going and have even signed up for two Oregon Coast workshops... bringing the kids (and another adult) with me.

And if I fail? If I don't make it to Oregon or I don't hit this overall goal of writing 200,000 words for the year?

It will *still* be a success because *any* writing with young kids *is* a success.

I'm gonna keep trying, I'm gonna keep plugging away because I've learned when I write, I'm happy. I'm a whole, more complete person. And that means I'm a better, more patient, more compassionate parent.

Because first and foremost, who I am is a parent.

I am a mother.

That is my primary job and role, twenty-four hours a day, and I *love* it. Yet, I still want to keep the writing going. I still want to be a professional writer. I want to be a healthy person who eats real food and gets plenty of movement. I'm also the primary speech partner for my kids. You heard me, *both* kids. We may not do something structured and routine, because that doesn't work for our family, but I'm still aware of this speech play, this speech work and weaving it throughout our normal lives.

I'm playing a lot of roles and I've got a lot on my plate (and we haven't even talked about my publishing business, one which I hope to at least get going by the end of 2017), but the truth is I'm just one person. There's only so much I can do when I have two young ones getting into all manner of fun.

So here I am, looking into 2017, and I'm going to do what I can. I'm going to try and then try again. I'm going to get up and keep going. I'm going to keep learning and keep writing.

In addition to The Year I Won't Sit Down, this will also be The Year of Writing and Learning.

Whether you're a writer or artist or have some other business dream cooked up in your heart, something that you *still* want to make happen in between the pauses in parenthood... you can decide what kind of year you'll have.

Create your own pauses. Don't wait for those moments to come to you. If this creative venture is important to you, find a way to fit it in. Trust me, you'll be happier for it.

For me, I'm excited. I'm ready to get going. I'm ready to tell some stories.

(Or I will be... as soon as my days don't start at 3:30 in the morning.)

THE REALITY OF LITTLE ONES

January 15, 2017
Kate, 4 years
Eric, 2 years

The realities of being a parent—a mix of cuteness, joy, and moments where my hair stands up like Doc Brown and steam blows out my nose. (Throw in two late-talkers and parenthood really gets interesting.)

What's amazing is I just wrote this last blog post, all raring to go, hopeful of my writing future, and ready to get my writing going and off the ground for 2017. I can practically hear the cheers and pink pom-poms behind me. All I need to do is start the writing and then...
    Then, last night, I got about four hours of solid sleep.
    My day started at 3:15. In the morning.
    I will probably stay in my PJs all day—maybe I'll even brush my teeth—and I'm hoping to God I will not be a screaming banshee

because I really need some peace to myself for a whole five minutes, *please*...

Teething. It sucks.

Thankfully, Eric's on his last set of molars (though how long it takes until they're freakin' finished requires more than a crystal ball, maybe a sprinkling of fairy dust and a good-size glass of wine, not to mention the required chocolate). Thank goodness these kids are super cute (I firmly believe, and many other parents of toddlers have confirmed this, that clearly this is a survival superpower of two-year-olds everywhere).

And this pretty much sums up the life of a parent-writer—certainly if your kids are under three. This time in our kids' lives, especially as we try to do a creative venture, means we need flexibility and acceptance.

I can try and force myself to do some learning, to take notes on the Research Lecture I've got geared up and ready to go... Or I can just say my goal for today is to keep breathing and keep myself as centered as possible because even I don't like being that crazy banshee with hair sticking up like Doc Brown in *Back to the Future*.

Plus, I know darn well from past experience if I try and do any kind of writing work or studying while the kids are interrupting me, oh man will I lose my shit. It's like my ability to be calm and roll with them kid punches these days is long, long gone. Just a distant memory.

Probably because of the lack of sleep.

I've learned it's better to just accept that today (or even just this moment) is not the time to focus on my writing or learning or even doing the dishes. It's better for everyone if I accept the interruptions and leave the writing for another day, another moment.

And I know, too, this crazy-hard time won't last forever.

Yesterday morning I felt fantastic. I felt energized. We even had a board game session with friends planned for Sean's birthday.

Then... we had to deal with five Eric poops... in a single day... and only one that ended up where it belonged (on the potty because, yes, we're still in the middle of potty training). Once was at farmers market and me, silly me, chose *not* to bring an extra pair of pants.

I've got no idea what I was thinking. Perhaps I simply assumed he'd already emptied his system of all things poop—and this *was* just a short walk from our home—or simply my lack of sleep.

Of course, Eric *insisted* on being carried so I ended up tossing my shirt and jeans into the 'Wash Now!!' pile.

After that adventure, Sean and I were stressed-out zombies. Whatever energy we had was zapped away, just like that.

One day, I swear, I'll write a nice, fluffy-bunny post about how great it is to have kids, to connect with them, to watch the world just open up before their eyes... but this moment is not that moment.

And that's okay too.

But really, to the people I see in the elevator who coo about how cute and adorable my kids are, who—after I say I haven't slept in five years—*still* tell me to enjoy them because the time goes by so fast...

Screw You.

No, really. Stop it.

Don't you think I know that? Don't you think I see and enjoy those beautiful little moments? Because I do. And my kids *are* wonderful—the problem is that feeling doesn't carry through for the whole 24-hour period in a day because this thing called *life* and *toddlerhood* enters the mix.

Maybe instead of giving lectures on loving my kids, you could do something helpful—like letting us off the elevator first. Or I should say, since my kids are already off the elevator, how about stepping aside so I can bolt after Eric. You know, something that shows you care instead of all the judgments and advice?

That'd be nice.

Yes, I think my filter is a bit short these days. (This whole only four hours of sleep is a killer.)

But really, as parents, we're doing our best. Truly. Sean and I are doing our best to be the kind of parents we want to be.

Parents who listen and understand and respect our kids' feelings. Parents who can empathize with their kids' feelings even though they're still getting in the car seat to play with friends and just get outside to *run*...

But in the meantime, kids... *please*, can you stop screaming or trying to hit my face? I understand the idea of the car seat isn't acceptable to you right now, but this *is* what we're doing and where we're going.

(Just imagine me taking lots and lots of deep breaths here.)

I won't even mention the whole 'keeping our home mostly free of dust and the food that, regardless of our herculean efforts, *still* ends up on the floor, bits and pieces and the dried Play-Doh now glued to the carpet like a hot pink mess' thing.

Or all the real food we take the time to chop and cook and prepare which is shoved away because what you really want is fruit and potatoes and the best steak parents can buy.

It's tough being a parent.

It's tough being the parent of a toddler who's got a very clear idea in his mind yet has zero ability to speak that mind and get those needs met. And, unlike Kate who liked figuring out the puzzles who were her parents and tried to communicate with us, Eric's more inclined to stomp and cry and hit.

It's also tough being a parent with some crazy dream of, you know, being a professional writer. (And you can just about replace that with anything you like—musician, artist, anything at all that involves reaching some dream you have that your cute little kids don't seem to give a shit about.)

Yet, we still love them.

And we still—even when all we need is just five minutes of quiet—can't help but reconnect when our toddlers wiggle their naked butts into our lap for a cuddle.

It's truly amazing how forgiving kids can be while we adults can hold onto our frustrations for hours (if not days, in some cases). But our kids, they're ready to cuddle.

They need that. They need that attachment to heal, to feel like they're loved and not alone (even if we are still rip-roaring mad). I like to remind myself of this (actually, I'm constantly reminding myself).

All those times when all I want is for my kids to go away so I can breathe for a moment, when I'm about to let the frustration flood out in tears—that's *exactly* the moment I most need to reconnect with them, to heal the rupture, to pull them into my lap and smell their hair. To feel their absolute trust and love for me.

And somehow, like magic, that reconnection eases my feelings of frustration, exhaustion, and really, just being overwhelmed.

This reconnection process is not always easy (I think it rarely is, at least for me, at least these days), but I'm glad I can at least be aware of these moments. I may not always act on it (or heck, sometimes I flat choose not to), and that's okay too.

Just like it's okay if I hold off on my writing plans and goals for 2017 until my life levels out a little. Or until I start getting a decent amount of sleep. Even if the fiction writing hasn't restarted yet, there are other things I can do. Like my online workshops or research for my historical novel set in Butte, Montana. Or just picking up a good book and reading for pleasure. And then... studying it.

Because my life *is* pretty intense right now and there's only so much a human body (and mind) can handle before it shuts down. Lights out. No one's home.

The other half is admitting that I *can't* do this right now, right at this moment.

Because I'm not perfect.

Instead I'm only one person trying her best, every day.

That's been my focus for these past couple of weeks. Looking back on the day when I first started releasing all these feelings and words onto the page (pretty darn unfiltered, I've got to say), our lives have actually gotten a little bit easier. We've gotten a little bit more sleep. Our life is leveling out, bit by bit.

But still, I'm not perfect.

There are only so many things I can do at any given moment. Like canceling my plans of hanging out with other moms, instead choosing to go to bed. Or skipping an indoor playground outing because the stress would be too much for me (and I'm still waiting for the day's poop from Eric, and trust me, he'd have no issue going right there, right in his pants).

Instead, I stay home... and I play with my kids.

I connect with them, playing *My Little Pony* with Kate and then throwing Eric onto our bed (he loves flying through the air, I tell you).

We had our speech-play sessions while simply living our life. It wasn't anything special, not part of any routine, just... our life.

And Grandma came over. After a month of her being gone, I think everyone needed that reconnection. It's especially important for my introverted kids (one who's talking, the other who isn't), to get that one-on-one time instead of being at an overly stimulating playground.

This physical connection, this straight-up *play* is so very important for them, more so than for other kids, I think. Because of their language delays, yes, but also because of who they are and what they need to feel whole and connected and healed. I see it in the way Kate and Eric express themselves, how they show their love for us, their joy and connection.

They don't have words so they use their play, their hugs, their smiles.

And I've got to be aware of that, I've got to be in tune with them. Turn that dial up to a hundred because that's how *we* communicate. This also means that my subconscious, instead of thinking up some cool story or idea, is focused on my kids.

It needs to be.

They don't have words yet (or at least many) to communicate their needs so I'm constantly reading their nonverbal cues, constantly following and listening to my intuition.

The truth is I feel better, too. After having these moments of connection and play, I feel less like Doc Brown's hair sticking every which way and more like myself. And with each moment of feeling like *me*, the urge to write, to tell stories, is coming back.

The key, I think, to being a parent and a creative is to *not* force the creativity. It'll be there when I'm ready. Because, right now, there's a reason I'm not writing (life being a bit intense, remember?).

Writing and storytelling—it's supposed to be fun.

Enjoyable.

The more I let go of my expectations, of circumstances out of my control (like sleep), the easier it's been for my life to level out.

To find peace in where I am in these moments.

I started writing this blog when I really, really wanted to tear my hair out, but now... I can feel it again. The writing is stirring. My little storytelling voice is peeking its head out and taking a tentative look around. Are we ready to start? Is it safe?

I think so.

If not at this exact moment, then soon.

I also feel myself returning to center, to being the kind of person I want to be. Patient and empathetic. To being my kids' speech partner again instead of wanting to lock myself in the bathroom. That's what my gut's telling me. All because I gave myself the permission to be a parent first (and survive!) and let that parenting take as long as it needed. I know it was the right call.

Especially when Eric grabbed hold and hugged me in that tight way only a toddler can—with his whole being and love. And that's when I realize the truth.

I *do* feel better.

Certainly, I'm not a saint or super-mom today (or tomorrow or like, ever), but maybe I'll do something else drastic and fun... like actually put some normal clothes on. Or just read a book.

Besides, I've gotten a good look at Eric's molars and, dear Lord, they've nearly pushed fully through his gums, so I guess there *is* a light at the end of this tunnel.

Days like this any tiny bit of success is a serious cause for celebration.

The writing, and all my big dreams for the future, will be waiting for me, patient, like always. Patient in a way that my two-year-old toddler can never, ever be. But that's okay because that's part of my role as a parent.

To be patient.

Or, at least, do my very, very best.

SURVIVING TAXES:

THE COLD, HARD NUMBERS AND THE STORY THEY DON'T TELL

January 19, 2017
Kate, 4 years
Eric, 2 years

How to pick yourself up and keep on going towards your Big Dreams... all while still being a parent.

I think the most challenging time for a businessperson who's also a parent (especially being the primary caregiver of two crazy-young kids), is just after the new year. I've already done the fun and exciting new year's challenges and set the goals I'm going to do my best to tackle. I even looked back at 2016 and saw just how much I *actually* accomplish.

It's exciting.

It's empowering.

And then it's tax time and the reality of my business comes crashing down. It's enough to pop my excitement-balloon faster than my two-year-old who full-body-squashes it (yes, a playful pastime of his).

As I said, I'm the primary caregiver for Kate, now four, and Eric, now two. You better believe most of my days (and nights) I've got my hands full.

Showers by myself? Ha. Some days I'm lucky to get them in.

Quiet, introspective time where I can think? New and fun and cool story ideas? Or maybe, when we're calmly walking around Disneyland, take a moment to study people as if they were characters, to wonder who they are and what they do based on how they're dressed, how they walk, their mannerisms, and how they react to the Disney world around them?

Yeah. Right.

Get back to me in a few years and I'll let you know how that's all going.

Writing for me right now means squeezing in stolen moments throughout the day. It's carrying a notebook in my already fully loaded purse (snacks and water bottles, anyone?). It means being very much separated from other professional writers and the little feedback I get is from my effort on continuing to learn, whether studying books by major bestsellers or taking online workshops.

My growth in writing is tiny.

In fact, you can't really even see this growth, my improvement, unless you get out a magnifying glass and squint your eyes... really... hard. Funny enough, this small, tiny steps of progress reminds me so much of Kate's journey with language (and where Eric is now). All we had with Kate were these tiny little nuggets, so small that to most people they were invisible and yet we treasured them because it meant she *was* moving forward.

No, I couldn't say, "Oh boy! She said a new word today."

In fact... it would sometimes be *months* in between new words and then we'd be lucky if she continued to say those words (the stubborn, control-orientated girl that I have). But when Kate looked up at us with a smile on her face after doing something cool with her toys (this is called 'visual referencing,' if you're curious) or when she listened and understood as I explained that another mom would help her with her jacket since I had my hands full with Eric—that was success.

This success was tiny, it was so small most folks would skip right over it, but for us and our journey, it was the exact opposite.

I'm doing this same process with Eric now, making notes of how he's sharing looks of excitement, not just with me, but with other moms. Of his very clear understanding when I say the word "more" and his continual babbling to get me to continue this tickle-fun game.

That is what success looks like... for him.

All precursors to words and yet, when most people see me playing with him like this, they have no idea what's really going on. Sure, I'm playing with my son and he's laughing like *crazy*, but I'm also 'working' on 'language' with him... all at the same time.

Who knew, right??

And right now, that pretty much feels like how my writing is progressing these days—it's so tiny no one can see it.

One word at a time or just even getting my thoughts and life back to a place where I *can* write fiction (please, please, please Eric... only two wakeups a night, okay? I can handle that!).

But tax season, though, really puts my whole life, my whole progress forward, my writing, into a cold, harsh light and it's really hard to not get discouraged.

When I look at my revenue for the previous year and look at my expenses... when my life and my writing is broken down into these cold, hard numbers, it breaks my heart. Because those numbers don't even begin to reflect what I've accomplished this past year or even what I *could* have accomplished if given an hour or two a day of actual writing time or publishing time.

What I *did* do in 2016 was write nearly 90,000 words of fiction. Plus another 29,000 words of nonfiction (basically, these blogs).

Right now, that's a whole bunch of words just sittin' on my computer, not making me any money. Because I haven't actually published anything new in a *really* long time. Maybe since Eric was born? I'd have to check and, wow, do I not have time to check.

I also started re-doing a whole bunch of my blurbs for previously published stories, but I haven't actually gotten to making those changes or price changes or rebranding my story covers. I haven't gotten to these things because I made being a parent a priority. After parenting, with the stolen bits of time I had, I made my *writing* a priority.

It's totally cool that I'm getting this great list of story titles with new worlds and new characters just waiting to get published (meaning I can also brand them correctly, all at the same time rather than doing it piecemeal), but it *still* doesn't make the process any easier.

To look at my 2016 numbers, my end of year earnings, and see... wow... a really low number.

Feels pretty shitty.

Not that I'm placing blame on anyone else other than myself. Or on my kids for taking so much of my time (which they *should*.)

You see, I *do* deserve a low income because, hey, I haven't actually put the time or effort into the publishing end of my business. Yes, I've been doing some learning and behind-the-scenes stuff, like finally getting the bones of my websites in order (okay... not even the bones, more like the outline of bones) and I took this fantastic 6-week course on blurbs. But again, it's not stuff you can see yet.

This is also true of my writing.

All the stuff I'm learning, all the pieces and all the growing I've done in the past few years, you can't *see* the effects of it. Certainly not in revenue (again... I have to actually publish this stuff first).

I also haven't landed any new sales to traditional publishing magazines although though I *do* have a reprint of a short story coming out, which is pretty cool (the story I sold at the last Anthology workshop I went to when Kate was eighteen months old).

So... no new sales...

But I've been getting almost-immediate, personalized rejections from the editor of *Fantasy and Science Fiction Magazine* (you writers out there know it's a big deal when an editor with possibly less time than me goes out of his or her way to write you a note about why your story 'missed'). I didn't get any of those personal rejections when I first started writing short stories back in 2011.

Progress.

Little, itsy-bitsy steps.

The only problem is sometimes it's just incredibly hard *not* to cave under all the negative, awful words of my critical voice. This voice is always waiting, like this five-toothed shadow in the creases of my mind, to tell me how bad I am, that I'm not improving, that my stories are slow and boring, and heck, I should just toss in the towel and give up because what's the point?

I mean... just *look* at my numbers! I'm barely selling at all. Clearly, I'm doing something wrong. Clearly, I'm not good enough yet.

Except... I don't give up.

Instead, I (somehow), pick myself up.

It has a lot to do with my stubbornness (where do you think my late-talker kids get it from?) but a lot of it is simply because I can't *not* write. The minute I start getting a half-decent amount of sleep, the stories just flare up in my mind and I can almost not sleep because they are just so cool and is sleep really all that important?

But fighting this negativity, fighting against these cold, hard numbers that only tell a fraction of the truth...

Is hard.

Honestly, I'm not sure how I do it, either. How I don't just fall into a gooey, icky mess even thinking about *all* the work ahead of me. *All* the work that needs to be done to put me where I know, without a doubt, I *can* be as a writer and a publisher, if I just had the time to do it.

Except... I chose to be a parent.

I'm even choosing to follow my kids' their interests in learning and education. I've chosen to be their primary language partner since both of my kids have a language disorder (well... Eric's still up in the air but he's definitely got a delay).

Yet here I am with my grand ole dreams about being a professional writer and independent publisher and that's probably just this side of crazy (or, to be honest, dead-on the crazy spot). What keeps me going, though, is this drive.

This complete desire to learn, to keep improving.

I *know* time will be easier to come by. Probably not *this* year—Eric is, after all, two years old—but I can look at Kate and see how independent she is, how I can get in my quiet time to my work.

Right now I'm in between typing up this blog and adding up my 2016 revenue and expense totals all while sitting outside of Eric's door making sure that kid stays in there to get the damn nap he so desperately needs. And did I mention I've got the laundry going too?

Yeah.

That's my life.

The life of a parent-writer.

At this moment, a parent-businesswoman, and believe me, my yearly revenue is very, very far from the truth of where I actually am, how much time and energy and love I've put into my businesses, how little sleep I've had in these past two years (or five if I'm being really honest here).

I have to keep in mind that each time I write a word of fiction, it's a success.

Even here, sitting outside Eric's door and doing a small snippet of my writing business, is a success.

I think that's ultimately how we succeed as parent-writers. Or parent-artists. Or parent-real estate agents (just substitute whatever you're trying to do that involves making some money).

We fit this in, our passion, our calling our writing.

We squeeze it in.

We have to.

Sometimes we cry (I cried a lot today... but being kept up since 1:00 a.m. two nights in row with a giant pile of laundry to tackle... yeah, crying is pretty much a given at that point).

Sometimes we have these clear moments of success, like every time I got an assignment back from my writing mentor telling me how I nailed it.

It's those tiny successes that mean everything.

All those cold, hard numbers? Well, I didn't make a whole lot last year but that goes a long way toward helping out with deductions because I *do* have my writing business set up as a business. I just have to get these things added up and done and off to our accountant, and then look forward to what I can do next, what *is* in my control.

A lot of my energy levels will depend on what I can't control, though, at least for the time being (I'm talking to you sleep... and my two-year-old). But hey, I *can* keep learning and I *can* keep writing, even if only in little bits. The rest of it—the big dreams I have for my businesses, for all the stories I'm itching to write and to tell—those will happen too.

At some point.

For right now, I'm just going to be this scrappy little mom-fighter kicking every ounce of negativity and critical voice as hard as I can because... because it's the only way I know how to keep on going, to keep even these small successes going.

And no matter what, I'm not going to stop.

Even if at times, like today, I need to pick up the phone and cry to my best friend or to Sean about how hard it is facing these numbers and the real truth of being a parent of little kids.

I'll cry and then I'll pick myself and keep moving forward.

Here's to another year down. Another year of raising a toddler and Kate, both late-talking children. Another year of small revenue but some really, really big successes.

Like teaching Kate the days of the week because she really wants to make cookies *today* and not Saturday and yet she keeps on asking, "Need more cookies now?"

And I smile and enjoy every single word.

NO SUCH THING AS "PERFECT"

February 14, 2017
Kate, 4 years
Eric, 2 years

The constant battle between everything we must accomplish instead of taking time for ourselves, our needs, and our own—essential—self-care.

If you've been following my blog, you've probably clued in that I'm not sleeping much these days (read: *at all*). And yet... life doesn't stop because my day started at 3:30 in the morning. The laundry still needs to get done. Food needs to be chopped, prepared, and cooked because feeding our kids (and ourselves) real food is important to us for feeling good and staying healthy. And let's not forget the endless wave of dishes.

You know, all that *normal* stuff that comes from living with kids.

So too comes the normal stuff when potty training a two-year-old... I'll just let your imagination fill you in on that one.

On top of all that parenting stuff, all the normal pieces that come with having kids, if you're like me and have got a late-talker (or two), you've got even more on your plate. You might be organizing and driving them to speech therapy appointments or maybe you've decided to just take on the speech work (and play) yourself because it's what works for your family.

That's right. You... the very person who isn't getting any sleep because of *both* kids.

There are moments when Eric does nap and I have the choice to play *My Little Ponies* with Kate (which she could do for *hours*) or I'm pulling out a book to read. Or playing video games. Or working on an online writing workshop.

I'm choosing to focus on my own self-care during those quiet moments. To fill my own cup so I can get through the rest of the day and evening, and chances are that it will be probably well into the next day (or several) before I get another peaceful moment of downtime.

I'm choosing to take care of me... and I'm feeling pretty darn guilty about it.

Correction: I'm feeling imperfect. Because there *is* so much more I can and *should* be doing.

Right?

I should be focusing more on Kate when I have those quiet moments, playing with her and connecting, doing the one-on-one time our speech pathologist wants us to do. Maybe fun activities and games that are of my choosing rather than always Kate's choosing.

Which all sounds reasonable but there's a whole lot more going on underneath there... my value, my worth.

I *should* be having one-on-one time with Kate, but not for speech therapy work. Instead, my focus should be on ways we can connect because when we connect, the rest of our day goes easier. *Kate's* cup is filled. She's feeling *my* love and when I do ask things of her, she's more willing to listen and follow along.

So yes, connection is important.

But Kate also needs me to *not* be a raging banshee and these days, that's getting really really hard. Massive sleep deprivation with maybe a teensy little end in sight (maybe?). Also Eric who only wants Mommy right now and will scream, nonstop, until his needs are met. And here I am, working as hard as I can to keep steam from flooding out my ears, to remain compassionate and empathetic. To not immediately jump into fight-or-flight mode but to stay present and connected.

To do *all* this I need to start taking better care of me.

It's like the flight attendants tell you every time you board a plane: Put your own mask on first.

And yet... it's still hard.

I've got this little voice in my head and it's constantly whispering and nattering, pointing out all the things I'm not doing and how things would be *so* much better if I were. I've got a list of activities and goals our speech pathologist wants me to work on with both kids and here I am barely getting through the day as it is. Even when I told her what we were going through (potty training and zero sleeping) her reply was for me to get help.

The comment just made me madder.

Are you kidding? Seriously??

Going through the system, whether through school or through our insurance (a blessing, truly, that we *have* options for both; I understand many other families aren't as lucky), but all this would greatly add to the stress. The overwhelm.

We would have to go through these systems to be seen by a decent speech therapist, one who actually understands the difference between a speech disorder and a language disorder and how to help my kids. We won't even talk about the emotional fallout the kids *and* I would go through as I fight for them, as I stand strong so others can understand my kids for who they are, to understand their unique difference. All for the effort of getting in actual, routine speech work time to save me less time and stress?

Sorry... but no.

This would *not* save me time and stress. This would be the exact opposite—for me, for our family.

How about I try and do my best at home and trust in my kids? Trust they understand what I'm going through and that I still love them?

That the little bits we get in... like Eric at the park, snuggling on my lap. How I started kiss-tickling him and he started laughing. I would stop and he would look at me, right in my eyes as if to say: I want more!! To which I said, "more" and kept on going.

Until I stopped and waited for him to look at me again.

Do you know what that was?

That was living. Living a life, connecting with my son, while at the same time practicing the speech techniques I'd learned from our speech pathologist. Is it not better to have these little tiny moments, dozens and dozens of these throughout the day compared to a set time with a speech therapist for thirty minutes? Maybe an hour?

Instead we have this time for speech and language play *the entire day*.

This is what worked best for me, for my kids and their needs. What I wanted to do was play with my kids.

Play... with language.

And clearly I'm not doing so bad. I have walking, talking proof in Kate that I've got this, that I can do this—our unique journey with language and learning to talk.

The other day I about fell onto the floor (thankfully, I was sitting on the floor to begin with) when Kate looked at me and said a full sentence in front of her grandma.

"May I have the iPad now?"

I didn't fully understand what she'd said, so I asked her to say it again. She did. She trusted her words enough to repeat them *and* she did it in front of another adult.

"May I have the iPad now?"

Yes, that's exactly what she said. Just picture my jaw smacking into our PlayDoh-crusted carpet. And you better believe I told her yes.

Did you see that *sentence???*

We don't overtly 'teach' our kids manners. I mean, with our

language-delayed kids, we don't tell them to say "please" or "thank you." Those are meaningless words to kids who rely heavily on visualization.

What do I mean by this? Well, the word 'apple' has a clear picture to it, right? But 'please?' Not so much.

So, we never bothered with manners... except... that's not fully true. We model it in our own interactions. Constantly. When Kate tells me she went potty (by saying "poo poo") and then we go and I help her wipe, I always say, "thank you" (I mean, she did go in the potty and then came and got me for help, which is certainly what I want so you'd better believe I'm telling her thanks!). Or when she actually does put her used bowl in the sink, I *always* show my gratitude (I get real tired real quick picking up twenty barely used bowls off the floor).

But the word 'may'?

That one surprised the heck out of me. Tells me right there that I'm not doing halfway bad with this manners thing because clearly she's getting it.

And yet... here I am still facing these moments of feeling like I'm a terrible mom.

Because I'm not perfect.

The other day, Sean and I were sitting on the couch while Eric was actually napping and Kate was quietly content with the iPad. I told him that part of me felt like I was a terrible mom because she was on the iPad so much these days, that what I should have done was use those quiet moments to be with her, to connect with her, to play a board game and teach her further things like turn taking (like our speech pathologist wants her doing).

But as soon as I let those feelings become words, said them aloud, I realized the other, deeper truth:

That I truly, *truly* needed this quiet time.

I'm not perfect.

There will always be something more I can be doing or something I want to be doing (or simply 'should' be doing). You'll notice I haven't talked about my fiction writing or my publishing at all...

even though I desperately want to get started on both. I know I can't.

Not until I start sleeping.

And it's extra hard to hear from someone else, the speech pathologist and professional we trust, someone who was a mom a long time ago and clearly remembers this stage, tell me that I should just "get help."

As if it's that easy.

For us it's not.

Sean pointed out that it's Eric I need help with, but Eric doesn't *want* anyone else's help. He wants me right now and he's pretty darn vocal about it.

This isn't to say my speech pathologist's advice was all bad or wrong, it just went in a direction we weren't comfortable with. Instead we've been asking for more help from the grandmas, and on those days when I've gotten almost zero sleep, I've started asked Sean's brother and sister to help. I even had a friend and her kids come over to play with Kate so I could rest and I'm working towards getting a mother's helper again.

So we're trying the ways that we can. (I know many of you might not even have family or these kind of resources around you and that's... that's just *hard* and lonely, too, I'm sure.)

But let's also be realistic here. When you have late-talkers, chances are you've got some pretty opinionated and stubborn little kids on your hands who darn well know *their* minds (and you're just not good at reading those minds). Whatever you decide—to get extra help or not—it's probably not going to be some simple or quick fix.

Parenting is *hard* work.

Parenting late-talkers is even *harder*. (Or any kind of unique differences your children were born with.)

Parenting is also about seasons. There are times when life is good and fun and maybe a tiny(?) bit easy, and then there are times like I'm living through right now when surviving the day is the goal. When getting to bedtime without losing my shit (at least not too much) is considered success.

I truly believe whatever your right answer is, it will be different from mine. It's quite possible my answer will be different tomorrow or the next day because life with our kids is always changing. We often have both joy and intensely challenging moments sitting side by side *at the exact same time.*

So let's be kinder to ourselves (this includes me).

Parenting isn't for the faint of heart. We can have this all-consuming love for our kids while at this same time (or the moment right after), want a break from being a parent. Like, "What the hell was I thinking??" kinda thoughts.

Because parenting is hard—and at the exact same time, it's amazing.

And you know what? Doing my best, doing what felt right every day, every moment... somehow the words eventually came to Kate. Even being my often inadequate and imperfect self, her words still came.

In fact, Kate's words are coming more, each and every day. Everything from asking "Can I have chocolate now?" to "May I have the iPad now?"

We don't need to be perfect; our kids don't *need* us to be perfect. All they need us to do is try and try again, every day. And to love them.

That's something I can do, imperfections and all.

RESTART THE WRITING

(AFTER A PARENTING LIFE ROLE)

March 5, 2017
Kate, 4 years
Eric, 2 years

When parenthood puts the writing on hold, at some point you need to shove the fears away, stand up, and get back to the computer.

So I'm getting to be pretty good about this restarting thing. Ever since Kate was born back in August 2012, I've continuously had to put the writing on hold for many, many different reasons and it's pretty much been for family reasons. The birth of Kate followed by many sleepless nights and teething, toddlerhood and potty training. Then along came Eric—

When you bring another kid into the mix life *really* gets interesting.

We had even *more* sleepless nights and discovered Kate was a late-talker. There was a good chunk of time, of several months really, where I was living in a pretty dark and mentally scared place. I had a lot of fear and uncertainty during that time and it was writing about my experience, first in fiction and then later in these blog posts, that helped me ease away from those fears and find the true joy in one, important fact:

Kate's my daughter.

Wholly and completely mine. Words... or no words.

We got through a lot of uncertainty with Kate and her talking, and not only did we get through it but we're a closer, more connected family because of it. The trust that we needed to put in Kate—for her to be who she was and find her words when she, and she alone, was ready—was huge. Huge. It's also probably one of the greatest gifts she gave us.

During that time of uncertainty, as I tried to find my footing as a parent and how I could best support Kate, I would pick up the writing... and then put it down. Because in each moment, that's what parenting and my own well-being demanded. I thought I'd gotten through all the really big hurdles of parenting small kids and it was *finally* time to dive back into writing...

Turns out, I was wrong.

Which I suppose is no surprise, really. Parenting is all about the twists and curves and the surprises you *didn't* really see coming. While Sean and I anticipated this next hurdle in our parenting journey, we didn't quite expect the way it came to be.

Turns out I've officially got *two* late-talkers—and I'm speech-play partner for both.

At least this time around I skipped the dark and scary part.

Unfortunately, I didn't get to skip the crazy, busyness of the holidays (and, for our family, throw in a ton of birthdays and anniversary celebration) and the bigger issue I really, really couldn't control:

Not sleeping.

Yet again.

Sigh. I'm certainly tired of not sleeping being a running theme through my parenting journey—it really messes up my big writing plans and publishing goals. I'm still in survival mode, still trying not to lose my temper, to not get frustrated with my kids for being exactly who they are (basically a two-year-old and a four-year-old).

It hasn't been easy, especially when I can't do the one thing that gives me more energy and more self-care than anything else:

Writing.

We were pretty much at the brink of me going crazy and we *had* to make some changes. So, we did. The kids' sleeping arrangements changed; they're now sharing a room (which they just *love*). Sean takes the first shift with Eric (meaning if Eric gets up, Sean puts him back to bed and not me). I get the second shift and start my day when Eric decides it's time.

And you know what?

It's working.

While our sleep (and therefore Eric's sleep) isn't perfect, the change has made a huge difference. I'm getting around six hours of solid sleep before Eric needs help, so I'm no longer the raving banshee I'd been for four months straight.

And with sleep came my urge and need to write, which in itself has its own hurdles.

You'd think I'd be an old hack at this. That I could just sit on down and let the words flow and *bam*, there's this super-cool story on the page and I'm sending it off to magazines, right?

Yeah... not so much.

I've done this restarting of my writing a half-dozen times (or dozen, really) since Kate was born. I know, without a doubt, that I can do this. That's not the issue.

The real issue is fear.

Fear to start writing again. That what I write will be this awful, uncomprehending mess (which my brain still feels like most of the time).

Fear that I won't do whatever story I write justice because all of my series characters and world-based series... well, they're just *important* and I'll probably mess things up so why bother trying?

And writing a novel?

Dear god, I can just feel my inner creative voice shiver at that thought. Never mind I've already written several novels (so I *know* I can do it). The real issue is one of focus—and again—parenting. There's no way I can stay focused enough right now to fall deep into one of my worlds, into characters I know and love, and getting down into their voices and opinions. And to have life go easy on me long enough to actually write and finish a novel??

Could life as a parent possibly leave me alone long enough for this to happen?

Each one of those concerns is based on fear. Fear put there by my critical brain to stop me from writing. To take the easy way out, to not put myself out there, to not set myself up for failure, to simply not *try*.

And yet... I know how to combat this. I've done it, time and again. (Too bad I couldn't skip over this fear stuff and get to writing, huh?)

This time, like all the others, I'm not going to let the fear and uncertainties stick. I'm going to try, and then I'm going to try again. One story may not work. I may need to redraft along the way or toss out perfectly fine words because they simply don't fit the story. (Stories which I'm slowly teasing out of my subconscious, out of my creative voice.)

You see, I know how to do this restart.

I know the tricks. I know what works for me. And I know how to succeed. I'm going to jump in with both feet and see where (and how) I land...

If at all.

I know, without a doubt, the greatest power I could give my writing is two-fold:

The first, as Dean Wesley Smith likes to say: "Dare to be bad."

I can do that. I can shrug off all those negative words from my critical voice.

So what if a story doesn't make sense? So what if all my words feel (to me) like this rambling mess as I slowly figure out what story I'm trying to tell?

The point is I'm writing.

Period.

Some readers may like the story, some may love it—or maybe it won't get read for a few years because I *still* haven't managed to bring the publishing part of my business back into my daily life. But hey, we're taking baby steps here.

The second power is much easier: write every day.

That's it.

Write *something*. Five minutes, five sentences, whatever, just *write*. (Fiction only, though. These blogs don't count.) I discovered last year that a writing streak is the single most powerful motivator in my arsenal for writing. I could manage the sick days. I could manage the days where I'd barely slept at all because that five minutes was a goal I *could* hit.

My ultimate goal is writing an hour per day.

I *know* I can't hit that every single day, but I can try. And I will ultimately succeed because I wrote *something*. Even a few words or sentences count.

The other part of this (and one I'm not so great at) is making quiet time for myself. Quieting my mind. Stop thinking about my to-do list or what needs to happen before we can leave for park day or Disneyland or adventures out in nature. Quiet time where I can let my subconscious peek out, can think about stories... about characters... about worlds. The act of simply stepping back and wondering and thinking... *what if...*

For me, this is hard.

If I'm doing dishes or cutting vegetables, I might prop my laptop on the counter and watch NCIS or turn on my phone and listen to one of the many podcasts I follow. Those are all important to me. They each fill my need for stories (watching TV shows) or learning (listening to podcasts), but I've also got to make quiet time a priority.

When I do, the act of writing itself is much, much easier because my subconscious has already tapped into my stories. At that point it's just a matter of quiet time alone, just me and my laptop, to put those stories onto the page, word by word. Instead of struggling to find my way to the stories, to leave parenthood and all its worries and the constant needs behind, I can simply step from one mode of being to the other. Almost like changing coats or putting on a different pair of pants. It makes the writing process easier, and truthfully, more enjoyable.

I have a long way to go towards my yearly goals, but I'm not going to worry about them. The only goal I have, right now, on this day, is to restart my writing.

I've done it before, and most likely in the future, I'll do it again. That's part of parenthood. It's how we parent-writers make it work.

You'll notice I always put the word 'parent' first.

My first and primarily responsibility is being a parent. My kids won't be this young forever. Eric won't always be a nightmare when it comes to sleeping (which, as I said, is *finally* getting better—our kids are sharing a room!!). And as I've said in previous posts, I won't be sending my kids off to school when they hit school age. I'll be homeschooling, following their leads and their interests, so I've *really* got to find a way to make the two work: parenting and writing.

Every day, every month, this process will look different.

For the past few months, it's meant putting the writing on hold as we dealt with potty training and sleeping and the final moments of teething (woohoo!!). Now, as parenting life settles out, it's time for me to conquer my fears. To look at those fears close and shove them out the door. To find ways to finally let my creative voice come out, play, and tell stories.

Good or bad, all I need to do is sit, write, and tell stories.

That I can do... even if I'm cleaning an Eric mess off the floor or the constant vacuum-fight between me and the ants because toddlers are *notoriously* bad at keeping food in their mouths (and great at getting said food on everything).

I can still write.

One day at a time, one word at a time.

I wrote this blog post two weeks ago, and let out everything I was feeling, everything I was struggling with. I'm happy to say that for two weeks straight, I haven't missed a day writing.

I finished one short story and started another.

Some days are crazy, like me writing 1,000 words in just under an hour. Other days were only five minutes or eight, but I got the writing in.

*I'm tuning in more to my creative voice. The quiet time to let the stories and characters come to me. This, turns out, is the bigger struggle. It's **hard** to put life (and all its distractions and needs and worries) on hold long enough to think about story, to get in touch with my characters, to figure out where the writing is going next...*

But somehow I do.

Each and every time.

LIVING DUAL LIVES
(THE PARENT/THE WRITER)

March 10, 2017
Kate, 4 years
Eric, 2 years

Accepting the seasons of parenting while still following your dreams.

The last time I went to an in-person writer's workshop was when Kate was eighteen months old. She's four and a half years now and well on her way to turning five.

That's two years of not getting my cup filled by being with other professional writers and the energy, the vibes, and all the craziness that ensues. Not to mention the learning that comes from such experiences. And all the reading we do. All that *great* fiction these amazing writers produce.

Wow do I miss it.

As much as I missed it, I knew without a doubt that this was another year I had to bow out of the annual Anthology Workshop hosted by WMG Publishing with Dean Wesley Smith and Kristine Kathryn Rusch. This was the first Oregon coast workshop I'd signed up for since Eric was born, and I signed up knowing there was a good chance I'd have to cancel.

Well, turns out I did—and I'm really, really glad I was honest with myself and accepting of the life I'm living to do so.

Or I should say: accepting of this season of my life.

The Anthology Workshop for 2017 recently ended and I'm seeing so many of my friends posting about how many stories they sold to editors (and stories they didn't sell). This workshop is a great opportunity where you get the chance to sell six different stories to six different editors. But just as important as those sales, you get to see *how* those editors think, how they feel about a story, their tastes and dislikes.

And the networking opportunities at these workshops? It's off the charts. Seriously. There are about fifty professional-level writers who attend and it's an amazing experience. It makes me tingle just *thinking* about it.

Once again, I had to miss it.

But this year was different for me. This year, as I saw the posts shared by the writers, the ones who'd gone to the workshop, I felt... lighter, almost. I didn't feel any regrets in my choice to not go. I didn't feel heavy or burdened or resentful even though I'd once again put my dreams on hold.

Instead of feeling sadness, I felt content. Happy, even. I was beyond thrilled for my friends and I didn't have a single, wiggly thought of, "Gosh, I wish I'd been there, too."

Instead I celebrated my accepting of where I am on this journey.

Eight months ago, I took a look at my life and seriously asked myself, "Can you do this? Can you write six short stories in six weeks? Right in the *middle* of the Christmas holiday craziness (and a slew of our own family's birthdays, mine included)?"

And let's not forget Eric, who would be turning two, and if you've got kids, you know darn well what two means (and not the terrible twos, but those are there, too). Nope, I'm talking *teething*.

The two-year-terror molars.

Not to mention Eric's continuous crappy sleep from the moment he was born. Sean and I could pretty much guarantee sleep would *not* be happening, right when I was supposed to be writing all those stories.

Turns out I was right—on everything.

The one thing I need more than anything, especially when it comes to writing fiction, is a clear head. A mind free to dream and play and simply *dive* deep into my stories; that was not my life right then.

So instead of feeling saddened, this year I accepted it.

I mean, yes, I *was* sad and I really, really miss being with other writers, seeing my own craft explode upwards and the possibility to sell my stories... but this year those were only passing feelings.

Why the change from last year to this year?

I'm not sure, honestly. Maybe I'm just maturing as a parent or maybe it's because I'm coming out the other side of this *really intense* season of parenting.

I'm starting to get sleep again. I've picked up writing fiction and I'm going strong with another writing streak. That's a huge success for me. So is this growing understanding that the life I've chosen—compared to other parents who have kids Kate and Eric's age—is *still* different.

I used to look at other writers around my age, who I was coming up with as a professional writer, and even though I wasn't supposed to I couldn't help but compare myself to them. I'd watch as these other writers shot skyward with their book sales, publishing more and more because his or her career as a writer was the path *he or she* had chosen.

And there was me, pushing hard just to finish a handful of short stories a year.

At that time, I was jealous because I *knew* I would be up there in the production, in the writing and the publishing...

If I didn't have kids. If I hadn't decided to give my life to two young human beings, to nurture and care for them, especially in the way and on the path we've chosen.

I'm not saying I felt this way all the time or for very long, but I'd be lying if I said I never felt this at all. The truth is I did because I'm human with big writing dreams. Those feelings and dark thoughts used to shake me to my core, made me question and wonder about the choices I'd made, the life I passed up when we decided to be parents.

More than anything, Sean and I had wanted to be parents.

Parents.

This year, all those feelings, all that feeling "less than" and "not enough" didn't hit me.

Instead I felt this nod and an acceptance to our life differences, me and those other writers. We all made different choices on our life path and I wouldn't give up mine in a heartbeat.

I know my writing will always be there. I know I will get back to it, bit by bit.

It hasn't been an easy road.

Heck, it's hard as hell, especially when the only writing feedback I get these days is few and far between. The progress I see in myself as a writer, in my craft, comes at a snail's pace compared to others because that's *all* I can manage with the season I'm living.

Even among other parents, I've chosen a different path.

My kids don't go to preschool, so I don't get this huge block of time to simply *write*. In fact, my kids won't go to regular school at all. Instead, we'll be life-learning with our homeschool group, going on adventures like camping trips or swimming at our pool or playing at the park.

One day, I'll be in a place where I can sit off from the group with my laptop and let the words pour out (in between the usual request for snacks and such). But I'll never have that chunk of time other parent-writers following a more traditional path enjoy—and I'm okay with that.

This path I'm walking won't be *easy,* but it's still the right choice for our family.

And yes, while Sean and I *did* choose to be parents, one thing we didn't choose is what that would look like.

Both Kate and Eric have language delays.

With Eric, we don't really know how much or even what exactly (he's still too young to know) and that's brought an extra level of parenting we hadn't expected. When Kate was Eric's age I was working through an incredible amount of *fear*. Fear at the darkness, all the doom and gloom everyone was pushing on us. I knew they were wrong. I knew they weren't *right* about Kate, but *they* were the professionals. *They* were the experts.

Me?

I was just a mom.

I worked through all that. I found my way—through fiction no less—to an incredible amount of strength and resilience I never knew I had. Or maybe I did but I'd never before had the chance to *live* it.

While we've come out the other end with Kate—which isn't entirely true as she has a long, long way to go before she "normalizes," we at least know what the heck's going on with her—here I am starting all over again with Eric.

This is part of the parenting journey I never asked for, but the one I have because of the child who picked me as his mom. I personally don't know of any other parent-writers who are walking this particular journey, parenting children with differences. I only know of a handful of families, mostly online, who've chosen to take on their speech work and play mostly on their own. We're not sending our kids off to our local school district for services or going through our insurance.

It's mostly just me.

And Sean.

And our family and friends around us.

Other parent-writers can leave their kids with family while they go off to workshops and I know that time will be a long, long way off for me. My kids are very attached to me; they *need* me around. I'm their voice, their anchor in a world that loves language and doesn't much care for nonverbal communication (which they excel at).

And me suddenly being gone?

Oh man, talk about a freak-out for them. And truthfully with who my kids are and where their language is at, they simply wouldn't *understand* me being gone for a week—and no one would be able to explain it to them.

I'm not someone who would put my kids through that trauma, so when the time is right, they'll just come with me. I'll have Sean or my mother tag along to babysit while I go and learn and network.

That's my plan, anyway.

Right now Eric's having a hard time being separated from me for even an hour, so going to an all-day workshop, several days in a row?

Yeah, *that'll* be a problem.

Maybe he's going through something developmentally right now and it's causing this extra anxiety. Or maybe it's just him.

So I'm looking to next year and I'm hopeful, but I'm also aware we might not be there yet. Maybe it'll be the year after—who knows.

If needed, if I need to cancel again, I'm okay with that.

Because this is my life right now. The needs of my kids come first, before my writing and my dreams—both will still be waiting for me.

And even that's not entirely true because I *am* still doing what I can. I may not be able to attend in-person workshops and conferences yet, but I can take online ones. Or I can crack open a book by a long-term, bestselling author and study what they've done.

So, it's not really a me versus my kids issue. It's just... that certain pieces of those dreams need to be shelved for the time being.

For a little while longer.

That's who I've chosen to be as a parent. I *really* am walking this different path. I can look at myself and look at other parent-writers and honestly say, "Their life is not mine. The choices they've made are not mine. And that's perfectly fine."

The choices they've made work for them and my choices work for me.

I could *not* send my kids to any kind of preschool because of who they are—their language issues and temperaments—and because of my own personal beliefs as a parent and a life learner. I just couldn't.

We're all different. We all make different choices. We all have different families.

And I'm okay with my little bits and snippets of success. I'm okay with sitting on the couch, Eric literally tucked beside me as he watches *Toy Story 3* while I'm typing away at this blog like a mad woman. I only have a certain amount of time before his *toddlerness* kicks in and he starts doing the usual: nudging at me to play, tugging on pants or fingers.

I'll take what I can get, these little moments of quiet.

Every little bit.

Somehow, over time, those little bits add up to something bigger. A finished blog post. A short story. Maybe even a novel. It might take me the whole damn year to write that novel, but I am working towards it—every thirty minutes, every day—and it will add up in the end.

I'll get there.

Along the way I'll get little reminders of the success I *am* having like this one: Allyson Longueira, of WMG Publishing, has chosen my story, "The F Factor," to be included in *Fiction River: Legacies*.

It's the only story I've sold to Fiction River, sold during the last Anthology Workshop I went to before Eric was born. Kate was eighteen months old at the time, and I worked as hard as possible, for six straight weeks, writing six solid stories.

I went out there and took some risks with that story. Opened up a part of myself I'd kept hidden from myself and my family. The story that sold was the one nearest and dearest to my heart.

The story also sparked a whole series and world. I haven't published the series yet, but one day I will. Meanwhile all the other stories I submit are inching closer and closer to professional sales. Only time—and my continued learning and writing, whenever I can, each day and each moment—will get me there.

My writing is my legacy, and so are my kids. So is this journey they've set me on.

This journey is so very, very different from anyone else's and one I wouldn't change for the world. I never planned on blogging about being a parent-writer or homeschooling or my kids being late-talkers with all the emotions that entailed and all the ups and downs that came with it.

And yet, this is the path I'm on. It's one I wouldn't give up or change, not for a second, not for the world.

One day soon, maybe this October or maybe the next one, I'll see my fellow writers in person... even if I have two kids in tow.

Regardless, this is my life. Mine and no one else's. No one's life will ever look like mine nor mine theirs, and that's how it should be.

We're all different, both as writers and as parents.

For me, though, this is the path I've chosen to walk, and I know in my heart it's the right one.

SELF-CARE FOR PARENTS

March 14, 2017
Kate, 4 years
Eric, 2 years

Improve your life, both physically and emotionally, by prioritizing your own happiness and self-care.

Last week I wrote a pretty open blog post about the challenges I've been living with for the past few months, everything from massive sleep deprivation to potty training while at the same time fighting this ridiculous inner battle between being 'perfect' and what I was physically and emotionally capable of.

And I realized I wasn't quite done.

See, while I came to the realization of *screw being perfect*, there's still more to the story...

Like how the heck I've handled my own self-care.

From the moment I became a parent, my life has been in the

hands of my kids. Most of my waking and sleeping moments have been controlled and dictated by them. First they're babies and then they're toddlers. They have needs that must be met (like... *now*) and we, as parents, don't get much of a say in all that.

Which is how it should be.

What was harder and has been a bigger adjustment, is not getting much say in the amount (if any) of quiet time my poor introverted self *required* for me to continue to function as a halfway-decent human being.

Showering by myself? Going potty without someone bursting in and crying or wanting an apple cut up *right at that moment*?

Nope.

I was also frustrated with the weight I'd gained over the holidays along with birthdays, birthdays, and more birthdays. My poor body, with all the sleep deprivation that had gone on for *months*, was pretty much freaking out any time I had sweets or sugars—which is the primary food group during the Christmas season (and I can't much blame my body for freaking out). I found myself in the position where I struggled to lose this slowly gained weight.

I recognized my issue was one of sleep (or lack thereof) and that I needed to eat as healthy as possible.

But *how* could I get back on track with my health? My sleep? How could I start putting my self-care forward with everything else we had going on?

The only things I had control over were exercising, what I ate (along with the quality of the food), and my own thoughts; that's pretty much it.

Instead of spiraling down into depression and negative self-talk, I asked for help.

I explained to my health coach the situation I was in and he got it. He understood what it meant to be a parent. He understood I couldn't devote crazy amounts of time and energy to making super-healthy meals that took, you know, thirty minutes or more to prep (as if I had that kind of time dedicated for prepping lunch — HA!). My health coach had also been living a life of sleep deprivation because he had a young child; like me, he was in the trenches himself.

The advice he gave me was something I could handle given my life situation. He told me to focus on making more food deposits than withdrawals. Meaning: put in the good, healthy food and eat fewer of all that sugary goodness. He also told me to keep my thoughts positive (which I was already doing) and finally to work on self-care.

He asked that I identify three things that were of the utmost importance to me in self-care and to prioritize them.

This... *this* right here is what my last blog was missing. Or not missing exactly, but certainly needed adding.

Whatever your life situation is—whether you've got a newborn or toddlers, or you're under a lot of stress and worry and overwhelmed caring for an aging parent—we all need tools to help us through it. Tools to help you survive your situation, your momentary life bump, until things, finally, *finally* start changing.

(This is especially true when you've got *zero* control over what's happening to you.)

Here's what I did:

I came up with three things that would help me feel whole and happy each day. I didn't need to do all three in one day, and some days I did none, but I could recognize which days would be the most difficult. Those were the days with lots of events and chores and plans. Those days I would need to make time in the evening or the next day for me time. Having this flexibility, both in my schedule and mentally, really helped.

My three things were writing (any kind of writing), learning (dear Lord do I *love* to learn; anything from researching history to craft learning and studying fiction), and finally... *play*.

Play consisted of video games or reading books or watching a favorite TV show.

In the past I had always regulated play to this *thing* that could only be done once my work was done. Which wasn't necessarily a problem... unless you're like me with a never-ending to-do list. I've since corrected that line of thinking.

Play is vital to my health and happiness.

Some days I'll play video games first thing in the morning with my cup of coffee, a kid cuddled up on either side as they play on their iPads and we're just hanging out together. Or I'll do my thing during Eric's nap or at the end of the day when they're both in bed.

Instead of filling that quiet time with more work or more house chores (or the million things I wanted to do for my business), I chose play.

Sounds really simple, right?

It totally wasn't. I mean if it was easy, you'd think I'd have figured it out before. But I couldn't even get to this place. I needed to shift the way I thought of 'play', realize that play *was* a part of my own self-care and happiness and *not* just this reward for getting through my day or checking off boxes.

Even though this acceptance, this shift in my thinking, was challenging and even though it took a while, I still made it happen because the coach's suggestions were simple: pick three things.

That's it.

It was something I, with my tired and exhausted brain, could hold onto. *In my head.*

I didn't need to look at my list or my calendar. I could remember all three options on my own. In fact, at any moment during the day I was able to stop and ask myself, "Have I done my self-care yet?"

Easy to remember. Easy to accomplish...

Most of the time.

But it really worked.

I chucked everything else that I 'needed' to do. I focused on my kids and what they needed (like baths—at least every couple a days—and feeding them, that's important, too). Anything else that wasn't essential I put on hold. All that other stuff, I'd get to it—once I took care of myself.

Once I started sleeping.

You're not going to believe this, but I'm starting to. Sleep, I mean. Actual real *sleep*. It's truly happening. Anywhere from five-hour stretches to *gasp!* eight hours.

Okay, eight hours was only once but I definitely don't want to jinx the upwards progress we're making here.

Is it glorious, though. And as I regain sleep, I'm picking up other parts of my life and I am—once again—writing fiction.

(Recognize a theme here between sleep, exhaustion, and the ability to write?)

Not only am I writing more, but getting through my days is easier, too.

It's easier to stay calm and present for Eric's two-year-tantrums (compared to previously when I got triggered and wanted to scream and yell right back). I've added our speech play back to the list—what I call 'connection' time. This is the time when I focus and play with my kids. It could be a short game of tickles and running into my arms or sitting down and doing a puzzle or a board game with Kate.

Bit by bit, I'm adding more play back into my life and every day I'm feeling richer and more whole because of it.

I'm still far from being a perfect parent and I have zero desire to *be* that perfect parent. No thanks. I like living in happiness, where some days my dishes sit until the end of the day before I get to them if that means I've allowed myself some 'me' time or connection time with my kids.

After all, it's not like the ants have discovered the house this season...

Yet, anyway.

The more I move forward, bit by bit, day by day, just doing what I can... life is actually improving.

We're coming up for air again and things are coming together. Eric and his potty training have had big successes. He went up to Sean and tugged on his leg before Sean put him on the potty and he actually *pooped*.

Some of you may not understand the enormity of this, but with my late-talker kids this bridge... Eric's needing to go potty and *communicating* that need...

It's huge. *Huge.*

It's a super big step for Eric and one that's taken longer than with most kids because of that communication barrier.

The pieces are clicking together. It just took our own (and really, my) stubbornness and patience, but hey, we're getting there.

Progress.

That's what matters.

So, if you find yourself stuck in crazy intense times with young kids (or... older ones for that matter, you're just not going to have the issues like the potty ones I've mentioned here), start prioritizing your self-care.

What can you do to take care of yourself?

Make it a priority and fit it in.

Somehow. Some way.

The truth is we've got to start taking care of ourselves as parents, particularly if we want to remain present and patient. Not only for ourselves—this is an *amazing* lesson to teach our children: taking care of our own selves *is* important.

For me I'm able to *enjoy* life and being a parent again. I'm able to take deeper pleasure and just plain joy in my kids, seeing their smiles, hearing the new words and phrases Kate's putting together every day with the amazing leaps and bounds she's making. And I'm seeing my little Eric grow as his language comprehension starts expanding.

And sometimes I simply sit on the couch with Kate tucked against my side and Eric sprawled completely on my lap, and just... enjoy them.

Enjoy the moment.

Every day, as parents, we do our best with what resources we have. Let's remember that. Let's forgive ourselves for not being perfect.

And instead just focus on the joy.

DOWNTIME

April 11, 2017
Kate, 4 years
Eric, 2 years

The desperate need to schedule quiet time at home in our crazy, fast-paced world.

These days it's crazy easy to pack our schedules. To fit in two and three outings a day, an art class or two, and heck, why not stop at the park with friends because it's a good chance to get energy out (for our endlessly moving kids).

Besides... what's a three or four hours of fun before bedtime?

Our days aren't just packed with a physical schedule. We have mental schedules as well. For me every moment of free-thought time is filled with audiobooks or podcasts (a favorite pastime for me while driving) or if I'm desperate for a TV show and plugging into stories, I'll prop my laptop on the countertop during the ridiculously, time-consuming process of cutting veggies or washing—I swear—the endless supply of dirty dishes.

(I had no idea we *actually* had that many dishes!)

It turns out, after all those events and outings and the stuff my brain's chewing on and sorting through... that's kinda a lot.

And it adds up.

Not that there's anything *wrong* if this is works for you and your family. What I'm learning is that time at home is critical, especially for my family.

We're a bunch of introverts.

If I schedule both weekend days with socializing, it means *everyone* is getting ready to have their own personal meltdowns and not just the two-year-old (he just gets the distinct advantage of actually being allowed to stomp and cry and scream).

These days, I'm starting to look at my schedule with more awareness. Yes, I *could* schedule swimming with friends on the same day as we have a play date at another's house... except I'm going to be exhausted, and yes, my kids will be having fun... but then *they'll* be exhausted (and cranky).

There's also my goal of being a more patient and empathetic parent with my kids who are constantly moving in and out of their own *BIG* emotions throughout the day. If I'm barely hanging on by a thread, there's a good chance I'm probably going to lose it and yell (and immediately regret it).

Yet even with my awareness, I still make mistakes.

Or maybe not mistakes, but choices.

Sometimes I am quite aware of what I'm walking into and what situation I'm setting myself up for while other times it's a straight-up —*oops!*

Maybe I scheduled a visit with dear friends and the next day I have a three-hour hair appointment (one of my few, amazing moments of alone time). Except I'll be socializing during both experiences and when I finally get home (with my nicely styled hair), I'll have a distraught Eric to support because I *abandoned* poor him in his complete and total, utmost need.

Meaning: I left him at home... alone... with Daddy.

A complete and total toddler tragedy, yes? But as soon as I walked in the door, I told Sean to check out and take a nap; he needed it (and earned it).

But the point here is that we all need downtime, even if some of us need more downtime than others. Your family will certainly have different mileage than mine. All four of us are introverts and we need that downtime—desperately.

These weeks I almost feel like some kind of battle-planner, making notes of the large events (Disneyland... the Aquarium... driving through downtown Los Angeles to visit grandparents or friends). After days like those, the next day must be a day of nothing.

Nothing at all.

Maybe a short afternoon stint, like swimming or inviting a few friends over (physical movement is essential for my two-year-old). Or maybe we can't do any of those things. Maybe we'll have a do-nothing day and just hang at home and play board games or do art.

Plus, I still got those damn dishes to do.

Then there's *still* me, doing this crazy gig (or at least it feels crazy), trying to run my own writing and publishing businesses, and I've got to get *those* things in the schedule, too. I need to make time in our lives for these things if I actually want to be successful, if I actually want to reach towards those big dreams and goals.

There are only so many hours in the day.

Even more important, I've only got so much brain computing power.

By the end of the day, I'm shot. Just... done. My brain's working on low emergency mode and doing anything creative at all? Or heck, reading a book? Even reading a book is a feat at times. And giant mental exercise like playing a board game (against Sean no less)? Not happening.

So... downtime.

It's critical. Perhaps more so for my family than yours, but when we find ourselves on the go so much, visiting with all these wonderful, exciting people in our lives and taking advantage of all the opportunities we're continually faced with, all the *choices* we have... I think we actually start missing out.

On the little things.

Like cuddling on the couch with me on my laptop working on this blog post, somehow managing to type with Eric sprawled on my lap watching *Wall-E* while Kate's pressed against my side, asking for help as she does the puzzles in on her iPad for: "My Monster Can Read."

Or those moments when Kate sets up her board game, *Unicorn Glitterluck* and says, "Mommy play? Come here, Mommy, play."

I need to be able to close my laptop with no worries or stress—what I was working on can get done later (because I've scheduled downtime into our week, meaning I *can* get it done later) —and play with her.

Then I'll play again because she had such a great time and now Daddy's up so we can all play together!

We're starting to move into art because Kate's interest in this area is growing and this is part of the self-directed, homeschooling journey we've chosen for our family—to follow their interests—so I certainly can't ignore her when she's giving me these big ol' hints in bright pink *My Little Pony* drawings, now can I? Or when Kate starts writing out numbers as her auntie rolls a bunch of dice for her *Dungeons and Dragon* character (hmm... I guess we're gonna start those game sessions early so Kate can join in too).

All this downtime isn't just for Kate or Eric.

It's for me, too.

When my brain is stressed, when I'm trying to gauge the timing of everything, the endless little lists that need to be completed before I can walk out the door with my kids (teeth? clothes? shoes? hair brushed... well, no one will notice and we're seriously running late), life can be *overwhelming*. So overwhelming that I can't possibly be creative at that moment.

And that's what I need to start protecting as well as making time for.

Being creative.

Or more to the point, daydreaming.

I used to be *so* good at daydreaming. Boring day at school? Boring office job? I had the coolest, craziest adventures going on in my head. But daydreaming also helped me fall into the stories I was writing... thinking about the characters... hearing their distinct and personal *voices*.

I know darn well that I *need* this quiet. If I want a shot at writing a story, I need to give myself the quiet time to simply let my creative voice come out and play. I need to turn off the podcast because I need to be bored. Bored enough to start hearing and seeing my stories come to life.

And I'm really, really bad at this, turning off all the directions and just let my mind be free.

There's so much I want to do and so little time I actually have and this whole daydreaming thing? It's *so* easy to put it off as 'less important.'

(Big ol' sigh right here.)

Which is when I get stuck on a story. The words flowing out my fingers grind to a halt. Sure I can keep typing—and every darn word feels wrong. Like the story is starting to spiral in some direction I can't see, where the story needs to go. That's one of the first clues I'm missing something. I lost the story or the character did something that they wouldn't have done. Or I didn't jump to the right place in time.

All I've got is this feeling, this creative gut-thing, and it's pretty little. It's just a quietly blinking red light.

If I'm too busy, if my brain is overwhelmed and overworked, I miss it... and then I have to go and cut about 7,000 words out of the new novel and redraft because I was missing the real important character emotion or some story element that *needed* to be there.

I'm still learning.

Learning about parenting, learning about how to be both a parent and a writer. I'm figuring things out (bit by bit).

It's taken a lot, a lot of trying and trying again. I'm still constantly looking at my schedule, looking over the previous weeks and what I accomplished and what—going forward—the kids and I could realistically do.

It's taken a lot of remembering that I need to be flexible.

(This flexibility is yet another theme through all my parent-writer posts.)

I've got a new scheduler that allows me to pencil in the week's activities and goals. It gives me space to write and I can flow through the week, even write in times for when something needs to start and whether it—*really*—fits in with what we've already got going on?

Seeing my schedule like this has helped me set realistic expectations. (A learning experience, for sure.)

I need to start getting videos of Kate and Eric to send to our speech pathologist. I've got a two-week block to get done and this *is* important. And it takes time. I can plan for that time now. I can go with the flow if one day the videos don't go well and I can try again the next day or the next.

For you—and whatever flow and downtime is needed for you family—take a good close look at who you are. Who your kids are or who your partner or spouse is. Be aware of temperaments and energy levels and driving time. Ask yourself: do you *honestly* have enough time to make dinner from scratch and get everyone in bed before the sun rises?

What about your own self-care? Your daily movements and exercises? Do you have the quiet time to dive deep into your writing, to let your subconscious come out and play?

This assessment feels like it goes double for us as homeschoolers. I mean there's *so much* we can do! There are so many opportunities, places to visit, classes to take, and why *not* jump into as many as we possibly can?!

Well, *you* can.

For my family, this totally won't work. (Again, learning through experience over here.)

If you find yourself craving some quiet time at home, why not take the afternoon to bake some chocolate-chip cookies? To let your two-year-old play in the flour, measuring out cups to his heart's content (knowing most of it will end up on the floor and not in the batter)? Or perhaps sitting and reading for yourself and watching to see if your kids come over because they want to cuddle and be read to.

If we're constantly on the go, constantly on the move, how can we allow for these quiet times when the real magic happens? That special connection when it's just you and your kids?

Or—for me almost as important—me and my creative voice?

We each need some amount of quiet, of this downtime, and it's really, really hard to see that time for how valuable and how precious it is. Plus, it can be hard to look at our schedules and start saying, "No." Start crossing off visits or museum memberships (because you feel this *need* and *responsibility* to use memberships).

Allow yourself, and your family, this quiet time and see what kind of magic happens for you... for them... for your writing.

Because this presence, simply being with them, is truly something special.

Like noticing that Kate had drawn butterfly and rainbow marks from *Fluttershy* and *Rainbow Dash* on our balcony with chalk (*My Little Pony* characters). At that moment, I had no idea how *well* Kate knew those characters, even picking out the exact colors from the chalk to match the character's colors (without looking to double-check). And yet, when I stopped moving and gave myself a moment to actually notice, to be present, and be in the quiet, it allowed me to glimpse her amazing little mind.

This, right here, is why we homeschool.

This, right here, is why I've chosen to be a parent—and this particular kind of parent.

I'm so glad to have paused long enough to see and experience this joy with her. (Then she *asked* me to take a picture and send it to Daddy, which we did.)

So think about your own busy, busy days and remember to hit the pause button and see just how many rainbows and butterflies your little one is dreaming up.

NEEDING SPACE

April 24, 2017
Kate, 4 years
Eric, 2 years

Please. Just five minutes of peace and quiet.

For me, personally, one of the most challenging obstacles of parenthood has been space. Space where it's just me and my thoughts. Quiet time that I use to think, reflect, and daydream.

I'm an introvert. I *need* this.

I need it for my writing because having quiet time, having space to myself, is when the ideas and those 'what if' questions come. It's when my characters perk up their heads and I can hear their voices and their opinions, see how they move through a world I've recently created or one I've been writing in for years.

It's this quiet, this downtime that has been one of the hardest adjustments since I became a parent because hearing a character's quiet voice is pretty darn impossible when I've got a toddler tugging on my leg and crying every thirty seconds. And if Eric isn't the one needing help or attention, his *sister* is.

Some days it's just constant.

Constant.

Now we all go into this parenting gig knowing it's not gonna be easy. At the same time I didn't know *how* challenging parenting would be—and often in ways that were pretty darn unexpected. Not to mention each kid has their different quirks and opinions and really, as parents, half the time it feels like we're up a creek and the only paddle we've got is this tiny twig that'll snap if you look at it wrong!

So yeah, sleepless nights? Diapers? The constant need to feed the little angels, and oh yeah, the *endless* amount of dishes?

I pretty much expected *that*. Sure, it's exhausting, but it's part of the deal of parenting.

What I hadn't expected was my need for space—personal, quiet space—where it's just me and my thoughts and I *don't* have to be a parent.

That one came as a surprise.

I always knew after Kate was born that I'd still be writing; there was never any doubt in my mind to this. I *need* to write. So, I knew I would.

And, I did.

But what I was missing, and what I'm still struggling with, is the quiet. That time to let my thoughts go and let stories work themselves out. To sit back and simply watch the world around me or think about some interesting story or idea question and see exactly where it takes me. And this quiet, contemplative time, of just being still and focused on my thoughts and my characters... it doesn't work so well with two-year-olds. Especially ones going through massive separation issues (meaning the only breaks I get are when Eric's sleeping).

Life with Eric right now is intense.

Intense.

I'm sleeping again (if I wasn't, I have no idea the level of crazy I'd be right now), but it's still challenging because Eric's needs are *so* constant and *so* intense. He has the patience of a typical two-year-old—which means *zero* patience. For Eric, this usually leads him to smacking or kicking me and needing to hold him close so we're both safe and he works through these *giant* emotions.

(When Kate was this age, she'd run off crying to her safe place we lovingly called her "crying castle," whereas Eric is the more... physical type.)

Every kid is different. Every kid has different needs at different times (so it seems, anyway). Everyone in our little family is feeling Eric's intensity right now, including Sean and Kate.

Poor Kate, who watches as I constantly deal with Eric's needs and his emotions and when she's needing me to show up, she's needing my support, I'm completely tapped out. It's all I can do to prop open my laptop and veg-out on feel-good TV shows. Kate's needing attention from me and I'm desperately needing a bit of quiet for myself.

Some days it feels like none of us are getting our needs met.

I've been struggling with this for a while now, balancing Kate's needs and mine and this rough transition we're going through with Eric.

I've been aware of this and thinking it through. I've done journaling, especially on my intense reactions to how Eric's acting and my own responses. Just as important, I'm focusing on how I don't like *my* reactions to his behavior. But it wasn't until I reached out for help from a friend, Michelle Charfen (who teaches the amazing Centered Parenting classes), that I realized exactly what the issue was:

My need for space.

The moment I identified my need as an actual, tangible thing, everything else I was feeling made sense. All the feelings of frustration and anger, how I was constantly short-tempered and always closing myself off emotionally... and how I was aware of these feelings, yet couldn't fix or change them. I couldn't because I hadn't actually addressed what the problem was.

Think of it like going to the doctor for back pain and being prescribed some pain medication. That's all fine and good—unless the pain doesn't go away.

We need to treat the actual problem and not the symptom.

Which... is what I had been doing in regard to my parenting and self-care and needs, how I would only look at the symptoms (my reactions and my feelings) and not look at the actual *cause* of those feelings (my unmet need).

And it's not just "I need space" either.

My particular temperament, my empath abilities and how strongly I feel emotions from others, how I take those emotions into my own body as if they're mine, it means that living with Eric and his constant *huge* frustrations drains every ounce of energy I have. I'm taking everything he's feeling into myself and then trying really, really hard not to act out on *both* our emotions.

Once I put all *that* into perspective what was going on really made sense.

So much of this was occurring *because* one simple need of mine wasn't being met—my need for space. It didn't matter that I was actually getting six hours of straight sleep most nights (shocking!) because I still wasn't in the emotionally centered place that *I* wanted to be in.

Now, though, with my new perspective I can move forward and start addressing the problem.

I need space.

At the same time Eric needs *more* of me.

He's hit some stage in his development where his anxiety has skyrocketed when it comes to separation. It's so bad that I can't even leave our apartment without him running after me, screaming down the hall with tears running down his face. It's really hard on the person who's left caring for him (generally it's Sean).

I respect Eric's need for me.

I also respect Sean's frustration when Eric is so very clear that he wants *nothing* to do with him and will cry the entire time I'm gone (that's what happened last time when I got my hair done).

And yet... I have my own sinking ship and I've got to take care of myself. I'm no use to anyone if I'm underwater with zero resources for anyone else's needs.

So... now that I know the problem... what the heck can I actually *do* about it?

Well, first off, there's no way I'm gonna figure this out in one try. And more than likely every day and every moment will be different from the next.

Come to think of it, I'll be working through this question for a long, long time.

If you're a parent, especially if you've got the toddler variety at home, then you're *really* going to understand what I mean about needing space. Even five minutes to myself on the laptop, writing an email or calling up a friend on the phone, would be a blessing. There are days when I can't even get thirty seconds of quiet *within my own head*.

That's rough.

And tiring.

And it really, really starts to grate on any patience and calm that I've stored up for the day.

I don't have to be perfect. I don't have to—nor could I *ever* be—the perfect parent or perfect writer.

I also know I'm not alone in this. I can and I *will* ask for help. Sometimes for emotional support; other times, for ideas and strategies, thoughts on how I can get creative in finding a way to meet my need for space.

That's what I did with Michelle when we had a really hard day. The first thing she did was remind me of how amazing it was that I had this *clarity*, simply knowing my need was a big first step. I had already done so much work knowing what the real issue was rather than me losing my cool and getting mad at the toddler.

I knew myself and I knew I was on the right track. This realization alone was immensely powerful.

My friend also reminded me it was okay that Eric felt the way he did, felt upset about being separated from me, and it was *okay* for me take time for myself despite his feelings, to walk away and give myself the space I needed.

It was okay.

Eric won't always be happy with the choices I've made, certainly not at this point in his life and it's okay that *he* feels upset. Someone else can be loving and present with him as he works through those feelings of sadness and as he's doing that, I'll be recharging my batteries so when I come back I'll be in a much better place to help him.

I need to practice my own self-care.

That means having a conversation with Sean, too, telling him how much I appreciate that he's taking on this hard time with Eric. To remind Sean how much I need this time.

Something as simple as "You take this hard hour and I'll take the other twenty-three."

It's not going to be easy for anyone as we work through this, but I can't allow myself to feel trapped, to feel like I can never leave the house without Eric in tow or can't meet another mom for coffee so we can connect about our parenting or homeschooling styles.

The great thing about having this conversation with Sean is I can find what needs of his aren't being met. I mean, I know what my needs are, but what about his? He might not even know himself and I'm sure there's something we can do, as a family, to meet more of his self-care needs.

After we have this conversation, we're going to need to start thinking creatively.

Maybe we hire a babysitter or do a child-swap with another mom (who's also willing to take on the crushed-heart of Eric) or maybe ask the grandparents for more help. There are definitely ways for me to find my own space within the restraints unique to my family. For example, the language issue means my kids need more support compared to other kids and their temperaments require that they fully trust this person before they're willing to be left alone with them.

Lots of questions and thoughts to consider, and while I don't have direct answers yet, I feel like I'm finally on the right track.

Because this isn't just about the long-term goal.

Some days I won't get that space. That's parenthood for you.

Some days it'll feel like I walked through fire, barefoot, and then hop-scotched back out the way I came without even a chance to breathe. Those days will need more in-the-moment tactics to keep me grounded and emotionally connected with my kids.

Focusing on breathing always helps... unless of course I've got the toddler pulling on my leg and crying (or hitting said leg). Try to do meditative breathing while *that's* going on.

Or maybe we get outside and get some fresh air, simply move our bodies and just keep moving.

I could, of course, call a friend or text when I'm at my wit's end... though that's hard for me to do. It's not easy to call someone up on the phone as I break down in tears and tell that someone how I feel like the WORST PARENT EVER (even as the toddler is pulling on my arm and doing everything possible to *get the phone away from me*.)

Or maybe I can just sit on the floor with my hand over my chest and acknowledge my feelings, let myself cry... and even this act of crying is okay. Seeing me cry and emotional will teach my kids it's okay for them to feel, too.

It's okay to feel this way, just like it's okay to give myself a little bit of forgiveness and love.

It's hard.

This parenting thing is *not* easy. There are days when the world is wonderful, when my little boy is my cute cuddle-bunny resting on my lap—and a switch flips and he's all-intense, all the time.

And through all this, here I am, still working at being a writer.

Every time I sit and put words to page, whether its these blog posts or in my fiction, I feel a bit of my spark come back. That shining bit of light that's me and only me. Not just the mom, but... me.

Something that is really, really hard to do when I don't get the space I so desperately need.

Then there are times, like the one I'm currently living in, where I acknowledge that I *can't* write right now. At least not fiction. Times when I go sit at the computer and it *feels like work*. The very idea of sitting down and making up stories feels like getting my teeth pulled—

I've learned over the past four years to put the writing down at that point and walk away. To keep the writing a fun, safe place.

We are right in the middle of some pretty big developmental milestones for Eric. Heck if I know what they are. I can only guess what's going on his little head, but there *is* something going on, some pieces of communication clicking into place.

I can see it.

I can feel it.

The rest of the stuff he's got going on... *intense* emotions, limit testing... oh man, is that sky-rocketing right now.

And for whatever reason, Eric's got it in his head that 2:30 *in the morning* is a perfectly acceptable time to start the day.

I *knew* parenting would be tough, but there have been some surprises I hadn't counted on. The need for space was one and another was that both my kids were late-talkers.

Yet... here I am, writing about parenting, writing about my late-talking children and our journey... none of this was anything I'd envisioned writing. It was never my plan. I never once thought of reaching out to other parents for help and guidance, simply so none of us would feel alone in this journey.

Yet here I am, writing to you.

I know there are others out there, just as lost and as sleep-deprived as I. We try our best to be good parents while trying to keep the core of who we are, our passions, our sparks, alive and burning (even if that burning is only a small glimmer of a spark).

THE INTRODUCTED PARENT

March 24, 2017
Kate, 4 years
Eric, 2 years

Managing our energies, resting when needed—this is especially true for our family of introverts living in an extroverted world.

Society, at least from my point of view, doesn't really give a shit about us introverts. You know, those people who get incredibly *exhausted* being around others, who feel completely drained when they go to big group gatherings, the kind of people whose idea of a day off (or heck, a vacation) is *staying at home.*

That's me.

Actually, that's my whole family.

We spent four wonderful hours on Saturday, socializing and catching up with long-time friends and their adorable kids (everyone had a fantastic time), but throw in two hours of driving (thank you, downtown Los Angeles) and for the rest of the weekend, each and every one of us were fried. From me and Sean to Kate and Eric.

Because we're introverts.

Going out and having fun means we need time to re-center ourselves, to settle in and fill up our cups at home. The day after a fun socializing event, we're usually on our iPads or playing video games together or reading books or coloring. Sure, Eric might be sprawled across my lap (he usually is), but he's also doing his own thing and he doesn't *want* my interaction. He just wants to be next to me.

The same with Kate.

I jokingly tell Sean I'm never alone because I've got one kid pressed against my side, the other on my lap, each of us lost in our world but still having this connection.

We each need our own space and ever since Sean and I made an effort to make sure *I* was getting some of my much needed space, everything slowly settled into place. Eric still has his big emotions and hard time with me leaving, but it's getting better. Maybe he's learning that Mommy will come back (because I do!). Or maybe I'm also better at managing our daily schedules and the activities we do. I'm sure I'm more aware of not just my energy and what I can handle, but the kids' energy and tolerances too.

The truth is everyone in my family needs quiet time, time to recharge our batteries and refill our cups (you can throw in your favorite description here).

Some of you might not understand this at all, might not how important time at home is for us. For others of you, you might be nodding your heads enthusiastically.

The problem is society and the expectations put on us as parents (not to mention everyone's got an opinion about parenting these days).

Think about it for a moment. Think about *all* the 'stuff' you're supposed to do to be considered a 'good' parent. Constantly engaging with your child through play or talking. Lots of one-on-one interactions. Lots of play outside, at the park. And all the feeding and care and necessary items associated with such outings.

And make sure your kids have healthy, whole foods for snacks and lunches and none of that drive-thru crap.

Which, of course, means the endless cutting of vegetables and bucket-loads of fruit (while at the same time praying your toddler doesn't get into too much trouble or, if you're living in my shoes, takes that very moment to potty on the floor because he knows darn well you aren't watching).

There are some of us who really, really struggle with that kind of chaos, especially when we're already depleted on energy.

We're simply not built that way.

Some of us *can't* go out to endless events, art classes, park days, and on top of that have one-on-one play dates (or go to school, if you're a schooling family). Oh! And let's not forget each of these outings lasts hours.

There are some of us who, when we stumble into our glorious home (sometimes with upset, crying kids because they're low on energy, too) all *we* want is to collapse on the couch and drink a glass of wine.

Or two.

And yet as a parent, I'm *constantly* bombarded with messaging all around me that I'm not doing enough, that what I'm doing isn't good enough.

What about the book time and reading together?

What about sitting on the floor, playing one-on-one?

What about the speech play for Eric? Did we have enough physical play? Did he get outside enough to run around?

What about Kate? She's Miss Constantly-Wants-to-Socialize. Guess what that means?

Going out.

And I'm using energy resources to help her and guide her while *still* running after Eric and making sure he steers clear of the street (on park days I'm usually clocking in a good mile's worth of steps).

And let's not forget the message that screen time is bad for kids. That we will damage our kids if they're watching too much TV or playing on the iPad or whatever. Now, you can have your own opinions about this along with the different research and the worries and the fears—I'm not judging you or your family or your values, not at all.

What I am saying is we're all different and we all have different *needs*.

And can we please, at least for the moment, lay off putting all this blame and guilt on people who are just exhausted? Parents who, truly, are trying their best??

By the end of the day I'm bone-tired exhausted.

After an outing I *need* my kids to be quiet, to give me some peace and quiet, even if it's just so I can get dinner together. It doesn't matter that all *I* want is to call it a night and go to bed at 6:00 p.m. with the kids. What's hard is constantly hearing the critical voices in my head, whispering that I'm this bad parent because my kids spent how many hours playing games or watching movies?

Guilt.

Shame.

It's all there and it feels like I'm constantly fighting them. Constantly fighting this message that I'm not doing enough. I'm not good enough. How, pretty much every day, being Super Mom isn't *enough* (or Super Dad, whichever parent or caregiver is at home).

On top of the usual parenting challenge course, we've chosen to both support our kids with their language and also homeschool. Right now, the homeschooling part is literally playing and living life. We'll color and paint, play some board games, but we're really following Kate's lead and where her interest takes us (like making word hide-and-seek books).

But...

It's the *one-on-one* time that's challenging.

Playing board games with Kate requires Godzilla-Eric to be napping (or that Sean's around to keep Eric's little hands from grabbing the scissors Kate's using for her word books). Or with Eric, speech play means Kate needs to be engaging in *her* things and willingly leaves us alone for a few minutes.

Why?

Well, for the speech part, Eric needs one-on-one time. Time where I'm able to pause, give him a chance to think through what I'm doing, what my words (or actions) are asking of him. He needs time and space to do this, which for him means comfort and a feeling of safety—

And the minute I start engaging and playing with him, laughing or clapping when he puts the shape into the puzzle box, Kate comes running over because *she* wants to play too.

Because we're having fun.

Which is all well and good except Eric is a "need-my-space" kinda kid. He gets frustrated when Kate starts putting her grubby hands on *his* shape pieces. And his only mode of dealing with frustrations is— no surprise— crying out and trying to hit her. (When you have no words and you're a physical being, it makes total sense that this would be your reaction.)

It's not going well.

Or I should say, it's not easy.

Kate has needs (she wants to play too!). Eric has needs (leave me the heck alone; *I* want to play with Mom. By myself. Without you.). And then, well, I have needs too (oh please, just give me five minutes of quiet and please, please, please I'd so love to write today).

For our family those needs are *also* tied to our energy and how much we have (or often, don't have).

Because we're all introverts I *really* need to have my awareness keyed to the energy pulse of each of us—myself, the kids, Sean... In the situation I just described with the puzzle box—and this is true of all kids, especially mine who are both introverts and late-talkers—I need to sit back and see *why* the heck this situation (Kate's interference, Eric's frustration) is happening in the first place.

Kate wants interaction and play of her own. With me.

Eric wants the same... but without Kate butting in and doing the puzzle for him.

Well, okay then.

Let's add *that* to the energy schedule as well as shopping at Costco and farmers market. Oh, yeah, we've got Grandma coming over, too.

It's a constant juggling act that (I'm slowly starting to accept and internalize is going to look different compared to everyone else's. The life choices we made (homeschooling, speech play) as well as the choices that were never in our power to make (a full family of introverts and two late-talkers)—all mean our home life *will* look different than most of the families out there.

There are choices we need to make, like screen time or only one outing a weekend (or day), that fit us and our needs.

And really, parents, we need to start accepting that for our kids to be happy and whole, *we* have to be happy, too. We need to start taking care of ourselves, to start putting our needs as a priority too. Because we can't be patient and kind, can't be centered and present, if we're constantly on that edge of exhaustion. We're gonna snap and yell and whatever.

Our needs matter too.

And for you introvert parents out there who know *exactly* what I'm talking about, you have double-duty because society as a whole doesn't understand us. Society likes the people who are constantly chatting and socializing, going out and having all these grand adventures. Well, that works for them and that's fine, but it doesn't always work for us. Or maybe it does but only in bite-sized pieces spread out over weeks and months.

And it's okay.

It's okay for us to be different.

For all of us as parents, though we need to be in tune with our kids and their unique energy, it's okay to be different.

Life is a juggling act, constantly checking in with ourselves and with our kids and our partners. Like how on the Saturday we saw our long-time friends, I made the choice to let Sean sleep in while I went to farmers market with the kids (which meant I had a wiggling Eric in my arms as I tried to pay). It was stressful for me but I did it because I knew Sean's needs were greater than mine in that moment. I also did the driving (that's also too stressful for him), but the second we got home? The second our kids were in bed?

I went to bed.

Because that's what I needed.

Being a parent is hard. Being an introverted parent is even more challenging. Introverted parents need to monitor our energy levels and that of our kids. For those of you introverted parents with extroverted kids, those kids who *thrive* on all the outings and socializing, oh man, do I feel for you. You've *really* got to be aware of your own self-care. (Truly, you guys are amazing!)

All I'm trying to say here is that it's okay to be different. It's okay to be a different kind of family because all of our needs are different.

We need to care for our kids, and we need to care for ourselves.

So, if you find yourself getting hit with all those messages—that you're not doing enough... that you're not good enough—keep in mind that a lot of those messages are geared towards an extroverted world.

And guess what?

That's not me. Or my family.

We do what works for us, what makes us happy and whole, and that means we *can't* be wrong.

All we can do as parents, day in and day out, is our best. To simply try... even if that means our world and our lives look different than everyone else's.

We try.

And then the next day, we try again.

PARENTING:
A ROLLER-COASTER RIDE

June 16, 2017
Kate, 4 years
Eric, 2 years

Getting through the ups and downs of parenting and shifting your focus towards the positive.

There really is no question about it: parenting feels like you're getting strapped into a roller coaster, shoulders pressed firm and hard to that rubber-plastic chair, and just holding on.

Sometimes for dear life.

Sometimes in utter and complete enjoyment.

And within all that, all those curves and loops, those corkscrews you barely saw coming, you have these wonderful moments of pause as you catch your breath and continue to climb higher (with the telltale *click, click, click* of the track), and you *finally* get a chance to see where you are.

How high you've climbed...

And how far you're gonna fall next.

Then you get to do it all over again.

But even *that* analogy doesn't quite work because it means that we, as parents, have no control. And while there are a ton of things we can't control such as sleep. (My dear children, could you please sleep through the night?) Or...is this really the time to get chicken pox and be housebound for two weeks ... or four since Eric's probably getting it next? When in fact, there are a ton of things that we *can* control, even if it doesn't feel like it at times (especially with the younger ones).

My little Eric *still* isn't a great sleeper, but he is getting better. Compared to six months ago when I was lucky to get 2-3 consecutive hours, we're doing light-years better.

I can't control Eric's sleeping—at all—but I can control me.

I can decide how much coffee to drink during the day, eat dinner earlier, finish my wine two hours before bed. I've started a bedtime routine, complete with candle, nature music, and an acupressure mat. Oh, and bedtime? Yeah, I'm heading into bed, lights off, by 8:30 these days.

I have to. My little guy thinks 4:30 a.m. is a *perfectly* acceptable time to start the day.

(I know, right??)

This new bedtime means I've had to cancel plans with friends, to say no to dinner dates and Parents Night Out.

Is it worth it?

Absolutely.

I'm getting a solid four hours of sleep and when I do wake up to take care of Eric, I'm able to go back to sleep faster than before. I'm also not as angry because I'm no longer living on that edge of being crazy and desperate for sleep.

I feel good, mentally and physically and I can tell my body is finally healing from the years of massive sleep deprivation.

I'm a *long* way from being done with the sleep ride—some nights are still just *bad*—and when both kids tag-team me? Dear Lord, meet

Zombie-Chrissy the next day. But overall, the sleeping is creeping towards better. I'm focusing on what I'm eating and on daily movement, and overall, I'm reaching my big reason for wanting to do all this...

To be a patient, calmer person with my children (and to be honest, with myself as well).

All these new changes are working.

I'm not yelling as much. I'm in a better position to be present and centered during those times when even the holiest of saints would have their work cut out for them (and you know what I'm talking about, you parents of two-year-olds).

I decided to focus on what I could control, and then, got creative.

Not that I'm always successful on the creative part. In fact, I'm still on this roller coaster ride when it comes to fitting in board games with Sean and my friends.

And fiction writing? I'm still figuring it out.

Still.

That's right. I've been at this parenting thing for four years and I still haven't gotten the magic answer, still haven't figured it out—I have a hunch that's a truth in itself. There won't ever be *one* right answer and whatever answer I find will change and adjust the same way the weather does.

And with my writing I'm still facing a high-ass brick wall filled with stuff that I truly can't control. Mainly, my son.

I can only fall into my worlds, into my storytelling, my writing, when I'm away from him because he's so intense these days and my poor subconscious spends any writing time I have shaking her little head saying, "It's not safe to come out yet."

I would *love* to write while the kids are sleeping. Except... I'm a morning person. Writing at night is a real, real struggle because by the end of the day I am *dead-tired* exhausted.

Okay... that means I've got to wake up extra early—before the kids. Okay, let's see if I can do that...

Wait. You mean, earlier than 4 a.m.? Wait a minute—I can't do that. I'm working like mad trying to *recover* sleep!

I know of other writers who drop their kids off with other moms and take turns with co-op babysitting. Kate is almost ready for that, especially if she trusts the mom, but Eric? Oh hell no. Nope. Not gonna happen.

A huge part for him has to do with language—I am literally Eric's foreign translator in this big scary world of rules and people who can't stop talking. The other part is his temperament. He is very, very attached to me these days and not even Daddy is good enough.

I *do* get that time away, despite the miserable experience it is for everyone else, but so far the compromise—Sean watching the kids for an hour while I take the rest of the day and night—is working for me and my mental well-being (and frankly my overall happiness). So long as I can get moving in time. So long as I can get the coffee done and get dressed and before I know it, Sean's heading out the door for work and we both didn't prioritize this time for myself.

As I'm writing all this out... processing through it... I'm also realizing I've only been focused on the reasons why I *couldn't* write or why I *couldn't* use the same methods of other parent-writers.

Once again, I need to shift my focus from what I can't control and move it back to the realm of what I *can* control.

Like I can make the effort, physical *and* mental, to grab my laptop, get dressed, and head outside to write while Sean's still home in the morning before work. An hour or maybe just thirty minutes. Let's say I don't even write, but just the act of getting up and getting some actual alone time... that's going to go a long way toward helping my subconscious feel safe again.

Add in the part about, "you don't have to write," because there are days when I can't.

We're still in this intense phase with Eric. Some mornings are hard. Crazy hard. To the point where I last as long as I can before bursting into the bedroom, bawling my eyes out, desperate for a break.

So Sean gets up, watches the kids, and I lock myself in the bedroom and just play with doing some book covers.

I play... and I get a bit of myself back...

I was able to finish that day and the one after that.

Some days are just *not easy*. (Not kidding... I ended up walking out of Disneyland with a crying, screaming toddler who was trying his best to hit me in the face all because he couldn't have the French fries he saw some lady carry out on a tray. Didn't mattered that I offered him other food or to go to a place that *didn't* have a line. Didn't matter one damn bit. He was upset and the only choice I had, after being present and calm with him, was to walk the whole mile back to our car.)

Then we have days that are totally fine and chill. Those are almost the worst because they are so deceptive... you think this is what the new norm is like, the new routine, and you start having these grand plans—gonna pull out my story and write, get back into publishing—which is about when the two-year-old decides to skip his nap.

For three days in a row.

Yep. We're also in the nap-skipping stage (imagine me crying in sadness right here).

It's one thing for me to tell this to you and quite another to see it. My mother-in-law just saw the tiniest glimpse of The Eric Meltdown, and we were actually having a *good* day, and she was like... no, I'm not real comfortable with you and Kate going on a ride at Disneyland and leaving me with him.

Sigh.

It'll get better, I know. Heck, every day it's getting better.

But some days are straight up like this roller coaster, the one you're strapped into and just holding on, doing your best to keep breathing and not lose your shit.

Some moments I'm successful, some moments I'm not.

I'm trying hard to forgive myself, to be patient and gentle especially on those days when I really, really need it, to let go of this unobtainable goal of perfection (you all know that doesn't exist in parenting, right??).

I'm not perfect... but I'm trying to be a good parent.

I'm still working on being a writer and because I worked on those covers, I got interested in this one series I hadn't written in for awhile.

So I pulled open this world's bible and started updating it and before I knew it, there's this little voice inside me, my own little two-year-old who really wants to jump out and splash in the mud naked.

One of things I can do, one thing that *is* in my control, is going with the moment when I feel it, jumping right on in and playing.

Just... playing.

I've realized, too, the more individual time I give Eric before leaving the house (or before I disappear into the bedroom behind the locked door), the easier it is on him. The more connection he gets from me, the joy of playing one-on-one, the better he's able to handle the short moments of separation.

So together, all parents—despite what each of us is going through, similar or different it doesn't matter—together, let's flip the lens around and look at what we *can* control.

What can you do to help promote your own self-care? To get the sleep you need, the food and exercise? The autonomy and creativity?

I feel *alive* when I write, but for you... for your kids, your family, *your* life, all of that will have a different feel than mine, different priorities. Only you (and your family) can figure that one out. I urge you to do the work, to sit down and think creatively, to shift your focus and put the power, the control, back in your hands.

And take time to acknowledge those in your life who are trying to help out (especially when it comes to your sanity). I realized I still hadn't done this enough with Sean. We'd played a board game and everyone was having a really awesome time... except for me (mostly because of the worst combination of random luck possible).

The next day, he listened to me and heard how upset I was, especially since playing the game meant I didn't go to bed until 11:30 (it was his Father's Day board game event). Later that day, I thanked him and told him how much I appreciated him simply *listening* to me. I needed that support, and I needed that hour without the kids because I was at my wits' end.

Thank the people in your life and thank yourself for doing everything you can, even though you will never be perfect, even though you may never get to all the things you want to do (like me and all my current writing dreams).

Then, shift your focus.

Look to what *is* in your control, because seriously, it just feels *better* to focus on the positive and what we, ourselves, have the power to change.

I may not have any control if my kids get the chicken pox (in the end, they didn't), but on the bright side I had to completely free up my schedule for potential quarantine. I can take this opportunity to connect with my kids, do painting and board games or roughhouse on the floor, all those little things that are so easily pushed to the side when I'm focused on cooking meals or getting everyone out of the house.

We're enjoying ourselves and having fun. You know, all those moments of why we choose to be parents in the first place... those moments when the roller coaster clicks up to the top of the hill and you're looking around in breathless wonder of how *really cool* your life is...

Right before you plunge back down into the next parenting adventure.

THE HIDDEN TOLL OF PARENTING

July 1, 2017
Kate, almost 5 years
Eric, 2 1/2 years

The hidden emotional and physical toll of parenting and finding ways to care for yourself. (Another post about self-care—because it's that important for how we show up as parents.)

Our bodies, as human beings, are crazy resilient. I mean, really. They can put up with a *lot* ...

Months (or years) of poor sleep, eating McDonalds Chicken McNuggets by the pound (at least that was me in my youth). The constant stress pouring in from every which way, from family, work, even getting on the freeway and driving to Grandma's.

At some point, though, our bodies slam the brakes on and say, "Enough is enough, dude."

Add children to that equation, to all the normal stresses our bodies and minds are currently under. Especially *young* children you can't reason with (or beg) who have their own very clear needs (clear in their minds, anyway) and really, really couldn't give a shit about your needs (like sleeping).

And while we're at this, let's up the ante and in add special needs differences just for fun.

All this is to say: parenting is not for the faint of heart.

Being a parent is the most beautiful, rewarding journey I've ever been on—and it's also the journey that's tested me beyond what I thought was physically and mentally possible.

And, I'm far, far from being out of the woods.

I realize my recent posts have this kind of desperate tinge to them, but what can I say? This is the life I'm living. It will get better, it will get easier, I know this and yet at the same time, right at this moment, life is hard.

There are days when I feel so completely alone, so trapped by the needs (read: Eric's *demands*), and I'm doing all I can to simply keep breathing (and somehow still being the parent I want to be).

Eric is literally smack-dab in the hardest part of his young years. He has the usual 'can't-wait-even-a-second' moments when he wants something, which usually results in a crying, screaming meltdown with hands (and sometimes feet) flying, doing his best to smack me.

Why?

Because he knows I don't like it.

He also knows I'm the safe person. He can physically react like this, can let go of control in his little body and just let go...

I'll be honest: it's getting better.

Sometimes when Eric hits those moments, he's a good foot or two away from me. It's like he's aware that while he *wants* to hit me, can't control the need for his body to lash out and move and react, he also has this awareness that he's not *supposed* to hit.

Why am I mentioning this?

Because every little positive step forward counts and when you're right in the thick of things, when all you can see of the forest are the pine needles sticking in your eyes, you've got to hold onto the positive things. Just like the potty-training bit, which is finally, *finally* coming together. We're almost there. Not that we're "done" (done in my mind is when I almost never have to think about it), but Eric's initiating on his own *and* he's communicating with us when we're out of the house and he needs the potty.

That's huge.

Huge.

Especially from a child who's been completely reluctant to use any form of communication... unless he darn well feels like it.

Ah, the stubbornness of kids. (And the intense, you've-got-to-be-kidding-me stubbornness of late-talkers.)

While I have some positive moments throughout my day, some little successes whether it's the potty or Eric engaging in play with Kate or me, those happy moments doesn't take away from how crazy *hard* life is right now.

For Eric, all his feelings, his intense toddler emotions are compounded by a *ton* of frustration because he has no functional words yet. He doesn't even have the word "no."

Eric's also not taking this middle of his two-year-old stage with the grace that Kate did. *She* saw the communication piece as this great giant puzzle... "Hmm, how can I tell Mom that I want to watch a *Tinker Bell* movie even though it comes from the strange red Netflix button?"

And yes, she'd figure it out. That was in her personality.

Eric? Not so much.

Like, really, *really* not so much.

If Eric wants to have four bananas for breakfast and I'm in the middle of saying, "No," (with good reason, I might add) there he goes. His switch has flipped and I've got to stop what I'm doing (usually in the midst of making an actual breakfast) and help him through those emotions. This means being present and calm (ok, I try *really* hard to stay calm but flailing hands certainly has an effect on my inner cool), to soothe him with understanding (and hopefully words he can understand)... and just ride it out.

I have to support him.

I can't get mad or leave the room. Or yell. Or let my own inner frustration (read: tantrum) out.

Time outs don't work for us (even if they're actually for *me* and I shut myself in the bathroom). They might work on some kids. Not Eric. He gets even madder and goes right for that thing he *knows* he's not supposed to do. Like banging the gate surrounding the very expensive electronics. Or climb *in*to the toilet.

You know, toddler things.

Your family is going to have different mileage here and, oh boy, do these two-year-old years vary.

Your family is also going to have different needs. I've got two kids and they each handled this stage completely differently. Kate ran off and cried in her crying castle; Eric wants to hit me.

Throw in *any* kind of special needs, from late-talking children to those with sensory processing issues and more, much, much more, these early years are even tougher. And for those of you parents who have children with even greater challenges, you have my utmost respect in the work and care you do.

I'm also slowly (sadly) realizing, there's not some magic technique or spoonful of sugar that's going to make these challenging moments go away or make them any easier. It's part of our kids and their development, as parents we've got to do our best to help our frustrated kids through the ginormous disappointments in life.

Like not eating as many bananas as you damn well want.

Why am I bringing all these challenges up? Why am I listing out each reason why life is so freakin' hard right now?

I just had a blood test confirming what I already knew: the sleep deprivation and stress has taken its toll.

I mean, I suspected this was most likely the case, but I didn't really *know*. I do now.

My blood work is wonderful. Really. Green all across the board from cholesterol to Vitamin D. Except I have inflammation. Inflammation that is directly related to sleep and stress.

Well, no shit.

I've suspected this for a while now. Parenting my two young kids has taken a toll on my body. But the question remains (and it's a big one): what the heck can I do about it??

It's not like I can decrease my stress by handing my son off to daycare (if you haven't been following my blog, just know this would not be a good move for *Eric*).

In March I cut almost all sugar from my diet. I had to. All the broken sleep (when we went through that terrible patch for six months) took its toll. I needed to stop the sweets and give my body a chance to heal (it did, and still is). My poor metabolism was shot and I was putting on a few pounds. Not a lot but enough that the negative self-talk in my head was adding more stress, not to mention I was feeling bloated and icky all the time.

Again, I focused on what I *could* do: not eat the sugar and focus on sleep.

Of course, I couldn't control how often my kids woke up at night, but I could control how much caffeine and alcohol I was drinking—I even made the bedroom more sleep friendly—and all that helped.

But what else could I do?

The guide this dietitian sent me was all great... except I was already doing most of it. It's not like I *want* to be waking up 2-3 times a night. It's not *my* choice. It's my kids' choice. You know, those little individuals I have zero control over.

I think that's what's so frustrating about this. I have all these wonderful recommendations to help with the inflammation, but it feels like half of them simply don't apply to me. Because I'm a parent. Because the *reasons* for the lack of sleep, for the stress, are *because* I'm a parent.

And a parent of a very frustrated, right-in-the-middle of being a two-year-old doing... you know, exactly what he's supposed to be doing at this developmental stage.

I know darn well the best medicine for us is time.

Eric needs time to grow and mature, to settle in with his language, with his sleep. I know in my heart that's what he needs except... what about me in the meantime? How much of myself, my own health, is getting sacrificed in the process?

Can I focus on my own self-care, on healing my own body, when the cause of the problem is my children?

The answer is no.

The answer is also yes.

There are some things I can do, small minor tweaks to help myself out as much as possible, but the source of the stress and the sleep deprivation, well, that ain't goin' away (probably not even when they're grown up with families of their own).

And sure, I've got the stress of Eric's frustrations, the instant explosions he's having these days, but I haven't even touched on the anxiety I feel about an upcoming video consult with our speech therapist. I mean, here I am, Ms. Confident when it comes to this late-talking journey and I'm still *scared*. Scared that she won't see the progress that Eric has made which has been huge for *him*. Yes, he's behind. No, he's not where other boys are, but oh my gosh, we're making progress. We're making these huge stride forwards, even if on the outside they only look like itty-bitty steps.

The point is they're there.

All of them.

All the visual referencing, how Eric will engage with people he trusts and likes in some kind of play or will show off to his aunt and uncle as he falls splat-face-first on the couch.

But I'm still scared that our speech professional will come back and put more worries or doubts in my mind. I don't need those doubts. They're not gonna help me. Not now. Not when I know we are already doing everything that Eric needs, and honestly, everything he'll *accept*. (A strange speech therapist he doesn't know trying to play with him? Prompt him when it comes to play? Oh *hell* no.)

All that above?

That's stress.

It's a hidden kind of stress, something that most people who look at me will never *see*. I generally don't talk about Eric in public. I'll talk about our overall challenges and simply surviving, but his speech journey has been different because he's a different kid than Kate. It's required me to really trust in his process and to recognize, too, that we *are* doing what he needs. Nothing more will make this process go faster for him.

It just won't.

Not with the kind of child he is.

And the truth is I can't have anyone else's doubts or judgments inside me. I simply can't. I'm already treading water, doing my best to support my kids in the ways that I know they need.

Which again... all this... it's taking a toll on my body.

Truthfully there's not a whole lot left I can do to make our situation with him, his current challenge, as well as my dreams for writing, better. I've been focused on thinking creatively, on thinking outside the box, but the challenges of my particular family means I can't just drop the kids off with a babysitter or a co-op or a daycare. Maybe in a few years, sure, but not now.

I know I'm not there yet, and while there are things I can't simply make go away (fear of the upcoming video consult), there are other things I *can* do.

Still, still, still focusing on self-care.

Sure, I might talk about all these great ideas and changes, but putting them into practice? Easier said than done. It's hard to break routines and behaviors; it's hard to break old patterns that put you, as the parent, last in line in terms of priority.

But I'm learning.

I am leaving the house every day, at least for thirty minutes. That's such a tiny thing, but so, so big. It gives me the chance to breathe. I mean really truly breathe... without spending every exhale wondering what the heck the two-year-old is banging into now.

I'll grab my laptop, a book, a journal. Maybe I'll do some writing, maybe I'll just sit outside, and again just... just breathe.

I'm also setting up times when a mother's helper can come over and play with both kids. This isn't going to give me any alone time, but it will take some pressure off. Maybe I can cut up veggies for dinner then or write an email that requires my whole brain. Or maybe I'll hide out in the bedroom and work on my publishing business while I have the help.

I guess what I'm saying is—I'm asking for help. Mostly from family at this point, but I'm asking.

I'm prioritizing *my time.*

When Grandma comes over for a visit, instead of doing the dishes or working on food, I'm going to leave the house.

Again, I'm taking time for me and only me.

That's not an easy thing for me to do, but I'm going to do it. Small, little shifts. Small changes in my mindset.

I went out to breakfast with a dear friend one weekend and I left feeling amazing. It felt like I was filled with this wonderful energy. I'll do that more too. Just getting away and connecting with someone who I know *will make me feel good.*

I'm going to surround myself with the right kind of people. People who add to my energy and happiness rather than take away from it.

Again, small little shifts.

This stress of parenting, especially right now, it's real. And I'm right in the thick of it.

I know I'm not alone. I'm not alone in feeling trapped, frustrated, at times even depressed. And those of you who have kids who walk to a different beat? You're not alone in all those feelings either.

I'm here to say, "I get it."

I can't get *exactly* what you're going through, but I empathize with you. And I applaud you. Truly. With all my heart.

It takes a courageous person to embrace being different, whether you have a special needs child, you homeschool, or you've chosen a different way of parenting than the norm. Or whether you're like me and following your passion, your dreams and creativity, while still being a parent and raising young kids.

At times parenting is a lonely journey and we have no choice but to keep moving forward, keep doing our best. The journey is hard and it takes a physical toll. It does. It takes a mental *and* an emotional toll, so let's all recognize that together. Let's all recognize that the journey is wonderful and it's really hard and draining, especially as every day we try our best.

Because you know when your little child smiles at you, you know, without a doubt, it's totally worth it.

Yes, yes it is.

But we, as parents, we matter too.

So, take the time to care for yourself. Do whatever it is *you* need to feel whole and healthy and alive. Maybe we can't do a whole lot, but even doing a little bit matters.

Just like you.

You, dear parent, you matter too.

FINDING JOYFUL MOMENTS

July 17, 2017
Kate, almost 5 years
Eric, 2 1/2 years

How to connect and find joy even during the tough times of parenting whether you're a writer—or simply trying to survive.

Let's be honest here: when life is hard, when parenting feels like the hardest, most thankless job on this planet, finding joy can feel like pulling teeth (or downright impossible). And yet there's something to be said when you take a breath, step back, and try to find some small positive nugget in this challenging trial you may be going through.

Because it works.

When you find that one little piece, the world doesn't seem quite so against you (or your children—who feel like they're plotting to single-handedly destroy you). Sure your day probably sucked, you probably yelled and lost your cool and there were most likely tears (from the kids *and* from you), but that one little piece, that one glimmering, positive thought, was like a beacon.

You were trying and still are.

You're doing what you can.

You are doing *something* in the direction you want, to be the kind of parent you want to be, in the way you want to be connected with your children. It's not a whole lot, but that little glimmer is hope. And sometimes all we need is hope to keep from falling down into those dark pits of sadness and loneliness. (Hope and a few good, nonjudgmental friends who are willing to listen while you pour your heart and your failures out to them. Those friends are essential, I'm telling you.)

Our 'job' as parents, this role we've chosen, it's twenty-four hours a day, seven days a week.

You may have no breaks. You may have no family around to lean on. You may not have money to pay for a babysitter or a mother's helper, to give yourself a small ounce of a break or the essential connecting time with your spouse or loved one (without having to referee a knock-down, drag-out fight between kids or catching the toddler and his chocolate/sticky hands before he runs wild touching *everything* in your house).

You may also, like me, have children who fall outside the normal, who walk to their own beat, who don't care about society and their stupid boxes and decided to create a box of their own (or hell, to just sit on top of the damn box).

This parenting role is *hard*.

This parenting role is also—and equally so—*joyful*.

I am constantly reminding myself of this. When the day is upside down and all I want to do is crawl away and cry (you know, one of *those* kind of days), I somehow try and remind myself to find the hope, to find one little joyful moment. Even when I'm upset, when I'm at my rock-bottom lowest, I have this little voice in the back of my head reminding me: if you connect with them, you'll feel better.

Sometimes, I'm in a position to do this.

Sometimes, I want to have a tantrum myself.

All that is good and easy to say, I know. As if thinking happy thoughts will magically turn your mood around.

Yeah. Parenting life doesn't work that way, but there are a few things I've found that do work.

Call a friend. Or text them. Or connect on whatever your favorite social media platform is.

But go to someone who is compassionate, who makes you feel *safe*, safe enough to reveal the awfulness of the parenting moment you've just survived (or are trying to survive). Connect with an actual adult, a human being who can wipe their own butt, and let those feelings out.

All of them.

You need to be heard and seen. You need someone to share this with.

When I call Sean at work he almost always picks up (if he's not in a meeting) because he knows I'm hitting the panic button and I need support. And oftentimes, that little bit is all I need.

Journaling is good for this too, and so is writing gratitude's—specifically gratitudes toward your kids. I try to look for the positive in any situation, even when the situations are really quite hard, to find those little glimmers in the middle of all that hardness.

I'll write out what happened, throwing in every judgmental thought about myself (and my kids) that I can think of to get how I *feel* on the paper. Then I step back and list the facts as if I were an observer without judgments, state what happened and why. I try to list what my feelings were in that moment and the needs I had that weren't being met. I'll do this also with the kids and what I think they were going through.

And then, just as importantly, I try to list ideas of what I could do differently next time.

This isn't to say next time will be perfect, but this exercise is really helpful in deconstructing the situation, helping me 'get under the hood' of why I reacted the way I did—and it gives me a plan for the future. Plans, though, especially with parenting (especially when the tactic you're taking hasn't been hard-wired into you from your own childhood) often fall apart.

This work I'm doing on myself, how I show up and parent my kids, it's a practice.

The simple act of reflecting and thinking forward will give me the barest hint of a roadmap, but one that means if I keep on going, keep on trying, I will find success.

I'd journal even more if I could, but finding the quiet time in this house, with my little Eric getting into *everything*, isn't working so well. I've decided to reserve those quiet moments for my own writing or my publishing business.

I've also found that removing ourselves from the house, getting outside for some fresh air, is huge.

To be honest, the house is generally the battleground that all these big emotions take place in. Which makes sense. We all feel safest there. It's also the place with a whole lot of rules (no, you can't stand on the entertainment table; no, we're not having four bananas [or chocolate] for breakfast). Leaving the house, getting outside, getting movement... satisfies a lot of our individual needs, even ones we may not be aware of.

Eric might *be* needing more movement. Kate might be needing space from her Godzilla brother. I just need to be left alone, goddamn it!

When we go on walks, we automatically invite connection between us. The kids running ahead of me, glancing back and smiling. Or jumping in place and then looking at me to show me how darn cool that was. All of those moments—eye-blinks, really—are chances to reconnect as a family, to get us back to center after a particularly bumpy moment. And with all seriousness, *I'm* the one who's usually most resistant to reconnecting.

The kids are like magic, I swear.

The second the front door of our apartment opens and they go running down the hall barefoot, all is forgotten. All is forgiven. I'm the one still carrying the baggage. Going on a walk or going to the pool gives me enough space, enough time to mentally calm down. It's enough to finally bring me back from that angry/frustrated place and when I do, my kids, including Eric, who is currently the source of much frustration, are waiting for me—with a smile. With complete joy and love in their face.

They've already forgiven me. They've already moved on.

Now I just need to act like a grown-up—or truthfully, more like a child—and follow their lead.

Yes, I know, this is easier said than done. If you've followed this blog, you know my son is hitting right in the middle of the two's and gets incredibly frustrated and physical (with me) when he doesn't instantly get what he wants. He also doesn't talk yet and that adds to his frustration. Sometimes it takes all of my control to *not* lose control (and some days/moments I'm way more successful than others).

But I keep trying.

I keep listening to that little voice: find the joy.

At least, I eventually do. I'm no miracle-worker. I'm generally overtired and overworked... and also so incredibly grateful to be home with my kids, to be helping them on their journey, one that is as different and unique as they are. Sometimes all I need is a thirty-minute break with someone else stepping in and managing the toddler.

Often, I don't get that.

Those days are about surviving and doing the best I can with the resources I have.

I try to be honest with myself—and kind. Kind because I'm not perfect, because I *am* tired and I *am* overwhelmed. After I take those deep breaths or go outside and get some much needed movement in...

I see the absolute joy in Eric's face. His complete love for me and his love of swimming and he wants to share that.

With *me*.

I get to see his growth, his expanding awareness of the world, how he'll jump on the couch and look at each adult in turn to make sure they saw just how awesome what he did was. Or his growing understanding (or maybe even just willingness) when we ask him to do something. Or how he's finally got this potty-training thing down.

Or Kate who's making leaps and bounds with language. How she's answering simple questions now and how she will go to Eric when he's upset, kneel down and rub his back and say, "It's okay, Eric. It's okay."

Little moments of joy... little moments of success... even when we're in the middle of some seriously hard times. Because, and I know it's hard to remember in the moment, the times won't *always* be bad. In fact, the very next moment can be an amazing one!

Parenting is all about the fluctuations, the movement. It's a straight-up roller coaster and it's hard, especially when there are only two adults doing everything... bringing home the bacon, cooking the bacon, the required house-cleaning, laundry, and never-ending dishes. And, let's not forget the actual act of *parenting*. You know, teaching and guiding our young ones to be kind, caring individuals. Talk about a tall order here!

As I'm often reminded, it's when we make mistakes that we have the most opportunity to learn. A mistake today, an unkind word or reaction today, means tomorrow you can do better. You can learn—about your kids, yourself—and find a new way, a new path, for tomorrow.

Give yourself a bit of grace, my dear parent.

We are doing our best, every day, every moment.

Oftentimes, all we need are those little moments, a little bit of space and quiet, to calm down and meet our children in that place of love and forgiveness. Because really, they're already there waiting for us. All we have to do is let go of our own feelings—all that frustration, anger, worry—and meet them with loving, open arms.

They always come running because they love us, for exactly who we are, as imperfect as we are.

Talk about a true gift.

AM I ENOUGH?

September 14, 2017
Kate, 5 years
Eric, 2 1/2 years

The ever-increasing bar of parenthood and the doubts that plague us all—whether you're walking a more mainstream path, forging a new path, or simply trying to be a parent-writer.

This is post isn't so much about being a parent-writer but mostly about being a parent and the constant question we ask ourselves:

Am I enough?

I've been struggling with this for a while now especially as the new school year starts, as new routines and schedules get hammered out and I try to find our new path forward. I'm also putting more focus and energy into the other areas of my life that I've put on hold to be a parent, and once again, I feel myself dealing with the question: Am I enough?

Am I doing enough?

Am I good enough?

This is straight-up tied to being a perfectionist, something I've struggled to let go over the years, to simply be who I am, to do the best I can and celebrate in what I *have* accomplished. And yet... every once in a while... my perfectionist finds a new way to creep in, to sneak into my subconscious, to create doubts and negative self-talk. A little, tiny voice nagging that I should do *more*...

Read more with the kids.

Play more.

Connect more.

And, of course, there's always *more* we could *do*, more to focus on, more to strive at being better...

A couple months ago, I dealt with how my perfectionist came into my writing process and it wasn't in the usual way either. It wasn't during the actual creation of a story, when I put words on page. I've learned to *trust* those words (and my unique author voice). I'd already dealt with *that* part so instead my perfectionist went and took hold of another part of the process: getting my stories out to readers.

I simply would stop dead in my tracks when it came to the editing process, the copyediting, and the publishing part of my business.

I was surprised. Shocked, actually.

I had no idea my perfectionist, my critical voice, had been sitting there and stopping my work from actually reaching readers. It's taken time, and it's still a process, but I'm currently working through this and am making *fun* strides with my publishing business.

And yet, that's one reason I'm now dealing with this question: Am I enough?

You see, as I focus on my business, I pay less attention to other areas of my life. Mainly, my family. I'm not connecting with the kids as much and we're not playing as much. Not enough board games or sitting down and doing art together.

If I step back and *look* at my life, I would (hopefully) see how silly my worry is.

I mean, I *am* putting attention and focus on my business—but that's part of *my* self-care. This is super important, this focus on self-care which I've learned (often hard-fought over these years). *I am important, too, and I've finally reached a point with Eric where I can put energy to these other important areas of my life...*

And yet the worries and the self-doubt are still there.

A huge part of the problem is that my brain, having lived through my own childhood and in this American culture for thirty-five years, *still* has all these labels, this hierarchy of what is deemed as important—

And what isn't.

Here's an idea of what I'm sifting through in my head: Sitting on the couch and reading books together or learning by playing board games (especially as a homeschooler) is deemed important. Swimming with friends for *hours*, playing with dolls, playing *Mario 3D World* with Kate, dancing with Eric—not important.

Which is ridiculous and intellectually I *know all* this. I do.

In fact, I've been working on letting go of all these thoughts and worries, what our world deems as 'learning' and 'education' ever since Kate was two years old and yet... yet here I am, still questioning the importance of play and joy.

For myself.

For my kids.

I know I'm feeling more pressure this year (and really, right at *this* moment) because technically, if life had gone the way I'd originally envisioned it, Kate would be in kindergarten. I mean, she's a *baby* five but, according to most states, she'd be in kindergarten and therefore,

Learning great things of importance! Learning things that are clearly not hanging out with friends and playing!

It's enough to drive me crazy. I *know* how I feel about education and self-directed learning. I *know* the value of simple play and social interaction... *which is exactly what she's getting.*

Right now. Every week. Every day.

And yet here I am mentally beating myself up because somewhere inside me, it doesn't feel like enough. That I'm not doing enough; that *I'm* not enough.

Which is my perfectionist speaking.

My perfectionist can look at the day we had, completely filled with trying to meet everyone's needs, of driving up and visiting with Grandma and Grandpa, playing with their big dogs (and helping Eric work through feelings of his safety and growing comfort). And then playing with older kids at the park. I can go over our entire day, and somehow, in some area, find myself lacking.

Here's what my perfectionist points out to me:

You didn't play when Kate asked you to. Why didn't you join her with painting? Or coloring Pinkie Pie's tail? You should put your own work aside. Stop typing up those notes for your online workshop; you're neglecting her.

(Never mind the fact that I facilitated *how* many days she's playing with friends, swimming and playing with dolls, even video games? Not to mention the outings this week, from rock climbing to visiting an ice cream art museum and spending a *ton* of quality, fun-time with Grandma??)

To which my perfectionist replies:

What about Eric??

Were you *really* connecting with him enough?

My perfectionist, with all her negative self-talk, doesn't stop there either. She'll point other things out—See? He's sorting those colored Legos on the floor. By himself. Why don't you join him? Why don't you use that as an opportunity to work on his sounds and his growing comfort with turning his voice on??

(Never mind that every moment he's awake I *am* aware of his speech, finding new and fun ways to play sound games that are natural for him and me. That we play tickle games and hide-and-seek games like crazy. But hey, *those* moments don't count.)

This is my own struggle, dealing with my perfectionist and the negative voice in my head that some days (like, right now) I feel like I'm in a constant, epic battle with.

You're getting a glimpse into all these thoughts I've got going on. I recognize them for what they are... and I'm trying to work through them.

I'm trying to pick apart the threads and figure out the *real* cause of why I'm having them in the first place and generally, if my perfectionist is involved, it has to do with fear.

Fear and protecting.

Clearly, some part of me is afraid of something or feels that I (or my kids) need protecting. Maybe from the great ways I can single-handedly Screw Them Up—

Which is just silly.

I literally just got off the phone with a friend who, after I told her about my week and everything we did (as well as mentioning my struggle with these negative thoughts) said, "It sounds to me like you're doing plenty."

Which I am.

I *know* I am. Helping my kids through their emotions, taking the time to connect, to empathize, scheduling fun outings with friends as well as stuff to do as a family (like rock climbing). Then there's keeping the house in somewhat order and the endless dishes, cleaned. Oh, and let's not forget preparing and cooking real food (at least most of the time).

I *know* I'm doing the best that I can and I *know* that my life, and my kids' lives, will look completely different than everyone else's. For example, a lot of kids Kate's age are focusing on school, on learning to read or beginning math, but for me, my focus is on continuing to help her with *language*.

I'm getting her out with friends, focusing on my modeling and recasting, having new experiences which are a fantastic jumping off point for more words to come, more language, more conversation.

That's *my* focus for her right now.

And what's super amazing is all the people in our life who matter most, grandparents, close friends, they all intuitively understand this, too. I'm not getting badgered about Kate's reading or anything else that might look school related. Instead, I'm getting smiles and looks of amazement over what Kate said or how she interacted with someone.

Other than language, I'm really tuning into what learning will look like for us as a family, and specifically for *Kate*.

As a family, we believe in self-directed learning. You might not, you might send your kids to school or you might follow a more classic homeschool approach. But for us this is what we believe in... following a child's interest, helping them by facilitating learning in an area they're excited about. It means I need to be aware of Kate and her passions, and when I see something, ask myself how I can help *that* grow?

For example, Kate's aunt was over the other day and she was rolling some dice to build a character for the *Dungeons and Dragons* campaign Sean's running. As she was rolling those dice, she was getting quite passionate about what numbers she was rolling. She was trying to create a sorcerer, so having a high strength number and *not* a high intellect number was bad.

Kate's aunt would get a set of numbers, write them down, and usually be pissed about some number not fitting into the sorcerer character she wanted to build. So, she'd start rolling again.

And again.

And again.

And Kate, who was interested, came over and watched. At first, she got a paper and pencil, and started drawing. Then, later, I noticed she was writing the *numbers*.

Thirteen. Four. Eight. An entire page of numbers.

I was *shocked*.

This was the first time I'd ever seen Kate write out numbers or even have an interest in numbers. But there she was, writing them all down. And the day after, while waiting for food at a restaurant, she started filling in numbers for a Sudoku puzzle all on her own.

So, I asked myself, *What can I do to help facilitate this interest?* I first tried rolling a bunch of dice with her and writing down the numbers, but she wasn't interested. She just started coloring. And that's when I had my realization of *why* Kate had been drawn to the numbers in the first place, why she started writing the dice numbers down with her aunt...

She was having *emotions*... about numbers. Those numbers *meant* something to her. They had meaning. They had a purpose. And these numbers were also fun (if it wasn't a fun experience, she wouldn't be doing it).

Kate wanted in on that.

I've already come up with some ideas of how we can go forward from here... like, when we play our weekly *Dungeons and Dragon* session, to start the game earlier. That way Kate can participate or just watch.

I've also picked up a role-playing book for *My Little Pony* (yes, there is such a thing) and am thinking about running a campaign for her and her friends. It will require some adjusting, but it'll give her the chance to have her own emotions about numbers, about game-play and cooperation, all of which, of course, will continue to build on her language. I even got a board game that mimics a playing style similar to a role-playing game that can scale for different ages. I've already put this in motion, inviting a few friends to come over, to try out the role-playing game, then get into some amazing board games I have as well...

And this, this right here, is why all my worries are just plain silly.

I *know* what I need to do. I *know* what I am doing and, gosh darn-it, it's enough.

I am enough.

I know this won't be the last time I struggle with these thoughts. I know it's just not my perfectionist at the wheel here. Self-esteem is playing a huge roll in my ability to stand up and say, "No. I *am* going to walk this other path and I'm going to be *comfortable* doing it."

The comfortable part is one I'm still working on and I plan on diving down deeper into what this means for me, in how it's manifested out of my own childhood and experiences, journaling and really delving into what's causing these different negative voices and anxiety.

Let me tell you, this self-exploration thing is a never-ending journey and it feels like every time I clean up one wire and one connection under my hood, I find a half-dozen more that need fixing.

And I'm okay with that. I like this feeling, the feeling of moving forward. Of learning about myself and why I tick the way I do.

As long as I try to balance my needs and dreams of being a writer and an entrepreneur with being a parent, I'll be struggling with these thoughts. I doubt they'll ever leave me... but as I said, I think I'll get better at handling this anxiety, this stress. I feel more confident in my abilities and in what I'm doing.

I also know parents who've chosen a more normal, mainstream life (meaning school but who are also engaged and supportive in their kids' lives) also have these same doubts. That they aren't enough as parents, that they need to do more, to give more of themselves for the kids to succeed.

I think it's a normal part of parenting.

Also normal: when you do something different than the mainstream... like homeschooling or being the primary speech partner for your kids or being an entrepreneur—

All these doubts will hit you extra *hard*.

Which means you have to keep beating them down...

Until the darn things find yet some other way to come at you to try to take you out at the knees...

And you go through the whole process again.

And again.

The truth is, I am doing my best to provide the right kind of learning, the right kind of environment and opportunities for my kids. No way in hell will our process, our life and learning *ever* look perfect—and no way will *I* ever be perfect. There will always be more I could add to my day—more connection time, more reading time, more social time. In fact, we could swamp our lives with *more* and still feel like it's not enough.

And that's just bullshit.

All I have to do is look at my kids, at their joy and smiles, look back to where we started out journey and where we are now.

Because the truth is—I am enough... just as I am.

WRITING WITH YOUNG KIDS

October 2, 2017
Kate, 5 years
Eric, almost 3 years

The ups and downs of parenting, of recognizing when the writing is impossible, and when—and how—you can find your way back to it.

The truth is ever since I decided to become a parent, I knew I'd have to tap-dance around my new (and enormous) responsibilities and somehow find time to write.

Taking care of my kids, feeding and clothing them, teaching them to be kind individuals who knew their own minds and beings. And the added challenge of both my children having pretty impressive language delays (both the speaking of and understanding of language). It's made for a different life, certainly different from the average parent's journey.

And all the while I've been writing.

Well, maybe not writing *all* the time.

Five months ago, when Eric hit his massive two-year frustration stage, I got almost no writing done.

I simply couldn't—even if I'd wanted to.

My storytelling brain, my subconscious, was hiding in fear of the overload and all the emotions that Chrissy-the-Parent was dealing with and helping the two-year-old through.

It was not the time for writing.

I've learned over the years, through trial-and-error and slow realizations, that writing around young kids really is a roller coaster. It's got lots of turns and loops and twists and *never* goes in a straight path.

I'm balancing my needs and feelings as well as those of my kids.

But as we slowly come out of one roller-coaster loop and start climbing upwards again, hearing the *click, click, click* underneath me, I'm breathing again...

And the writing, like magic, comes back.

Because this whole time it's been waiting.

I always knew I'd keep writing. I knew that I wouldn't be writing a whole lot with a newborn around (ha... little did I know how easy *that* stage would be), but I knew I'd keep writing. When I told this to one friend of mine, who already had a child of her own, I remember her looking at me with snotty amusement.

She, of course, wasn't a writer.

To be fair, I wasn't a mother yet either.

I'd thought, as I went into this parenting journey, that I'd have some sort of a schedule. That I'd figure out some timing that would work between baby, house, and husband.

Turns out, with kids there's no such thing as a schedule. Or a consistent schedule. (If my kids could read this, they'd be snorting in laughter.)

The one constant with kids is there is no such thing as a constant.

And consistency? Forget it.

Sure, life might have a routine... for a week or two or three. Hey, maybe you're lucky and you get a whole month of routine. But then someone gets sick or has a slew of bad nightmares and you find yourself with a child pressed against either side of you and your own sleep goes right out the window.

Such is the life of a parent-writer... of kids under five, anyway.

And those of you (most, I imagine, reading this) have your kids in daycare or preschool or maybe they've already started kindergarten. You'll have a lot more routine simply because school starts at a certain time and that's when you Must Be There. And while your kids are in school, you'll have some bits of quiet, uninterrupted time to get your word count in (after you've returned from dropping them off or doing some desperately needed grocery shopping).

I've chosen a different path, one that suits our family and our lifestyle. We've chosen to homeschool and follow a more self-directed learning approach, which is really great and exciting (for all of us), but it means I've got another hurdle to overcome:

Writing with my kids *around.*

For me, gone are the days of sitting in a room making shit up... at least *alone.*

I still get some quiet time in. Sean watches the kids for an hour while I go write in the clubhouse. I get some self-care time in (being alone and writing) and I get the word count in. Or when Grandma Charlie comes over and wrestles the two kids on the floor (she's usually on the bottom).

However, coming out of five months of not writing and helping Eric through his *Big Emotions*, I was having a really, really tough time restarting the writing.

I wanted to write... but the drive wasn't there. And every time I'd go and get a couple thousand words in, my critical voice would sneak in and derail the whole thing, which triggered my creative voice who then refused to write.

Suddenly writing felt like work again. Which for me is a big, flashing neon sign that my critical voice has taken over.

This has been another part of my writing-parenting journey, a realization that has come slowly... along with ways to pull myself back up again.

There are times when my subconscious can relax, can come out and play and tell the stories it wants. Then there are times when I need to shutter those writing doors and post a sign saying:

Gone Parenting.

I'd just come out of this stage but hadn't yet flipped that door sign over. I was trying to write, trying to find my way back into a story I *knew* I wanted to write...

And I felt totally and completely stuck.

Enter Dean Wesley Smith and his novel writing challenge. Dean is one of my writing mentors on the Oregon Coast, along with his equally amazing and supportive wife, Kristine Kathryn Rusch. They've both known me from before I became a parent. In fact, before Kate was born she'd already 'attended' three workshops with Dean and Kris along with two more after she was born.

(Eric has yet to meet them—I'm hoping by the end of 2018 we can make that happen.)

Dean put out a call for a couple of brave souls to write three novels in three months and he would be our first reader. Succeed or fail, you'd get two online workshops for free.

And then I felt it... this little spark of excitement.

My first legitimate thought: Could I do this?

I knew *how* to make it happen.

To eat that kind of elephant, I needed to focus on one day at a time, on how many words I needed to get in each day rather than looking at the whole entirety of the novel.

I did the math, came up with 3,000 words a day. Then I looked at my day... and realized to do this I'd need to not only write while the kids were around—but also after Eric went to bed.

I usually *never* write in the evening. I'm a morning person. I'm at my best and most creative early. By the end of the day, I'm usually a brain-dead zombie (another reason we haven't played many board games this year).

But aside from the logistics, the real heart of the matter was one of mindset. I would have to go at this with complete joy. If the writing felt like work in anyway whatsoever, I couldn't do this.

I had to let my creative voice be in complete control... and I had to recognize the signs when it was starting to shift.

Let me tell you, writing with your kids around is pretty much a big-ass mirror showing you who's in control: your creative voice or your critical one.

(I'm really not kidding here... I could be writing away, typing like crazy, with Eric sitting on my lap... or getting frustrated and yelling about the umpth-teenth interruption over the broken train track.)

The promise to myself had to be recognizing the moments for what they were. If the kids were having a hard time, were needing extra attention, then I needed to close the laptop and focus on them. I wouldn't get frustrated because what I wanted to be doing was writing.

Instead I needed to let it go and tell myself, "You'll have another chance later."

I'm still early into this challenge, but so far I'm learning there are actually quite a few chances throughout the day. It really helps that I haven't overbooked myself like crazy, that I'm not rushing from one event or play date to another.

Of course, being sick has had a bunch to do with that.

Yep. Day 1 of the challenge and I've got a nasty throat cold and am heading off to bed while Nyquil does its thing. And yet, somehow, even with three of us with colds, I'm getting in those 3,000 words.

The other mind shift I've made is the time I spend *with* my kids.

Okay, you're probably thinking, "What are you talking about, Chrissy? You're with your kids all the time."

And you'd be absolutely correct. But seriously, how many times are we actually, fully and completely, present with our kids? *Not* thinking about our grocery list or what time dinner needs to start so we can have an honest-to-God decent bedtime?

Instead of telling myself to be sure to get on the floor and play trains with Eric or *My Little Ponies* with Kate, I'm focusing on the hundreds of individual moments. The opportunities for connections. Like running in circles around the living room, falling on the floor in a laughing tackle. Or letting Eric hang from Sean's pull-up bar and laughing hysterically.

I'm connecting with my kids and laughing and living in joy.

The more I do this, the more I focus on small, authentic moments throughout the day, the more my relationship with them deepens. It grows stronger. Which also means later in the day I'm able to open up my laptop and write. Even with them around.

(Talk about a different experience than a year ago when this was the last thing in the world I could do.)

What often happens, too, is Eric will run over, laughing and asking for a moment of connection, a kiss from me, a shared look of love, and then back he goes back to what he was doing.

And all the while I'm still in my creative voice.

I'm a long, long way from figuring out this parent-writer journey, but it feels like I'm onto something here, something I've known for a while I needed to figure out.

How to write with my kids around.

No, I'm not going to get long stretches of quiet time writing by myself because that's simply not the life I'm living. Instead, I'm living a life with my children right beside me and I wouldn't want it any other way.

And here I am, slowly finding ways to write the stories I desperately want to tell, the novels I've put on hold for a long time. My kids and Sean and I—we're figuring this all out together and at this moment in time, on this stretch of our roller-coaster life, we *are* figuring it out.

It might be a different story tomorrow or the next day or the next month, but we'll keep moving forward because that's simply what you do as a parent and a writer—because not writing isn't an option.

BEING AN EMPATH

(AND RAISING THEM)

March 19, 2018
Kate, 5 years
Eric, 3 years

When you and your children—literally—feel the emotions of others and take them into your body. How being empaths, for me and my kids, has affected these early childhood years and therefore my ability to write.

The idea for this blog has been on my mind for a few months, that I'm an empath and so our my kids (and what that's meant for their late-talking journey), I've been hesitant to write these thoughts down and share them with the world. I think because this is very personal to us. At the same time, we live in a world that largely doesn't understand people who feel this way, who deeply feel the emotions and energy of the world around us.

Or doesn't care to.

You see, my kids and I are empaths. For most of you out there, just the word itself is making you scratch your head and go, "What? What does *that* mean?"

You might immediately think it's the same as being an empathetic person, where your heart easily goes out to another. Being an empath and being empathetic are quite different.

An empath means you literally *feel* another person's emotions, their happiness, sadness, grief. You feel all of it inside your own body. You absorb those emotions—even physical sensations and ailments—energies, into your own body. The energy comes from other people, but other places, too.

Sometimes it's hard to even know if what you're feeling are your emotions—or someone else's.

There's a lot more to being an empath than my brief little paragraph, and many others explain it better than I ever could (along with all the layers and different types of empath a person can be). I recommend Dr. Judith Orloff and her recent book, "The Empath's Survival Guide." This book has been instrumental in helping me understand myself and my kids, as well as shown me protective measures we can take to protect our energy.

(I will include some other resources I've found helpful at the bottom.)

Up until a few years ago, I didn't know I was an empath. But when I looked into it, it was like a piece of myself, some deeper understanding and awareness, *finally* fell into place.

Who I *was* made sense.

Who I was as a child made sense.

I was the child who was quiet. Shy. Sensitive. I felt things intensely and I learned from a young age I needed to protect myself from all the feelings and energies (and anger) around me.

I learned that in order to survive, I needed to be perfect.

If I didn't make mistakes or fail, then I wouldn't get yelled at. I wouldn't feel the judgment of teachers. When it came to physical or emotional pain, I'd learned to almost cut it off from me, completely divorce the pain from my psyche and not allow myself to *feel*. Because in feeling, I would want to feel and connect with others and *that* was not allowed.

So, I wouldn't put myself in front of the class where everyone would not only look at me but would stare and see just how odd and awkward I was. And me being me, I would *feel* every bit of emotion and thought and I would clam up tight, not letting an inch of myself through.

Looking back... I understand now.

I understand why my earliest memory was one of sadness and trauma (especially in the eyes of a three-year-old). I understand why I never had true, close friends in school and why I never fit in. Why I always felt alone and different. Why I was drawn to the kinds of relationships I was in and the holes in my life they were trying to fill. And how, somehow, I pulled away from a narcissistic relationship and reclaimed my own strength, rediscovered who I was...

How I found my own way back to my true self and to my writing.

With this new perspective—that I'm an empath—my life makes sense. It's like finally having that one missing piece of a puzzle and *now*, now I can see the picture for what it really is.

It makes sense now.

I make sense.

And sure, there's still so much growth and learning to do, but I'm seeing the world and myself in a completely new way. This awareness is a complete gift, especially as I turn and see my kids in this same light... and their own piece of the puzzle falls into place.

You know what else empaths are crazy good at?

Non-verbal communication.

And who are the two kids that chose me as their mom? Late-talkers.

Kate didn't talk until four and Eric's on target to be similar. And yet... it just baffles me when people ask how my kids communicate because my kids communicate with me in a hundred different ways. And me being me, I can instantly zero in on what my kids are doing —the situation, the context, the cues they've given me...

And know instantly that Eric's thirsty or that Kate wanted blueberries.

Or now when we're at the park with our homeschool friends and Eric starts looking around for me (because somehow I moved past the stage of him constantly running to the street), I can *hear* him calling for me. I can *hear* him looking for me.

All without him saying a word.

My kids are empaths as well.

Exactly how strong they are, I don't know yet, but I do know they both have strong empathetic traits. And I know that Eric's even more sensitive to the world than Kate. (At the end of this article I will have links in case you're curious about your own kids and being empaths.)

My kids were born with the same low barrier as I was, this lower filter to the world and its energies. Where other people have a higher threshold of tolerance for this energy, we simply don't. And my kids being so young... oh my gosh... it makes sense now. They haven't yet developed all the protective strategies I'd learned on my own—which weren't necessarily good ones but did help me survive, like the perfectionism and being shy and shutting down.

It makes sense why my kids act the way they do, in particular as late-talkers, and why I've always needed to be so aware, so in tune with what they are feeling. This allowed me to sweep in and take them in my arms when they needed it or protect them or guide them. They were never the kind of kids you could let cry and they'd 'get over it.'

Oh, no.

They'd keep getting upset. Keep getting ramped up. To calm down they needed to be held and loved; they needed a feeling of safety and security.

Kate might run off crying into her room, but you'd better believe she's running back out twenty seconds later so I can hold her and be with her through those feelings. After her special friend leaves from a fun morning of play time and she's upset and crying, brushing off her feelings and telling her to "get over it" doesn't work.

Instead, I sit with her, my arms around her and let her feel that sadness. And when she's ready, I ask if she wants to read the picture book, *The Invincible String*, which is about loving someone and being with them even when they're far away.

The pictures and words there help her understand.

My compassion and willingness to sit with her helps her understand even more.

All this is especially true when it comes to Eric.

Oh, my.

Everything I'm saying here goes double (or triple for him). Even as a baby, he *felt* the energies of the world. So much of our struggles, of what we went through when he was two, made sense. His sleep? That elusive sleep Sean and I were holding our breath for years to finally happen? Eric couldn't fall asleep or stay asleep because his body kept moving and jerking, as if it simply couldn't settle down on its own, couldn't get all that energy out of him. He'd get so frustrated he would cry. Like, big-time cry.

And you know what? That hasn't changed.

He still needs us, even as a three-year-old, to help his body settle. He climbs into our bed after a few hours of sleeping on his own. He nestles between us with his feet tucked under either Sean or me, or he's got his whole body pressed against us (last night I was the designated 'calm presence'). He still wakes up crying out and angry, he still flails with his arms, so frustrated and mad because gosh darn it he *wants* to sleep and he *can't*.

Words don't soothe him.

Only touch does.

We've been on our own journey when it came to Eric and his sleeping, and we've gradually stopped fighting his needs. We've slowly accepted this part of who he is, and I say slowly because parents can be pretty thick-headed at times, even when we're being conscious and mindful parents.

Now, though, now I understand *why* he does this and *why* he needs it. And I'm taking this new insight into the rest of his little life.

And suddenly, it all makes sense.

Like how when Eric gets upset during the day, with his full-on crying and screaming and flailing arms (and legs) the *only* way to calm him is by picking him up and putting him in my front toddler carrier. That's right. I walk around farmers market or Disneyland with a three-year-old on my front. And you know what? He almost always, instantly, calms down. With both of our heart centers touching, my heart to his, he can pick up and draw from my energy and patience.

He settles in.

He relies on my energy to help protect his, to help shield him when the world gets too much for his little self.

I no longer try to sit and hold him when he's like that. I no longer try to be that calm person helping him through those emotions in the way I used to. I still am that calm person (or certainly *try* to be), but the very first thing I do is pick him up and hold him. Eric's now at a place in his own maturity that he understands this. He understands his own needs and that to calm down, Mommy needs to hold him in just this way.

I've stopped fighting that.

Or maybe fighting isn't the right word, maybe it was me resisting... but even that doesn't feel entirely right. I'm aware of exactly what Eric's needs are... how I can best help him *and* that I need to completely remove him (like far, far away) from the thing that set him off in the first place.

If he can see whatever that was that set him off, you better believe he's just gonna keep getting re-triggered. (He's very persistent and opinionated, my Eric.)

For these past three years, I've been learning from my son, trying to understand him and his specific needs—which have been much, much more intense than Kate's ever were.

It was like she was complete training, complete preparation for me to have Eric.

How, when we go into a particular house, just pulling up to the curb he immediately starts crying and fighting in his car seat, how he already can feel the sadness and depression sitting within that house. He can feel it, so clearly, so immediately, even as I pull up in the car.

And looking back... I remember that Kate was the same way at this age. That she, energetically, didn't have the same protection as others did, that she was able to more easily *feel* what others felt, *feel* what the world felt.

She had the same reaction as Eric now does.

And here's the interesting part, at least for my kids and my family, it wasn't until they started settling in, until they started having a more centered relationship with the world, its people, its energy, that they started talking.

I am by no means saying this is why they didn't talk until later (or that this is the reason for your kids, either). But my intuition knows, with 100% certainty, that being empaths has played a part in it. That, for my kids at least, talking simply wasn't as important as building their little barriers.

Talking wasn't a priority for them.

Handling and filtering out all the emotions and energies and feelings, *that* was what they needed to put their own energy and learning towards, not talking.

And as my kids have needed me less, needed less of *my* energy to protect them and regulate them, the talking has started coming. Slowly, like someone putting a single toe in the water before taking it back out again. Yet for them, for my kids, there's a correlation.

It's making sense now.

Bits and pieces of the puzzle, of my kids, have been falling into place. I'm still exploring what this all means, especially as a mom of two late-talkers, and you'll see me working through all that and reflecting it here in this blog. I encourage you to do the same, especially if any of this rings true for you and your kids. Your kids will absolutely be different from mine, just as Kate and Eric, while similar, are completely different kids with completely different temperaments.

As parents, though, I feel the more we shift our focus, to really look and see and experience the world through our kids' eyes, the more we can understand. The more we can guide them and support them in the unique way that *they*, as individuals, need. For us not to look at them as someone who is 'shy' or 'sensitive' or has 'something wrong' or something that needs to be 'fixed'...

Let's altogether shift our focus and simply see our kids.

Let's accept them, quirks and all, differences and all, and learn to treasure that uniqueness. Let's see them for the unique gifts they are and the gifts they're giving us, as parents.

And it's not just for us, either, it's for so many others.

One of the many pieces that resonated with me the most in the *Empath Survival Guide* was how empaths are called on to heal the generational wounds of our family and our past. This has never felt truer than while raising my two kids. They've called on me to be a better person, a person who constantly learns and relearns and reflects back on my own life and journey. They've given me the gift to grow. The gift to learn. The gift to find my own strength and my own power.

I can't see the whole picture yet—of me or my kids—and frankly, I'm not sure I ever can or will, but all this feels right.

It feels right—

For us.

And as we settle into this new understanding, as I learn more of my kids' needs and my own, the more my energies are freed up—and the more I'm able to let my creative voice fly and write.

If you want to know if you're an empath, Dr. Orloff has this wonderful quiz right here: https://drjudithorloff.com/quizzes/empath-self-assessment-test/.

If you want to know if your kids are empaths, go here: https://drjudithorloff.com/quizzes/is-your-child-an-empath/.

Another great resource, which was the start of my own awareness, is the Happy Sensitive: https://thehappysensitive.com.

THE RIGHT PATH

February 20, 2019
Kate, 6 years
Eric, 4 years

When your life and family looks different from everyone else's. The strength —and joy—needed to stay true to yourself and your family even when, at times, you walk alone.

It's been awhile since my last blog post—no, really it has.

But I haven't forgotten you.

I haven't forgotten you wonderful parents who are on this journey with me, parent-writers, or simply parents raising differently wired kids, late-talkers or kids who simply walk to their own tune (proudly and with such conviction, mind you). Or parents who are struggling as you scour the internet, desperately trying to find a message or two of actual *hope* rather than one of fear.

I'm still here, but yeah, I went underground for a while.

A couple of reasons for that.

The first is life actually got a bit easier this past year, enough that I could breathe (a little) and I put some real energy and time back into my fiction writing and publishing business. You can go to your favorite bookseller and put in my name and you'll find quite a few titles with rebranded covers and blurbs, not just the ones I'd written back before Kate was born but a couple of new ones.

(Although, fair warning, there are more than a few older titles I still need to get to—but I'm the tortoise in this race; I'll get there.)

But truly, last year simply felt *good*... for me.

I'd put a lot of time and focus into my own self-care, from exercising and movement, camping and being out in nature, to my writing.

The writing was just huge.

These past few four years I've put so much time and effort into the learning side of things, in my craft and my publishing, and I'm finally starting to see it come together.

It's been a very slooow journey but also rewarding.

There's also another reason I went quiet: I needed to.

Something I've learned from writing this blog, from sharing my journey with these two differently wired kids, one thing I discovered is that part of my purpose was to be honest and real, but also hopeful. If I'm going to write about our journey, even if it's something I'm still struggling with, then I need to have found a bit of peace with it—a centering, if you will.

And this past year, well, I've been very focused on Eric and his slowly developing path.

The truth is when it comes to my little Eric, I needed the space to grow in my own strength and resilience. I needed the ability to hold him close and I needed to do some more growing of my own—and I did that.

Actually, I did a lot of it... and I have no intention of stopping (which is a darn good thing because that's what Eric is needing of me).

I just finished reading a book by Father Richard Rohr, "*Falling*

Upwards" and towards the end he talked quite a bit about shadow-boxing. This idea that you're constantly fighting the shadow side of yourself, the forgotten and denied qualities in yourself, the parts of yourself you've put away in order to fit into our world and society. This is work we'll be doing for the rest of our lives.

This past year I was shadow-boxing.

A lot.

You see, to stand in this space, to be fully present with my kids and accepting of who they are, of *trusting* in who they are—takes a great amount of bravery. Bravery—especially when it means walking a path that no one else is walking, standing alone against so many—isn't something that comes easily or naturally to me. I've had to dig really deep, look hard at a whole bunch of my fears, and question everything.

What Brené Brown describes in her in book, "*Braving the Wilderness*" (which I cannot recommend enough), is exactly what my journey as a parent, an advocate, and as my kids' voice, has felt like.

You see, I *am* stepping off the path.

I'm stepping off the tried and true and well-beaten path of so many others, and I'm walking on my own path... both as a parent and also as a parent-writer. I'm heading into the wilderness, where I often feel alone, but I stand there anyway.

I stand in my truth and in the truth of my kids.

I don't know what our journey will look like in one year or two or five. I don't know when exactly Eric will start talking except that it will happen and it will *only* happen at his time and at his pace.

That's a lot of trust to put in such a small person and that requires a fuck-ton of bravery, especially when you turn around and look at the world we live in.

We have our trusted speech pathologist and even she, who knows Eric, knows his temperament and how trust and control is absolutely essential to his developmental process, had moments of concern. Not of Eric's progress but of someone else seeing him, evaluating him.

Our specialist *knows* what we're doing is providing the ultimate environment for Eric to learn and growth with his language.

She *knows* this, but someone else? Someone who didn't take the time to develop a trusting relationship with him, to really give Eric the space to show everything he knows and where he's at, could come into our lives and do harm. Someone who thinks they were doing good work but actually doing quite the opposite.

We live in a very litigious time and I'm very aware of the perceptions and judgments and concerns of others when they see us out in the world—much as I try to not let those judgments bother me, I still have to be aware.

To protect us and my kids—because our path *is* different from the traditional, mainstream way of parenting and raising kids who are different.

This is one of the big reasons why I keep in contact with our specialist, why we keep to our regular doctor's visit: Proof. Insurance. Covering our asses for others who don't understand, who think they can come into our lives and that they know everything.

(If there's one thing my kids have taught me, it's that we know so very, very little.)

But what this often means is that I often feel vulnerable.

I'm scared.

I'm out there in that wilderness, often alone, teaching my kids differently than everyone else. I'm parenting differently, I'm allowing them to feel their emotions (yes, even the upset and the frustrations, so long as everyone is safe), and, wow, is it interesting to see all the *adults* who can't handle such outward displays of emotions. You see, when you exist with your kids differently, people notice...

And often when they notice, they don't generally have anything kind to say.

Rarely am I met with kindness or curiosity. Rarely, though it does happen, does a stranger come up and touch my arm and say, "You're doing great. Thank you."

It's hard and it's scary, but I'm doing it anyway.

This past year, bit-by-bit, I've learned to stand in my discomfort and the shame that's trying so hard to send me skittering back to the conventional path.

But I keep standing there... and, even more importantly, I'm learning to speak up.

I'm learning to speak up—and to call others on their words, judgments, and opinions (because no, when people say something to me it's not for the benefit of my kids or me—it's generally out of *their* own fear).

My children are different.

They are exactly who they were meant to be and I will trust in that.

So when we go to farmers market and Eric is so frustrated and mad because goddamn it, he wants one of those twist potatoes but I'm saying no because we're watching our money and it's just too expensive—and he loses it. Many would call it a tantrum. Laying on the ground. Crying. Kicking and screaming because he's so frustrated. Everyone is always safe: Kate, Eric, people walking by, because safety is a priority for me.

But this is also a priority: to recognize and allow our feelings.

Eric's feelings. Kate's feelings. My feelings and Sean's, too.

So, when Eric's having his frustration, when he's letting the whole world know he's pissed in the only way he's able to communicate, I allow him to have those feelings. I kneel down from him or across the way (we're talking ten feet here, as I'm usually in line to pay for something else at the market), and I hold out my hands to him.

Patience. Love. Understanding.

He will calm when he's ready and accept my arms and my calm.

But sometimes, well, he doesn't want to because he's *pissed*. Understandable, right? Think about your own life and emotions. Wouldn't *you* be ticked if someone tried to shove aside your feelings of anger before you were ready? Hell no!

So why the heck do we expect this of our kids?

I don't.

Or I'm trying not to. I'm working on it.

But I'm also working on my voice. That particular day I had no less than four different people stand right next to Eric and look around for me—and those weren't looks of concern but *judgment*.

Frustration. Annoyance. Those people were mad that my son was having his emotions and *they* were the ones who couldn't handle it.

(And to clarify: Eric was in no one's way. We were outside and the market wasn't crowded at all.)

I literally had to tell those people that I was right there. To *not* touch my son. To leave him alone.

They weren't helping.

These people who, again let me repeat—were NOT interested in helping *Eric*—they wanted to help themselves. I told them they weren't helping. Kneeling down, complete adult strangers, and thinking their words would get him to stop with his big feelings of frustrations.

Right. Strangers? Eric?

No way in hell.

But Eric got through that moment. He calmed down and let me tell you, it didn't take nearly as long as it would have a year ago or certainly two years ago (hell, even six months ago). But what was more important to me was when I stood there in my space, in my strength, and told others, "*No*."

More than that, I was telling them their judgment wasn't helping. And did it feel empowering. To take my stance as a parent and allow Eric to have his emotions, to work through them, and when he was ready, to calm. And these outsiders, these strangers, had no business forcing him to move past it before he was ready. (I will also say there is a complete double-standard—if it's Sean out there with Eric, *he* doesn't get the judgment and the looks that *I* do.)

My growth hasn't just been in these hard and difficult moments. It's in seeing the little moments, too—those bits of success and progress—and holding them close. Sharing the success with family and close friends so they can see it too—and they do. Like the other day when I walked in from my morning writing session and Grandma Charlie said to Eric, "Look. Mommy's here."

And Eric, his eyes, they flicked from Grandma, back to me, to Grandma again.

I saw that moment... and I also knew, deep down, what else it meant.

Eric has never said, "Mama" before and yet... he knows I'm 'Mommy.' Often with kids who are late-talkers or who are differently wired, you just never know until you know.

Well, now I know.

I'm 'Mommy' to him.

He knows this, without ever saying the word, 'Mama,' he knows this—and I know he knows it as well.

And because I share our experiences and our journey, because we have such amazing, wonderful grandparents, when I shared this awareness my mom noticed this moment, too. She'd seen his eyes go to me and she understood what it meant.

Everyone in our family, especially when it comes to Eric, has learned to focus on the small moments. Those little baby steps forward...

My journey this year hasn't just been about Eric, either. It's been about Kate, too. We've started on what would be first grade for her and our path of learning looks very from everyone else's. Very different.

I mean, really, just about everything we *do* is different.

My kids climb trees and boulders and spend their days at the beach where they get their fingers in the wet sand while a pod of dolphins swims by in the distance. My kids play video games and board games. My kids play and play and play some more. They go on outings with their friends. They go camping to Joshua Tree or Sequoia, sometimes with friends but oftentimes with just me. They also go to Las Vegas for my own learning as a publisher and a writer. They go to Disneyland where they've learned patience and to accept you can't get everything you want (ahem... I'm still learning this myself).

Everything we do looks different.

It's like we have our feet on a whole bunch of wilderness paths and sometimes it's damn *hard* to keep back all the judgment, too easy to keep letting it sink into your subconscious, to make you doubt, to sap your hope and joy...

Joy.

And that word right there, that feeling, of simply being present and in those quiet moments... this is what I keep coming back to.

Joy is my barometer.

Joy tells me if what we're doing is working, if it's successful or not. If my kids are in joy, if they're happy and healthy and learning—whatever way or shape or form that learning might take—then I know in my heart, in my soul, we're on the right path.

With Eric, we're still growing and discovering.

I know in my heart there is no label that will fit him, nothing that will fully describe who this little boy is. I have a feeling he's the type of soul our professionals haven't seen before (or if they have, haven't *accepted* who these children are). And for Kate, well, let's just say her journey as a late-talker has been a gift.

A gift.

I'm not sure I would have thought that when we started this journey—actually, I'm *certain* I wouldn't have—but that word, 'gift,' is also completely true. You see for us, for *Kate*, the late-talking was largely because of her temperament, because of her intense anxiety when she wasn't perfect or 100% accurate or sure.

And guess what?

She's talking now but she's still the same person. This anxiety, this temperament, it's a part of who she *is*. Having this understanding —seeing it, accepting it—has allowed me to do so much more for her as we move forward.

I'm seeing this anxiety as she learns to write... to read... do math... and dipping her toes into the strategy of board games. Or when she's playing those crazy hard, advanced levels in *Mario 3D World* with Sean and she just wants to him to do it all and the little light bulb in my head goes off.

Ahhh. That's what it is. That's what's happening here.

Her anxiety. Her sudden desire to freeze and run the other way because it can't be perfect, she can't do it 100% right and that causes her so much stress.

I say Kate's late-talking has been gift because it's given me the tools to guide her in all these other areas. To live in this world and grow in a way that's comfortable and supportive to her, rather than simply tossing her in with all the others and pushing her to 'just deal.'

My main goal, my main focus wasn't ever to help Kate to talk. It was to help her trust in her words. To allow for mistakes and that these mistakes were okay. And guess what? That's exactly what I'm doing with the rest of her learning.

These snippets here, these little moments and insights I've shared briefly, sum up where I've been this past year—and what I've been doing.

I've been growing and stretching. I've been learning and allowing my kids to guide me. And honestly, that's what it's really come down to...

Me.

My growth. My learning.

So much of my stress and worry has stemmed from *my* fears and I've had to take some good, often uncomfortable looks at them.

I have so much I want to say, but this blog is already running a bit long so I'll leave you with this. I'm far, far from being done with my own learning, but the real truth I've come to see and hold inside me, especially when I'm faced with doubt and judgment or uncertainty is this:

My kids know *exactly* who they are—it's me who's still trying to figure it out.

So long as I keep listening, keep following and guiding, I know we'll stay on the right path—even if it looks different from everyone else's. And the more I do this, the more I find my own joy and let joy lead me forward, the clearer the path is to my writing and my dreams...

My goal for being both a parent and a writer.

. . .

My heart tells me it's time to write again. To tell more of our story and offer my hope—as well as my fears and insecurities (and believe me, there's quite a few tumbling around in there).

Many parents have reached out to me this past year for advice or simply needing a kind presence. To connect and be heard without the usual judgment or shame, both which seem so common when you have differently wired kids or because you've decided to walk a different path. Thank you—you know who you are—it's your presence and your continual reminder that my words brought you hope that's pushed me to write again. And frankly, because I still have so much I'd like to share and so much I'd like to work through together.

CELEBRATE OUR DIFFERENCES

March 23, 2019
Kate, 6 years
Eric, 4 years

Let's stop comparing. Let's change the narrative of what success looks like—as parents, as writers. Instead let's celebrate our differences and our life stories—even when those stories are different.

Each one of us faces our own unique challenges.

Not one of us are created the same. Not one of us follows the same path. And our families, the situations we're presented with—the challenges and rolls of the dice—are just as different.

No two of us are the same.

If you have children, I'm sure you've noticed they're different from each other—sometimes surprisingly so.

This also means that you can't compare.

Truly, you can't.

You can't compare two siblings and you can't compare families; you certainly can't use your observations or opinions as some measuring stick and think it's going to get you accurate results on whatever it is you're looking at—everything from parenting to writing to success. Your ego (or even mine, at times) might think you can and that comparing is actually a good thing—but it's not.

Comparing and measuring flat-out doesn't work.

Because again... we're different. It might look like you're comparing apples to apples, but one might be a Pink Lady apple and another might be a Granny Smith or a Gala. You can easily bite into one and enjoy the heck out of that taste, but another might be perfect for baking and not so much for eating (unless you're into the slightly sour/tart taste and if so, good for you!).

My kids are the ones who first taught me this shift in thinking when it comes to comparing —and not comparing—on a deep, intuitive level.

Back when we'd attempted to go through early intervention with Kate, back before she wasn't even three years old, I witnessed how the evaluators only cared about certain results (caveat: this was my experience; yours, if you've gone through this process, might have been totally different and wonderful). For us and our experience, the evaluators only cared about the results listed on their little sheets, the specific answers that would indicate if there was something wrong or what age-range Kate developmentally fell into.

For them, it didn't matter that Kate, even at two, could give directions all the way to Grandma Charlie's house (a good forty miles away with lots of freeway in between) or Eric who, as I was checking into the Golden Nugget in Las Vegas (we'd stayed there several months earlier), promptly took my mom's hand, walked her out the front doors and proceeded to take her to the Container Park—a whole seven blocks down Freemont Street. He remembered *exactly* where to go (and no, my mom had no clue where she was going).

My kids wouldn't have gotten any 'points' on those evaluations.

For our particular evaluators, it didn't matter that my kids, both with receptive language delays, wouldn't have even *understood* what was being asked of them. (They are also the strong-willed type so the chances of Kate or Eric actually *doing* what was asked of them was... slim at best.)

The amazing gifts my kids had, these little differences that made them who they were (crazy good memory and visual spatial awareness), wouldn't have shown up on those tests because those answers didn't count.

Instead, the tests would have indicated there was something 'wrong.'

Because, at least in our experience, those evaluators and their tests hadn't been able to see the whole of who Kate was. Because she's different. Because she's not like any other kid who's walked through those doors (and this goes double for Eric).

As I've learned, there's nothing at all wrong with my kids. They're just different—and I love that about them.

Hell, *I'm* different.

We are each individuals, each with our own unique framework and mind and body for living, and what works for one family absolutely won't work for another. We're individuals with our own thoughts, feelings, temperaments—heck, we each have different experiences from our childhoods that we carry around and this *certainly* shapes who we are, even at this very moment.

Why is this coming up for me again?

The idea for this blog has been knocking around in my head for a few months now.

Back in October I went to a business workshop and something one of the speakers said really irritated me. Like—*really* irritated me.

She had gone through an ordeal that put her in the hospital and she absolutely had a full plate (including a toddler at home and a baby on the way). Despite what life had thrown her way, she'd managed to write several novels.

This, by the way, is amazing. Wonderful. I am happy that she was able to do this, that writing and storytelling helped her through (what I'm guessing) was a tough ordeal.

What I *wasn't* okay with was her sitting up there and saying to all of us, "So, if I can do that, write all those novels, then you can do it."

Her intention, I will say, wasn't wrong and it wasn't bad. Her intention was to shove away any excuse some of us might have for not getting our butt to the chair often enough and writing enough. Everything else was just excuses because if *she* could do it, then we could.

Which is the part I call bullshit.

Which is the part of her story, of her sharing, that rubbed me wrong—because it wasn't true.

At least, it wasn't true for *me*.

Sure, it might be true for this writer, she's a completely different person than me with a completely different life experience.

I'm not only an introvert, I'm also an empath. This means when my kids are with me and having a hard, *emotional* day, I'm doing my very best to stay grounded, to help them through that emotional wave (or tsunami). I'm doing my damnedest to remain the parent I want to be.

Some days, some weeks, that's the most I can do. To even show up and *try* is success.

When I went through that dark and scary time, back when we didn't know what was 'wrong' with Kate, I couldn't write at all. I was terrified. In my heart I knew there was nothing 'wrong' with Kate and yet that's all the professionals kept telling me and I had to slowly, slowly find my grounding again.

To tell the doctors, "No."

To insist that I *knew* who my kids were, on a soul-knowing, gut-level.

I couldn't write at all during that time. I just... couldn't.

Even though I desperately wanted to.

My focus was on my kids; my focus was exactly where it needed to be. There was simply no space for my inner two-year-old (which is what I call my creative voice) to come out and play.

There have been times in my life where I didn't have the space to play. And yet, for me, the choices I made were exactly right—

For me.

After the presenter finished her talk, I met another woman, an expectant mom in fact (I'm guessing the universe nudged us together). She revealed to me she was now terrified of trying to be both a mom and a writer because she knew, on her own gut level, that she couldn't do what this other mom had done, so why even try? Why try to be a parent and a writer?

This expectant mom understood how her mind and body worked and it wasn't the way this other writer had gone up there and said, *this is the way it's done.*

This presenter's words not only rubbed me wrong on the parenting level—we are *all* different and we've been all dealt a unique hand of cards—but I also realized this same idea didn't stop when it came to parenting. It had to do with health as well. It had to do with the health of your whole family—including aging parents.

Maybe you are caring for aging parents and the emotional upheaval *that's* putting you through.

This really hit home for me when I went to the Anthology Workshop and I got a chance to hear other people's stories; not just their *fiction* stories, but their life stories as well. Wow, was it a success what some of those writers had done, simply showing up and turning in their stories.

Just... *wow.*

Caring for ailing parents or perhaps caring for their own health and unnamed sickness and the fear that comes up with *that*—of not knowing what's wrong with you. That's scary. That's hard. And for someone else to stand up there and judge, to declare a blanket statement that if you can't go and write three or four novels when your inner life is in such turmoil... that's *wrong.*

And again, it's bullshit.

Here's what I've learned on my journey, especially with these kids who are so different:

We, as humans, live in the gray.

Sure, there are some constants, like don't hit and hurt or kill people, be respectful even if you disagree (I'm just pulling these off the top of my head). But you know... there is something to speaking your truth. Something to standing up, even if you're respectful, and telling another, "*No*. What I've learned is what's true for me—even if it isn't true for you."

Or what's true for me *right at this moment* may not be true a week from now.

Our lives are fluid. They're constantly changing. We're (hopefully) constantly growing. And we need to have allowances for those differences. My story is mine and *your* story is yours and is true for *you*.

We need to have allowances for this.

We need to have kindness and respect for each other.

The more open we are to these allowances and differences, the more I think we can reach some pretty amazing heights.

And sure, my life is challenging at times and my journey with two differently-wired kids has had its ups and downs (and you've read all about it), but I also know that someone trying to be a new parent, to find her way through anxiety, is leading a completely different life than me.

I know, too, that I have this incredibly wonderful and supportive spouse. Sean has always stood by my writing, all the years of time and money, of coming with me to these workshops so I can be both a writer and a mom, even using his vacation days to do so. He's fully onboard and believes in our different approach with our kids and education, teaching them to go out into the world itself and learn by living. Even the choices we've made with our parenting—I'm aware not everyone has this and believe me, I am *so* grateful for Sean.

I can't imagine what it's like out there, doing something so different and not having the support of the person closest to you.

Or if that closest person to you has health issues or any of the thousands of other life rolls that come our way...

Our lives are different from each other and that's a good thing.

So let's be kind, please.

Let's not fall into the comparison trap—and believe me, that's *not* an easy thing to do.

I just sat in a roomful of amazing writers who I was cheering for and whose stories I loved, but it's still hard to sit there and hear the reasons your story wasn't chosen. And on the flipside, I also got to see the amazing work those writers did, stories that I loved or didn't, that got bought by those editors...

And then I got a chance to hear a snippet of their lives, of their actual stories, of how they even got to this place, this moment. They wrote these stories for the workshop. They did their best and showed up.

We're not supermen and superwomen who can finish everything on our to-do lists, flawlessly and perfectly, who can juggle several different balls at once and never drop a single one—seriously, I don't know this person. This person doesn't exist and if they do, I can pretty much guarantee you they're not living in the joy.

They're not present in the lives they're living.

So, let's stop this narrative. Let's stop trying to be perfect—and comparing ourselves to what we think perfect should be or even what success should look like.

Let's just go out there, do our best, and fall down a few times (like I certainly did at the workshop—at least it *felt* like I did). And then, let's pick ourselves up and try again.

Let's celebrate our differences and our kids' differences.

Let's celebrate how our lives are shifting and changing, taking each of us to different places and in different directions. Because we're all different and that's what makes our stories—whether fictional stories or life stories—so damn amazing.

And then, let's share those stories.

The only way to change the narrative, the only way to shift the 'this-is-the-way-it's-done' mentality, is by opening up and sharing our stories.

I'll start with me.

My name is Chrissy Wissler. I'm a writer, a mother, a wife, an empath—and every day I struggle to show up and do the best I can.

There's so much more I want to do, so many more stories I want to tell, adventures to live and experience, but some days, some weeks, are just *hard*.

Really hard.

Some days all I can do is the basics. Some days it feels like I can take on the world. Some days it's a struggle to find the energy to smile, let alone write a story. And as hard as those moments are... I'm learning that it's okay. It's okay to rest. It's okay to just take a moment and reset and... breathe.

Just breathe.

Because what really matters is picking myself up off the floor and trying again.

That was me this week.

Picking myself off the floor, sitting down at the computer, trying to find the fun again. Or showing up and breathing and doing my damnedest to stay calm while the four-year-old is completely incapable of regulating his emotions and is letting stuff go (I'm fairly certain he's currently focusing on other areas, like language). So yeah, that was me carrying him out of farmers market in one arm, protecting both of us, while pulling the wagon-laden with groceries in the other. When he's like that... it's rough. It's like being continually slammed with an emotion truck that doesn't let up whose driver doesn't, even for one second, take his foot off the gas. When Eric's incapable of finding his calm, I need to try—for the both of us.

So that was me this week.

I showed up and... tried.

I did the best that I could with the energy that I had and no, no I didn't hit my weekly writing goals and... and that's okay, too. Showing up, sometimes, is success right there, though it's often hard to keep that in perspective. But I need to remember that. I need to celebrate these little wins, these little bits of progress. It might not be the four novels, but it's still success—

It's *my* success.

So, how about you? What stories would you like to share? What stories of yours would you like to *celebrate*?

A JOURNEY OF INNER GROWTH
FAILURE, SHAME, AND SUCCESS PART 1

May 8, 2019
Kate, 6 years
Eric, 4 years

Uprooting old beliefs around failure and success... in my writing.

I've been doing a lot of inner work these past few months. Lots of stretching and growing, lots of times where I've been really, really uncomfortable as I dug deep into myself, into my past, trying to understand where some really old thoughts and feelings had come from and finally, *finally*, I'm coming out the other side of this process.

Not that I'll ever be done. This is just peeling back the layers of an onion and I suspect I'll be working on that onion for a long time to come.

This will be a series of posts—and I suspect I'll be adding more as I peel back those layers.

A writing mentor of mine calls these kinds of posts 'process blogs' and I love that term. This is me, working through my process, putting together all these different bits and ideas from both my brain and my heart (read on to see why I put 'heart' in there).

Even though these posts will be specific to *me*, I have a hunch there will threads here that resonate with you, wherever you are on your journey, whether you're a parent (or not), a writer (or not), or whether you're striking your own path on some venture or life's journey.

Regardless of what that looks like for you, I hope (as this has done for me) what I write here will give you cause to pause, to take a closer look at your life, and maybe, just maybe, ask yourself some deep questions, like: Where did your beliefs about failure and success come from? Are those beliefs aligning with who you are and where you are on your journey? Heck, are those ideas even *working* for you?

(Here's a small spoiler: they weren't for me.)

That's ultimately what this journey has been about, this uncovering if you will.

Failure.

Shame.

Success.

What are they? How am I defining them? I'm getting down deep into the core and understanding of what my beliefs surrounding these three—failure, shame, success—mean for *me*.

The 'me' of right here and now and not the 'me' five years down the road when my kids are older. Not the 'me' of my childhood and how I was raised, by my parents and by school and by culture, but the 'me' walking on this path, right here, right now.

Why in the world did this all come about? Why couldn't I leave well enough alone?

Because part of living for me is to always keep growing, keep changing, keep deepening my sense of self and healing those old shadowy places inside me. And this time (honestly, like all times), it wasn't like I asked for life to get hard or anything. As usual, the challenges of life just sort of happened and I had a choice:

Bury my head in the ground or roll with those changes and see what turned up on the other side.

So, I rolled and I kinda... sorta... maybe... kept my balance—
ish.

All this shifting and changing, well, it started right around the same time Daylight Savings started here in the U.S. (pretty much the bane of all parents, readjusting our poor kids to some arbitrary time schedule). It was also during this time that my critical voice got cranked up super high.

The Anthology Workshop I attended in March in Las Vegas played a big, big role in that (which is a normal occurrence after a workshop like that). And because things weren't hard and turbulent enough in my inner life, Eric decided it was time to step his toes into the language waters.

Which is wonderful and joyous and—

Really, really intense.

See, language leaps usually correlate to a drop in (read: zero) ability to emotionally regulate. And that means I need to pause everything, to breathe as best I can, trying to not get triggered myself, and sit with him as he rides out those emotions.

Needless to say, my ability to write, to go down into the creative space of my subconscious, was pretty much nonexistent.

But it wasn't *just* the situations in my life, the life rolls and bumps and bruises I just mentioned. There was also much, much more (here comes that first layer of the onion) and I finally got a glimpse of the long shadows and beliefs about my writing and publishing career I've been carting around for years.

For me, as these things start to surface, my process of uncovering, of understanding, begins with feelings.

And, as I've discovered, it's almost never the first thing I think it is. Yes, that first feeling, that first hint is real and true; it's usually not the bigger, underlying issue.

Instead, it's my first clue in the mystery.

And right around this time, after the workshop and Daylight Savings and Eric saying a few words here and then (and counting), I got hit with a ton of bricks that came in the form of my beliefs around failure.

In truth most participants in the Anthology Workshop got hit with failure. When you write six and seven and eight different stories, hoping to sell to the anthology that's buying, you are going to fail.

You will.

But even that statement isn't entirely true. If you look through only the narrow lens of, "Did my story sell?"

If you look at it *that* way, well, yes, a lot of us failed.

But that's not the whole truth. *That's* the shame and those old beliefs sneaking their heads in, that success *only* counts when you get an actual sale. But what if that editor loved the story even if they couldn't buy it? What if one of the other editors loved it, even if they weren't the ones with a checkbook at that moment? Is that still a failure? Really? Truly?

So, if you widen your lens, widen your thoughts and ideas about success, about failure, the story itself changes, doesn't it? The story you're making up in your head, usually about you and your self-worth, changes.

That's something to think about.

Something to hold deep in yourself and wonder, to question. Especially when it comes to questioning the reactions you get at this workshop as the days wear on and your protective armor, the thing that was keeping you safe and protected, gets chipped away, falls apart, piece by piece...

And there you are, vulnerable.

Except this time there was something else surrounding me in this struggle and it wasn't until the last day of the workshop that another piece of *my* understanding fell into place.

As you advance in your craft (in my case, my writing), you start becoming a stronger, better storyteller.

That's the nature of how it all works: keep practicing, keep studying, keep learning and over time you get better. But here's what I didn't know: as you grow your storytelling chops, you start taking risks. Your *stories* take risks. They do something different, something you've never done before. They're reaching higher and higher, right for those stars (or a fastpitch softball snapping towards you) and—

And you fail.

A lot.

Because maybe your craft isn't quite there yet, maybe it's not quite at the level for whatever story you're reaching for, so you take a swing with that story and all you hear is the loud thud of that softball smacking hard into the catcher's glove.

You missed.

That time.

And maybe those stories were almost there, were almost strong sales but instead just barely missed the mark—and when you're in a room filled with amazing professional writers you better believe the quality is just amazing.

But... and here's what I didn't understand at the time... are those moments, those stories, those risks you took really failures?

Are they?

Risking yourself? Pushing boundaries? Going to a place you haven't been before because you've been too scared or nervous? Or maybe you went and told a story that's incredibly vulnerable to *you*, a story that literally came right from your heart and now there you are, putting it out there for others to see, read, and judge?

What if they don't like it? What if that story from your heart misses?

I wrote a story like that.

It was the one story, the one out of all eight I wrote for this workshop, the one that would have broken my heart if it didn't sell...

And it didn't.

Not at first. Not to the editor who was buying for the anthology I'd written it for.

Instead, Dean Wesley Smith bought it for *Pulphouse Magazine* after this first editor rejected it.

Here's the thing: I knew that story would sell. I knew it. Maybe not that day, but eventually. To someone. Somewhere. Because that story was all emotion and it came right from my heart and by God I was crying while I wrote it so I knew there was something there. I know good stories come from vulnerability and, wow, was that story vulnerable.

Looking back—even in that moment of writing it, I knew I'd succeeded simply by having the guts to write that story. Success was sitting down, shoving my critical voice aside, and saying, "I'm going to write this story. I'm going to go *there*. Even if it hurts. Even if it's scary and I'm putting myself out there in this way."

Writing the story was success.

Writing even a fraction of *my* story—of raising kids who are different, of finding my strength to stand up and believe in them, to trust in them while the rest of world, our society, wanted to shove them into boxes and the hell with the consequences (my kids, well, they're the kind of beings who kick said-boxes to the curb)—was a success.

Writing the story was success.

Sitting down and even attempting it was success. Even if that story hadn't sold to any editor at all, it was far, far from being a failure...

Except that one story was the only story I sold at the workshop.

There were other stories where I took risks, where I pushed myself to try different forms, different historical time periods, a different, edgier voice—and many of them just flat missed. Other stories weren't quite finished. There's even one I'll put in a drawer and it'll never see the light of day nor will I try again.

Can you imagine? Day after day of being in a workshop like this? Sitting there surrounded by intense emotions (and a shit ton of fear) as everyone waited to get feedback on their stories? To see if they'd succeeded or failed?

My personal history, my past, especially from playing competitive fastpitch softball, had a hard, hard time handling this... this failure. You see I'd been trained by my parents, by my coaches, even by myself, to criticize and analyze every single movement, every pitch I threw, every time I swung the bat...

Every mistake and failure. And every success, too.

And all that old training, well, it hit me—hard.

You know the feeling, the one where you want to run to the bathroom and shut the door and cry? To not let anyone catch a hint of how deep you're hurting inside because showing them, showing anyone at all, would be too vulnerable? That this... vulnerability, this emotion, these tears, aren't allowed? When all you want is to hide and keep your hurt close, your heart closed off, and not let anyone see?

Yep. That was me.

But thankfully, right as that feeling smacked into me, that urge to run into the bathroom and hide, I knew what it was.

Shame.

For the past year I've been reading and working through shame and my own history of shame thanks to Brené Brown and the amazing work she's doing (I highly recommend you read any of her books or watch her TEDtalk or her show on Netflix). So, as I felt that intense need to run and hide and cry in the bathroom, I was aware of what this need to run and hide was...

And that layer of the onion peeled back a bit more...

Shame.

I was in shame and I knew the only way to get rid of shame is to shine a big ol' light on it. I couldn't go and hide—shame loves it when we hide. It thrives in the shadows and the darkness and the only way to expel it is to talk to someone about it.

So I did.

I didn't run and hide, but I turned and asked for help (and this asking for help is another big deal for me—you *never* asked for help in my world).

And as I slowly worked through this, as I slowly brought out the feelings and blazed a big shining light on them, I realized there was much more going on than just shame. This whole time, shame had been hiding the truth about failure. It had been disguising the real pain, the *real* fear hiding underneath it.

At first, I thought my reaction, this shame around failure, had everything to do with perfection. All those years of playing softball and playing at such a competitive level, surely that had to be the cause.

Then I dug deeper and deeper...

Because my reaction in this moment, from the first desperate urge to flee to the bathroom, and later my inability to let go, to stop these sudden, desperate waves of pain and the need to cry...

That intense of a reaction meant this pain was old.

Really, really old.

It also meant I had a choice. I could look at the pain closer or I could ignore it. Because even though I'd dealt with it at the workshop, even though I pulled myself back up and confided in others and talked through these feelings and this shame, I felt in my gut I wasn't fully healed, that there was more going on.

I came home and there, on my nightstand, was Brené Brown's book, "*Rising Strong.*"

This was *exactly* what I needed in that moment. To pick myself up off the floor, to rise up even though I felt beaten and bloody and head-down in the arena. I even went so far as to go through the worksheets Brown offers on her website because I *needed* to get down to the heart of it, this hurt that was so old and deep.

It was in doing this work—as I tried to rediscover the fun in my writing, to convince my creative voice that it hadn't failed, that I could come out and play again and it would all be okay—that I finally got a hint of what was really going on.

Of just how big and deep this old hurt, this old belief, really was.

And, of course, life likes to throw a couple punches at the same time.

So there I was, feeling raw and vulnerable and very much like a failure when Eric decides it's time to work on his language and trust in his voice and words—and out the window went his ability to emotionally regulate.

(I say this lightly but my goodness, that couldn't be farther from the truth.)

My full focus during those moments was on him, on staying calm and present, on not allowing myself to be triggered as his primitive brain took over and the littlest, littlest thing became this explosive frustration.

What do I mean by that?

I mean moments like this one: "No, you've already had one bag of gummy bears; you can't have another."

Picture a full-on, full-child frustration filled with screaming and kicking and attempts at head-butts towards Mom (because Mom's the safe person he can 'lose it' with).

I had to let go of all my goals and challenges and streaks for my writing. Simply being present with him took an unbelievable amount of energy and focus.

I had to stop writing.

I had to take the pressure off my writing and simply let it wait until life got easier again.

During this time, I slowly, slowly realized these feelings about my writing, the shame I felt from the workshop, the idea of perfection and failure, was only scratching the surface of what was *really* going on. That it actually went deeper... these feelings, this shame, it all stemmed from success...

Success with my writing.

I had this idea, this old belief about my writing, about what I considered 'success' in regards to my writing, that did not—could not —match the life I was living.

The life I had chosen.

For me and Sean. For my kids.

For my family.

This was the truth that had been hiding in the shadows the whole time. It was success and my *idea* of success, that was the problem, that was inconsistent and did not match with all the choices I'd made.

I finally had a glimpse of what was really going on.

Now, I just needed to figure out what the hell I was going to do about it.

Again, because this is so deep, because this is so involved, I've decided to make this into a whole series of blog posts and I've a hunch they'll keep going, way past the ones I wrote during this particular season of a life roll. There's always more to learn, always more to understand, another layer of onion to peel back. Because this process, this learning, is very much like an onion (which can be quite annoying at times). As in: "Oh shit. I thought I'd worked through this already!?"

It's a feeling and a sentiment I'm becoming quite familiar with as I walk this different parenting path, this different approach to learning—and to just living life.

WHAT 'SUCCESS' REALLY MEANS
FAILURE, SHAME, AND SUCCESS PART 2

May 8, 2019
Kate, 6 years
Eric, 4 years

Uncovering deep-rooted beliefs about success... and letting go of what's no longer working.

As I mentioned in my last post, it was looking closely at my feelings surrounding failure—and my intense reaction to it—that triggered the realization that it wasn't *actually* failure that was the issue...

It was success.

Specifically, how I defined success.

This idea of success—and my definition of it—was something I'd learned from my parents and my community, from schools and society. It was always inside me, many layers deep, with roots going to places in my life and psyche I had no idea of until I took this hard, uncomfortable look at it.

And when I did?

Well, the answer—and the truth—was pretty darn clear.

'Success' was getting in the way of my happiness regarding my writing. All these ideals and images and beliefs were keeping me from fully aligning with the life I wanted to live with Sean and my children.

I'd found the tip of an iceberg with that failure; peeled back that first layer of the onion. I had no idea how far under the surface that ice went, how deep these ideas about success went inside me... and the only way to understand, the only way to heal and move forward, to be fully aligned with the writer and mother and person I wanted to be—

I needed to lean in closer.

Closer to the pain. Closer to hurt.

So, I did.

You see, as an independent writer and publisher, part of my business is to be aware of, well... the business. Looking at the different models of other successful writers—ah, you see that slip up there? How my first reaction was to write the word *'successful?'*

Yeah, that ice goes down pretty damn deep.

So now I'll purposefully change the wording and say, 'financially successful' writers.

Those writers, well, what did they do to make their writing success happen? How many novels (especially in a series) did they write? How much time and money did they put into things like marketing and changing delivery models and thinking about licensing (and the many ways licensing alone could—and *would*—change my business model)?

And here I am, the parent of two young kids.

Kate, who just turned seven, and Eric not yet five. We're homeschoolers and self-directed learners. My kids, who are differently wired and march to their own pace and tune, and Sean and I, as parents, who willingly and lovingly allow them to follow and be their truest self (even if it's not always easy).

I came to the slow and very uncomfortable realization that everything those other writers did? That what all those ~~successful~~ financially successful writers did to put themselves in that exact position...

I can't do it.

At least right now, for this season of my life, I can't do it. Writing four novels a year would be damn, damn hard. It's not that I physically can't or don't have the motivation or ability to do it (if you know me personally, you know I'm determined and focused and really have an ability to dig my heels in when it's something I'm really shooting for). But my motivation and ability, that wasn't the problem.

The problem was time.

The problem—and if I'm being honest, it's not a 'problem' but my reality and my truth—was I already *had* a full-time, demanding job.

I couldn't put in the time and money and effort these other writers did, even if those writers were also parents of young kids, because my world, my reality, was completely different from theirs. What my kids demand of me is different than what they experience. The energy it takes, the inner toll to keep showing up and doing my best. If you have kids in similar situation or maybe you're a new parent and this is the first time you've ever felt the deep exhaustion of being sleepless for a year (or longer) or maybe you have aging parents who need the heartbreaking kind of support that I haven't yet faced...I'll bet you know what I'm talking about, in your own way. The energy. The all-consuming focus we sometimes must give to those we're caring for and the simple fact there are days when feeding them and (mostly) clothing them is simply 'good enough.'

And that 'good enough'?

There are days when that's all I shoot for.

Just show up and do your best. Show up and ride out those intense emotional reactions and hold your own triggers, your own past, at bay while you've got a screaming four-year-old in the chiropractor's office and you feel trapped (cause half the reason you're there is for your own adjustment) and all you want to do is cry.

Right now, my full-time job isn't writing. It's not writing these blogs. It's not doing these acts my soul absolutely loves and craves.

My full-time job is raising my kids.

And success? My definition of it? This belief I'd been living with for over thirty-seven years? It didn't line up to the truth I was living.

It didn't line up to *my* truth.

That meant I had a shit ton of work to do—inside myself.

So, I got to doing.

Now, as I was alluding to above, there's a shit ton of effort and energy that goes into raising kids, regardless of the way you do it. But when you step off the conventional path, whether it's school or educational choices, whether it's a more conscious way to parenting, whether it's taking your differently wired child and saying, "No," to the current systems...

Whatever your path has been, whatever choices you've made—especially if those choices are different from the collective whole—when you brave your own wilderness and give yourself up to the uncertainty of what the future will look like... that's hard. Real hard. And it takes an emotional toll.

Yes, it's worth it, but there *is* a cost.

See, my kids are different. They showed up in this world knowing exactly who they were. They are sensitives and empaths, introverts and much, much more. I can feel it in my bones; I know it in my gut. And because of their differences, they've called on *me* to be more. To show up as a different mom than how I first envisioned myself. They still call on me to grow comfortable in my uncertainty, to trust in them and their path even when no one (but them) can see what that path looks like.

To trust in them, to love them, to follow their joy. We had no idea when they'd start talking, but kept holding their hands and loving them and supporting them, so when they were ready, when they were comfortable, we could guide them along the path they, and only they, needed.

I always wanted to be a mother, but my idea of 'mother' was pretty normal. I'd always known my kids would go to school. I'd always expected Kate's first word to be 'mama'... and yet there I was, waiting four years to hear that beautiful, beautiful word for the first time.

Four years.

With Eric, it's been even longer.

As a writer (and this whole time, even on my path to motherhood, I've been a writer), I would eagerly listen to other ~~successful~~ financially successful writers who were parents and listen for advice that I was *clearly* missing. How they could go and do it all. How these other moms also breastfed and also got about zero sleep for the first year (ahem... make that five years) of their kids' lives and maybe they homeschooled, too...

How did *they* do it?

How were they writing and parenting *and* becoming financially successful?

That's when I slowly began to realize my truth: that what they were doing, what allowed them to walk two demanding paths at the same time (and chewing gum, apparently), wasn't going to work for me.

I heard of one writer who went to a three-day conference and left her eighteen-month old at home with her mom. I'm honestly happy this worked for that mom—it wouldn't have worked for me. Never.

Not only was I still nursing Eric at that age, but I was the person who kept him centered and calm. I helped Eric regulate his emotions and extreme sensitivities to the world and its energies. Even now, with him being four-and-a-half, I'm still that person. He'll hold my hand and gently rub his fingers up and down my arm. Or touch his foot to my arm or leg and do the same thing.

Also, I was Eric's voice (and Kate's too, frankly). And because of how close and connected I am to both my kids, I understand their needs better than anyone else... without either kid saying a word.

That's my role.

That's my *job*.

None of this is me saying parents who've chosen differently for their families are wrong or they made a wrong choice—far from it. It was their choice, made in the life they were living, with the kids they'd been given.

And this... this was mine.

When I went to the Anthology Workshop in Las Vegas, the one

that set me on this path to uncovering my iceberg of failure and success, I didn't go alone. My kids came with me, and my mom came to watch them. She supported me and allowed me to follow both my dreams of parenting—and writing.

(I'm aware, too, that this act of even going to a workshop, of staying in a hotel for a week and having childcare is a privilege. It's *my* privilege.)

For my kids, for who they are, being separated from me for eight days was never an option. They need my support in ways other kids don't (and yes, there are absolutely other children in this world who need far more care and far more energy than mine and I greatly honor and respect them). This whole time, since I became a parent, I've been walking two paths: the path of a parent, the path of a writer.

But what I hadn't really done was to look closely at my own expectations regarding "success."

I needed to look at the reality of enough novels for my book sales to really take off—usually around twenty books, twenty-five books—and then I needed look at the time and energy needed to *actually* write and publish said books. Add in the marketing and learning of the business in order to achieve that financial success I was reaching for...

And realized I couldn't.

Realized that—for the life I'd chosen, the one I loved and fully embraced—I could *not* achieve this expectation in my head, the one that was labeled 'financially successful.' I just couldn't do it... at least right now. Not while my kids still needed me in the many, many ways they did.

It was a hard, painful moment and I immediately felt like a failure.

I'm talking *Failure*. This great dream of mine, of being a writer, something I'd wanted since I was thirteen, was done. Over.

I'd failed.

I couldn't do it.

At least that's what all the negative voices in my head, all that self-talk and shame, were screaming at me.

I'd made a conscious choice of putting my writing career on hold to be a mom, but then the two kids who'd chosen me required more of me. To support them and help them in deeper ways than most kids, I needed to put the writing career off even longer.

I was still writing. I was always writing, even if only a little bit (something that non-writers in my life had proclaimed would stop completely once Kate was born—they were certainly wrong). Sure, there were times when I needed to let the writing go, to have it wait off to the side as a place of safety and joy until I could breathe again. But even then, the writing couldn't be my primary focus.

It couldn't be.

And that meant, by the definition of success in my head and heart, the definition I'd been raised with from society and from my parents—earning a living wage, carrying my share of the financial weight of our family, being independent—all those feelings and thoughts that went into the word "success"...

By all *those* definitions, I'd failed.

That thought, that word 'failure,' took me right out at the knees.

It was the first—and only—time I've even remotely considered giving up. Giving in. I didn't because I knew my soul wouldn't let me—but it still hurt like hell.

I didn't shy away from the pain.

And let me tell you something, if you're ever in a situation when you feel something that intensely, that painful and sudden and completely unreasonable (see all my comments above about negative self-talk) that means it's old. When the pain hits you good and hard. Like going from zero to sixty and suddenly you've been gut-punched and breathing is just about out of the question...

It's old.

In my case, I couldn't stop the tears.

They. Just. Wouldn't. Stop.

So, I stopped trying. I let myself feel all that pain while at the same time I kept hold of the negative self-talk, the shame in me that desperately wanted to take over. Shame is a powerful thing and I recognized the words it loved to throw around:

"Worthless."

"I'm not good enough."

Any time I'd catch a hint of those words, I'd stop them. I'd tell myself, "This is shame; that's all it is. I *am* good enough."

I'd keep on feeling, but—this is important—I'd keep feeling without the downward spiral of shame. I'd feel, but I wouldn't let the shame take over.

It was during this whole process I realized what I needed to do.

I needed a new definition of success. Not the definition handed down to me by society and our schooling system, but *mine*. A definition that lived the values and the choices I was living, something that was not tied to financial success but real, honest-to-God success.

What *was* that? What did it look like... *for me*?

I already had done this type of work for the rest of my life, living with kids who'd already pushed and challenged me to be more, to be greater. I'd done it everywhere else in my life... just not with my writing. Not completely. Not fully.

(If I had done this work, I wouldn't have sprawled out on the floor with two boxes of Kleenex.)

It was like I had no idea how hidden and deep this idea of success went. I had no idea it had permeated all the way to my writing, something I'd protected and kept safe from (most) financial pressure. I'd always worked to keep my writing fun and yet... my *expectation* about results, about success, hadn't changed.

And it needed to.

If I wanted clarity with my writing, with my journey as a connected, conscious parent, as a homeschooler and self-directed learner, as a parent of two differently wired kids, I needed to get this expectation straight. If I wanted joy and happiness with my writing, to be in a place of peace, right down to my soul, I needed to do this.

And since, for me, joy has become the barometer of living life, it was about darn time I made this happen.

It was then—when I was down in that darkness and slowly pulling myself back up, slowly telling shame to take a hike—that I got pissed off.

Pissed. Off.

There was no way I could hit this impossibly high bar of being a "financially successful writer" *and* the parent these kids needed me to be—and here's where I got pissed—who the hell ever said what I did as a parent had no value?

Who the hell in our collective society said that the *only* worth a person had was about money? Status? That the work I did as mom (and perhaps you, as a caregiver of any sort), didn't count? That we had little or no value because the work we did was invisible, unseen? Because it didn't contribute to the gross profit of our country?

Fuck it and fuck them. I'm tired of playing by their rules and the rules of society and at least for me, inside me, I plan on changing those rules.

So, I did.

In the next blog, I'll walk you through how I did that, how I made that shift inside myself to live a happier, fuller life. Yes, it's personal to me but I hope by sharing this journey it can offer you insight and clarity for yourself. Or at the least knowing that whatever journey you're on, you're not alone, that you have value even when, in the eyes of society, you are valueless or worse: invisible.

We don't necessarily have the power to directly change society. We do have the power to change ourselves. And who knows? Maybe we'll start our own ripple of change towards living a more whole, happier, joyful life...

REDEFINING SUCCESS

FAILURE, SHAME, AND SUCCESS PART 3

June 2, 2019
Kate, 6 years
Eric, 4 years

You figured out what's not working—great! Now it's time to replace these ideas and beliefs with what you do *want.*

I've found when I put questions out to the universe, when I'm in need of guidance or support, guidance usually comes—not that it happens right away, mind you, and not that I get some thunder and lightning moment, either. Instead the guidance is gradual, almost like seeing signposts along the road or if you're hiking, those metal tags they attach to trees so even when you can't see the path in front of you, you can still find your way.

And these past few months—a good chunk of the year, really—I was trying to find my way with my writing career. First it was finding my way through failure and shame—those old beliefs I'd been carrying around—and it was only through looking closely, I discovered neither failure or shame was the heart of the issue...

I discovered that my hurt and pain, the fact that I wasn't aligning with the life I wanted to live, had more to do with success—and how I was defining success.

For my entire life, success has been directly tied to money. To independence. To being able to support myself or the least, carry my fair share. And yet here I was in this situation where my hands were almost, quite literally, tied.

You see, in order to make money as a writer (or the kind of writer *I* wanted to be and not someone who spends half their days marketing), I needed to write more books. I also needed books in a series... which isn't easy as my magpie creative voice *loves* to dance from one series to the next. The real problem, however, is—at this point in my life—getting consistent quiet time and space to really dive into those stories is hard.

Really, really hard.

And the kids are my priority. They, as I explained in my last blog, are my full-time, twenty-four-hour job.

Simply looking at this truth, that my kids *are* my job, my priority, meant that my barometer for success with my writing *couldn't* be about the money. If it was, if all my hopes and dreams for my writing hinged on being financially successful, well, then I'd failed before I ever got started. I simply didn't have the time or energy required to make that idea of success happen.

Why not?

I'd already ear-marked my time and energy and space to being with my kids, to helping and supporting them, to helping them grow into the unique beings that they are.

So where did that leave my writing?

As it stood, with this old definition of success still in place, it meant I was a failure.

And I wasn't.

I *knew* I wasn't.

Whenever I talked with my mentors or other professional writers, the last thing they ever thought of me was as a failure. In fact, they'd look at me and be in complete awe of what I was accomplishing. They'd tell me I was amazing and courageous, all this inner work I've done, all this healing of my own childhood so my kids could thrive. And yet...

Yet failure was always there. Shame, too, was ready to sneak back in and I had to stand firm against both.

Which... as I write these words, sounds easy. It sounds like all I needed to do was change my idea of success, my definition, and everything would be fine. It'd all be right as rain.

Except it wasn't easy.

It was hard. And painful.

I'd just finished a workshop where seven of my eight short stories didn't sell (and a few stories didn't work at all) and shame was right there. Right there waiting in the shadows, ready to take over if I gave it an inch (and it totally would).

I knew the real problem.

I knew this wasn't actually about failing to sell those stories, but about success. Success and the ideas of success I'd unknowingly, over many years and through society, put on my writing. How the hell could I merge the two—success and writing—to fit into this life I was living with my two unique kids, the life I'd happily, joyfully, chosen?

I needed help. I needed support. So I reached out to a friend I've known for years, a friend who isn't a writer, and she listened to that call when I could barely stop crying and finally said to me, "I don't understand. I've read some of your stories. I loved them. To me, stories that people read and enjoy... that sounds like success to me."

My friend, who wasn't a writer.

My friend who wasn't plugged into the indie publisher world, who didn't know about all the thousands of things I should/need/must do to be a financially successful writer.

My friend, who is a reader, and as a reader, she loved my stories.

Success.

And that, right there, was the start of the shift for me, this gradual settling in as everything slowly changed. Slow because all of this was very, very deep in me (and not in the least bit comfortable). I needed to change my whole world view, not just in writing, but in all areas of my life—especially my views about jobs.

All the times I'd met Sean's coworkers and they'd ask what I did for a living and the shame I'd feel, the embarrassment, when I'd answer I worked in an office or in administration instead of saying what I felt in my heart was my true calling: that I was a writer. But how could I claim that status? That title? After all, I wasn't "financially successful" so how was I different from everyone else out there who was writing their one book?

And then, when I became a mother?

It was like all the work I did became invisible. Became valueless.

It's really no surprise I'm wrestling with these old beliefs in regards to my writing, certainly not after the past seven years of being a mom and feeling unseen, feeling valueless because so few people ever saw the value of the work I did...

The work I continue to do.

Then, of course, there are all the myths surrounding the life of a creative person. I'm sure you know a few of those myths: You can't make money as a writer/artist/musician. If you try, you'll be a "starving artist" and would have to waitress to pay your bills.

I've known since I was thirteen that I wanted to be a writer.

Storytelling, daydreaming, they literally saved me from hours of complete boredom in school and I started putting those silly fantasy stories to paper. But I never pursued it. Never pursued this dream, this career until my adult life (just before I became a mom).

Why?

Because time and time again, I'd gotten the message you couldn't make a living as a writer. That writing was not, and could never be, a full-time job. And so, like many others, I pursued a more acceptable college degree that would lead to an acceptable, steady, reliable job (which it didn't—though to be fair, I barely tried).

But I think all the way back then, during my eighth grade year, was when this idea of being financially successful really took hold. It's also one of the many reasons Sean and I have chosen a different path to learning with our kids, a self-directed learning approach, following your passions and interests so when you're an adult and ready to go out into the world you actually know who you are.

As I look back on my childhood and see those missed moments, those missed opportunities, I also see the things I've carried with me as an adult were the things I was passionate about. The places my family visited over the summer that I loved and enjoyed. From trekking glaciers in Alaska to Yellowstone National Park and Butte, Montana, with all its deep history—all of those moments, those experiences, eventually became stories and novels and series I've written.

When you think about it... that kinda sounds a little like success, doesn't it?

I'm sure my parents think so when they read my Cowboy Cat novels. I'll bet they're feeling a lot of joy knowing on that particular family trip, at that moment, something special happened for me... special enough for me to write about the place, the history, twenty-five years later.

That sounds an awful like success. It sounds like joy, too, joy through living.

There I was, wrestling through these old beliefs, these old ideas, trying to find a new way of looking at success and not really knowing how to do it—when the universe answered.

It was like every moment I needed a new stone on this path I was creating, there it was. Waiting.

A 'Goop' podcast episode popped onto my feed literally as the kids and I were camping in Yosemite National Park and I was writing Part 1 and 2 of this Success blog-post series. And then another came podcast through, this one from Krista Tippett in, 'On Being'. Then another and another. And I slowly built this new path of success.

My path.

And your path? Yours will probably be different. Your path will work for you—as it should.

What were some of the stones I was offered? How did I lay out my new path to success and happiness, fit it in with the life I was living with these two unique kids?

I'll start with Krista Tippett and an interview she did with Abraham Verghese and Denise Pope. This particular episode was one of my stones on this new path to success—How Do You Want to Be When You Grow Up. You can find it here.

This entire episode is wonderful, but the first part that really stuck out for me was about six minutes in, when Pope talks about the research she's done with kids in schools regarding success. She would ask both the kids and then their parents what they thought success was.

For the kids, they would answer: money, grades, test scores, where you go to college.

For the parents, they'd answer: happiness, well being, giving back to society, loving and being loved.

Krista Tippet commented that when she hears this it tells her that, as a society, we are *really* good at teaching this one area (money, test scores), but not the other (happiness and being loved).

Which, Pope says, is true.

From the moment kids walk into a school, what do they see? Awards cared for behind glass cases, the honor students on the wall. How about when we tell Grandma about our SAT scores and how well we did? We often *don't* talk about what we may have done to help society. We don't talk those other areas of happiness and being loved and helping others.

I highly recommend you listen to the interview or read the transcript because she goes into much greater detail (and this is doubly so if you're also struggling with this belief around success and achievement). When I heard this interview, when I heard what Krista Tippet and Denise Pope were talking about, I sat up and took notice.

Because everything they said—was true.

In general, we don't teach our kids how to value their wellbeing and the wellbeing of others. Sure we kinda teach this, it's the quieter story, the quieter focus. Our main focus is on teaching them how to win ('winning' also means you're beating out someone else). We're often not taught how to empathize or how to have hard conversations, how to listen and be civil even when we greatly disagree. We don't teach our kids to even have a conversation about success and its meaning—and how they can possibly shift this value.

I kept going deeper with this question of how to shift the value I'd placed on 'success'...

And the universe, well, she kept on answering.

I mentioned the Goop podcast. In this one (another time I sat up and took notice) was an interview between Gwyneth Paltrow, Demi Moore, and Arianna Huffington, "On Redefining Success with Age" and you can find that here.

Arianna really knocked it out of the park for me (about four minutes in). She talks about how in our society there are two metrics for success: money and power, which she describes as sitting on a two-legged stool...

And sooner or later you fall off.

But Arianna discovered a third leg of the stool that includes these elements:

1. Well-being—because without your health and sense of vitality towards life, nothing else matters.
2. Wisdom—this core center of wisdom, something we have to slow down to actually be connected with.
3. Wonder—how do we notice the beauty around us?
4. Giving and Giving Back

Arianna also talks about failure and building your own inner resilience, which really struck a chord with me. I wouldn't be here right now, doing this inner work, if I hadn't looked at where I was and realized I couldn't go in that direction anymore.

I could have thrown in the writing towel over what (on the outside) looked like failure.

I could have tossed my hands up and walked away from writing completely. Could have simply waited until my kids were older and needed less of me before I started writing again.

I honestly believe if I'd done that, it'd have been a tragedy.

For my soul. For my readers.

Also, too, for my kids. It's important that they see me—as their parent, as a woman and a mom—carving out this time to make myself a priority. *That* is a value I want both my kids to carry with them into adulthood.

So instead of walking away, I'm still here. I'm still growing and stretching and building my own resilience that will take me one step closer to my success...

My success.

Mine.

And yet... why is it so hard for me to shift this belief? Why am I struggling? Why is there such resistance inside me, especially when it comes to this one area of my life?

I look at my kids and how we've defined success for them and their journey—joy, wonder, curiosity, empathy, kindness—and yet when I look at myself, I resist this same definition—at least for my writing. I'm resisting this allowance to myself, for this to be the same measure of success... for me, for my writing.

How to make this happen, though, this allowance, this new measurement of success, that's the key. I need to shift my mindset and awareness, almost retrain these old, old beliefs deep inside me.

As I've learned, this process, rewriting and retraining these old beliefs, won't be quick and easy. This has been a slow shift, this slow allowance of grace toward myself; loving myself for exactly who I am and this path I'm walking—even though it's different.

Letting go. Forgiving myself.

Choosing presence and joy over what makes the most financial sense such as foregoing writing another book in a series because my heart is calling me to write these blogs or explore my sci-fi softball world deeper with a novel and seeing where that takes me...

In the Goop interview, Demi Moore's advice is just as invaluable as Arianna's. At the 7:40-minute mark she says, "Who we are is not what we do—it's just something we do."

And when someone asks that dreaded question, the one that always made me feel less than, not good enough, the 'what do you do for a living' question?

Demi has a beautiful answer: "To value myself enough to know that this inner work, at the end of my life, will probably be the most important work I ever do. Success is now out of the beauty and quality of how I live, where my relationships are more important, and what I do comes second."

Wow, did that feel so good to hear, that all this inner work and growth I've been doing, stretching and heading into some pretty uncomfortable directions, has value.

True value.

That these strong, independent women are shifting the conversation away from money to this deep, inner work.

But let's be honest. When you first meet someone and shake hands and someone asks what you do, they're *really* not interested in hearing about stuff like inner work. "Yeah, I've been wrestling with some pretty old beliefs about failure and success—oh, and shame, too, can't forget shame. I'm trying to shift all that crap away from my writing because I'd really like to be a happier, more whole person."

As a woman I'm very aware of things like money and status and how important all that is when it comes to the value others see in me (which is something Arianna and Demi talk about). That as women, if we don't value our relationship, the relationship we have with ourselves, how can we value anyone else?

There's so very much in this podcast, so much that resonated with me such as when Demi said she didn't really start to understand this, didn't really get it until she said to herself, "Let go. What does it matter? What does it matter what someone else thinks? It's okay. Nothing is really ever that bad. It's okay."

It's those moments of awareness, when I'm right in the middle of a shame storm (as Brené Brown calls it) and the negative self-talk comes roaring in (like what I experienced at the Anthology workshop that initially sent me on this path of success discovery), that I most need to remember this:

Let go of what others think. Stay caring and focused on my own joy. My own ideals for success.

This whole time I've known the truth; I've known the answer.

Right now, it feels like I'm digging success out by the roots. Like it's pulling and grabbing hold of all manner of things because it's just that deep.

And it doesn't want to let go.

But I *am* changing. I *am* shifting—and yes, I'm still learning. But I'm hoping by putting down another piece of my path, another stone on my path of being, I'll keep going in a direction that fits better, better for who I am and the life I want to live, this new and different life I'm offering my kids.

It will take time for each stone to settle, before that stone is sturdy enough for me to stand on so I can put down another.

Then another.

And as I moved to yet another stone on this path I was creating, I kept asking for help and guidance. I turned to my writing mentors and asked what success could look for the writer I was right then, the one who couldn't write as much as she wanted. Do you know what they said?

Take the pressure off my writing. Take the numbers and money off my writing. Keep it fun. Keep the writing a place of joy.

Success, they told me, is in raising these amazing, unique little souls.

They were so right.

Success is simply getting to the writing when I can and having fun. Success is just showing up and trying. Doing my best.

I don't know about you, but all that feels so much better than balancing on a two-legged stool. It'll take time. It'll take work to shift my mindset from one of money and sales to...

Joy.

Wonder.

Wisdom.

Presence.

Well-being.

But wow... all that is sure worth living for and if I lived my life in alignment with those principles, those beliefs, I imagined I think that was a life worth living.

A life with no regrets, but of joy.

Pure joy.

And maybe, too, by choosing to life my life in alignment with these beliefs, maybe I'll create some ripples. Standing here, talking about these ideals, this new way of living and envisioning success, living these values for my kids and their friends and others to see... I wonder... will I create some changes? Will by this small act of *my* choosing to live in alignment with joy and hope and presence, help shift our collective conscious, help shift our understanding about money and success? Could I?

Because success *is* more than money and this definition *will* be unique and individual for each one of us, just as we are unique individuals.

If you ask me, that sounds like a life worth living.

That sounds like a joyful, *successful* life.

IT TAKES TIME

FAILURE, SHAME, AND SUCCESS PART 4

August 17, 2019
Kate, 7 years
Eric, 4 years

When you're working through old pain and old beliefs, it takes time. Time to let go. Time to heal. Don't expect to get it right the first time—but keep trying, keep moving forward, and see where your path takes you.

I wish I could say that this whole process is a one-and-done kind of thing. You go and do the work, dig down deep and sit in a whole bunch of uncomfortable feelings that most people take one look at and hightail it in the opposite direction...

Except it's not a one-and-done deal. It's a process, one I'm still involved in and still working through as I make my way back to my writing—and frankly, just time for me.

Chrissy, the writer. Chrissy, the person. Not just Chrissy, the parent and caretaker of all things invisible, emotional laborer for her family.

Part of my process in coming back to the writing is tapping back into the publishing industry, listening to my favorite podcasts and reading blogs about business. Sounds easy, right? Like all I need to do is just hit 'play' on my phone and there goes Mark Leslie's interview with Kristine Kathryn Rusch and it's all good, right?

I tried listening this week.

Twice.

The first time I had Eric screaming and upset in the car because I didn't realize the last time we'd gone on our camping drive to Lassen Volcanic National Park (a *really* long-ass drive) we'd set a new routine of having iPads for the drive, and here I was, now heading south to see the Perseid Meteor shower and—oops.

No iPad.

Needless to say, that moment wasn't a safe one to listen and learn about the business of writing. I tried again later the same week, this time while washing dishes, and immediately teared up and got this tight pressure in my chest.

I stopped the podcast, stopped the water, and look closer at those feelings. I held them close and let them be what they needed to be while at the same time I tried to understand what the heck was going on.

Hadn't I worked through this? Hadn't I gotten to the point where I was ready to jump back in (okay, maybe not so much *jump* but at least put my toes in the water)?

Except I recognized the feeling in me: fear. I was scared to listen to the podcast. Scared to listen to the Creative Penn. Scared to read all of Kris Rusch's business blogs because I knew I'd hear all about the latest changes and shifts in indie publishing, things that I would need to do for my business and yet... couldn't do.

Not at that moment, anyway, because of the life I'd chosen.

Chosen to parent these kids in a conscious, mindful way. Chosen to sit and be with him in the aisle of Costco while Eric cried and let loose about how mad he was that I wasn't buying the gummies he wanted (that Grandma always brought) and even had a Costco employee come up and say how she did that once with her parents and never again.

(By the way, it was at that point Eric stopped screaming, buried his head in my lap, and cried. And the employee? She immediately said, "Aww..." Because in Eric's actions she could see how sad and hurt he was and now... now he just needed comfort and love from his mother.)

It is *really* hard to stay present in the midst of such big emotions. So hard to not take them into myself and be swept up by them or have my own triggers reaching back to my childhood.

I've chosen to not only homeschool, but to follow a completely different path of self-directed learning. To trust fully and completely in my kids with their language, their learning, to be completely who they are...

And frankly part of me is terrified to even try, to try and be in this space where the things I love, the things I really want to do, can possibly, maybe, happen.

Like fiction writing.

Like working on the next cover for my short story or Cowboy Cat's latest novel that's patiently waiting for me to go through the copyedits.

I'm scared about the study-along workshop coming up and the writing I'll do for it—I'm afraid that the time will come and my creative voice won't be able to write.

I'm just... scared.

So, I'm sitting in these fears. I'm letting them be with me while at the same time not allowing the shame in (and it's seriously sneaky, by the way), not for one moment allowing myself to believe that I'm not enough...

And standing there in my kitchen, soapy water on my hands, water turned off, I identified these fears and looked closely at them—where they were coming from and why—and no surprise, it was all tied to success again. But as soon as I identified, as soon as I saw this fear of failure and success for what it was, that tightening in my chest eased.

Not a lot, but a little.

Enough.

Enough for me to have the space to—once again—identify and name what success meant for *me*.

Like earlier that day when Eric wanted his iPad he said, "iPad."

And later he did the same with apples.

Two words he'd said at camping because camping is this comfortable, magical place for him. Camping requires a ton out of me along with a lot of prep and work and there he is bringing these words home with him. How he trusted himself and his voice and us enough to bring those words home and use them.

Success.

Success is even *going* camping in the first place with my two kids. Sometimes with other moms, a lot of times by myself. In fact, after sharing a recent blog post about our favorite board games to take while camping, a mom commented, "Not all superheroes have capes."

She was talking about me. About how what I did, what I was continually doing, was amazing. That it was...

Success.

So why is it, why—after all the work I've done—is that pesky fear still hanging around? This old belief and myth of success, and why does it have such a hold over me?

Because it's old and it's probably been there most of my life. It will take time to shift my thoughts, to keep putting down this new foundation and this new way of seeing—and living—success, especially when it comes to my writing.

Because I am successful. Back to what Demi Moore said in her interview with Gwyneth Paltrow, "To value myself enough to know that this inner work, at the end of my life, will probably be the most important work I ever do."

The fact that I'm choosing to show up and be the parent my two unique kids need of me, that I'm trusting in my intuition where they're concerned—and trusting my intuition about my own path and my own future—even with all of society's pressure to conform and be like everyone else.

That's success.

And for me and my writing, success will be showing up and trying. To sit and learn and have fun.

Fun.

That's what I'm going to do; that's what I will *try* to do. Show up, sit, and see what happens. If I'm feeling the fear, I'll sit with it for a while, look closer and question it. Ask if this fear or feeling I'm holding onto really needs to be there.

And if the joy and fun isn't there?

It's okay to walk away. It's okay to try again later. It's okay for me to simply show up and try the next day and the next.

Starting today.

Today I'll sit back down at my writing computer, breathe, and see what happens—follow the joy.

Because I can do that.

I can show up and try and see where this path—*my* path, as a parent, as a writer—takes me.

AFTERWORD

THE JOURNEY CONTINUES

March 11, 2020
Kate, 7 1/2 years
Eric 5 years

My journey as both a parent and a writer continues... and it's far, far from being over.

Looking back at where I was almost eight years ago, when I had the joy and privilege to welcome Kate into this world and then later Eric, there's no question about it:

I'm a different person.

I'm still Chrissy, yes. I still hold the core of who I am, but I've also changed and shifted. I've gone deeper into myself—because I had to. Because that's the kind of parent my kids called on me to be.

I'm still growing, still changing, still healing, still me...

But I'm also *more*.

No doubt about it, my kids have been my greatest teachers. They've taught me to smile more, to be in joy more, to welcome and accept our world that's simply overflowing with differences. I've seen how trusting in them with their language, in trusting that they knew

Afterword

themselves and what they needed, has led to them being so joyful, so full of life and wonder. I'm now seeing the same when it comes to their learning and how much I can keep learning from them.

The real beauty is this change didn't just show up in my parenting, it's showing up in who I am as a writer—and now in my fiction.

I had a sense of this, but it didn't really come to light until I started writing stories for the 2020 Anthology Workshop hosted by WMG Publishing. The stories I finished and turned in, the stories I was reaching for, striving to tell, to simply do justice to the depth of emotions I was trying to convey, just... *wow*.

One story truly was mine and Eric's story.

I cried the whole time writing it (bawling is the more appropriate word), spelled checked it, and sent it off without another glance. If I had, I would've changed it. I would've messed with it.

I knew I had to leave that story exactly as it was, trust in what I'd written, trust in *myself* as a writer.

So instead I texted a dear friend and told her I was scared to death of sharing this story with everyone (not to mention this story would be talked about in a room full of fifty professional writers). If I had even *allowed* myself to think about any of this, I would never have emailed the story. Or written it in the first place.

But it was a story that *had* to be written.

I felt that right to the core of my being. Whatever happened, wherever this story ended up, didn't matter. The writing of it, *that's* what mattered most.

I'm beyond thrilled to say this story sold—but it wouldn't have if three other editors hadn't pushed for why it *needed* to be in this particular anthology.

(You can read the story in *Pulphouse Magazine: Messed Up* later this year.)

Story after story I wrote for this workshop, each one going for some deeper understanding of emotions, of our society—even our society in the historical past (another story which sold!).

The Chrissy of eight years ago couldn't have written those stories.

I simply hadn't been tested by life yet—not really—not with the

Afterword

kind of soul-deep trust I've been called on to develop since becoming a parent. I've needed to look closely at my own reactions, to see and understand the threads to my childhood and my past, and many more threads that aren't all mine but are actually lineage hurts and pains. I now see the world has changed and shifted, has simply gone deeper...

Because I'm parent.

And all of this is now coming through in my stories. I hadn't expected that at the time, all those years ago when I attended my first Anthology workshop and was three months pregnant with Kate. And yes, I saw signs of this change in me and my fiction... little hints... little whispers...

But when you're isolated from other professional writers, when you're not necessarily getting a lot of feedback on your stories (are you even improving on that one or two stories you'd managed to write in a whole year??). The truth is you don't *really* know where you stand until you dive into the deep end and see how well you swim.

I'm getting a pretty darn good clue about my stories and who I am as a writer, but I'm not there yet. Plus who I am is shifting and changing, even the types of stories and genres I'm being drawn to now are changing.

But from a craft and professional standpoint, I'm not there yet. Not by a long shot. Two of the seven stories I'd written for this workshop sold, the other five that didn't were close.

Close.

I can't even begin to tell you the relief I felt even in this—as a *writer*.

This has been a long, long journey for me as a professional writer. A dream that started when I was thirteen and here I am now... getting there... getting closer...

This dream I'd happily put on hold because being a parent mattered that much to me. A dream I continued to put on hold because of who my kids were, to give them the support and love they, as individuals, needed.

All those early (and hard and joyful) years of parenting, I kept writing. Kept studying. Kept learning. Some themes have remained constant through the years, and some would come and go like waves. Constantly changing schedules, finding a balance between writing and parenting, self-care.

And then there were the themes that *actually* got me through those challenging, intense moments: mindset, shifting my beliefs, letting go.

You got a glimpse into my journey as a parent-writer with young kids—differently wired kids—and I'm hoping you can now glimpse (or hear) this giant sigh of relief because I'm getting there... and my writing is moving forward.

It's so unbelievably hard to see your progress when your life as a writer moves... so... *slow*. You wonder if you're getting better at all. If any of this even matters or if you'd be better off binging on Netflix or *NCIS* or *Once Upon a Time*...

I'm here to say it *does* matter.

It may not seem like anything at all. It may seem like no matter what you do you're not moving at all... you are. Even if you can't feel it. So simply trust in it.

Trust in your love of stories.

Trust in your creative voice.

Trust that it will come back when it's safe to dive back into the writing again and trust, too, that you will know when that time has come. But in the meantime, give yourself grace. Forgive yourself for not hitting your daily word count or sticking to the schedules.

I think that's the biggest advice I'd have given myself. That I didn't have to commit or walk in stride with those other working professional writers (who did—or didn't—have young kids). They're not me and I'm not them.

Different lives, different situations, different people.

I would tell myself to simply do *me* and do the best that I could. And even when I couldn't, when I'm in the middle of those hard, hair-pulling days, to simply let the writing go.

It will be there waiting.

And every time... it was.

Afterword

The other thing I wish I'd done earlier was change my ideas and beliefs around 'success.' If I'd done that... wow... I would've been so much happier, so less rigid and resistant to my life and circumstances as a parent. Giving myself *grace* would've come easier because I would be measuring my progress through my own barometer of success rather than strictly a financial one.

I didn't, though, and clearly this came about when I was ready, when I *needed* to hit rock-bottom in my writing journey before I could finally break free and start creating my own ideas and beliefs about success. But if you can skip that fall (or at least not fall as far as I did), do so. Please. It will save you so much anxiety, so much stress. You will have a lightness to you and a presence and a focus with your kids if you can do this work. Because at the end of the day I truly believe mindset is everything.

Mindset in how we see ourselves as parents, mindset in how we see ourselves as writers. Allow yourself to be different, to not be like me or any of the other writers (or parent-writers out there).

Go be you.

It has been my utmost privilege to share a part of our story and journey with you. I originally wrote these blogs so other parents wouldn't feel alone like I did, especially when you're in the thick of parenting babies and toddlers and you can barely breathe let alone finding the space and quiet to write.

My hope, too, is to shift how we view each other, especially in terms of being both a parent and a writer.

There's room in this world for all kinds, all shapes.

To have writers who can maintain their productivity and those who simply go away for five years or ten—or writers like me, introverts, empaths (add in whatever description you'd like), but writers who decide they're going to walk a different path altogether as both a parent and a writer and somehow—still—keep writing.

Whatever you decide, whatever path is yours and yours alone, please keep writing. Stay flexible. Keep learning. Let go of any mindset or beliefs that no longer works for you...

And always, always follow the joy.

Afterword

This is the single greatest lesson my kids taught me: if you follow the joy, you're on the right path.

AUTHOR NEWSLETTER

To keep up with Chrissy Wissler's new releases as well as information about her other works, please go to ChrissyWissler.com and sign up for her newsletter.

ALSO BY CHRISSY WISSLER

Cowboy Cat Mystery Series

Women's Justice

Mother's Justice

Romance Novels

Home Run: A Home Run Novel

Stealing Second: A Home Run Novel—Coming Soon

Second Chance: A Romance Video Game Novel

Finding Dreams: A Romance Video Game Collection

Fantasy Series

Searching for Sanctuary: Novel

Dragons in Preschool: Short Novel

The Blessings Bridge

Hidden in Time: Novel

Hidden in Lore: Collection #1

Hidden in Myth: Collection #2

Hidden in Legend: Collection #3

Young Adult Series

Swing Away: A Little League Novel

All or Nothing: Collection

For more information about Chrissy Wissler's other works, go to ChrissyWissler.com

ABOUT THE AUTHOR

Chrissy Wissler's writing has garnered praise both from readers and professional writers. Readers love her characters and the emotional grip she engenders.

About her novel *Home Run*, *New York Times* bestselling author Kristine Kathryn Rusch said: "Wonderful book, chockfull of unexpected surprises. If you like sports novels, you'll like this—even if you don't like romance. If you like romance, you'll like this—even if you don't like sports novels."

Chrissy's short fiction has appeared in the anthologies: *Fiction River: Risk-Takers, Fiction River Presents: Legacies, Fiction River Presents: Readers' Choice, Deep Magic,* and *When Dreams Come True.* She writes fantasy and science fiction, as well as a softball, contemporary series for both romance and young adult, and historical mystery.

Before turning to fiction, Chrissy also wrote nonfiction for publications such as *Montana Outdoors, Women in the Outdoors,* and *Jakes Magazine.* In 2009, *Inside Kung Fu* magazine awarded her with their 'Writer of the Year' award.

She has continued writing nonfiction about parenting, writing, and children with differences. She also writes articles about playing board games with your kids, which you can find at HomeschoolBoardGameClub.com.

For more information about Chrissy Wissler's other works, please go to ChrissyWissler.com and sign up for her newsletter.

For more information:

www.chrissywissler.com
chrissy@chrissywissler.com

f facebook.com/chrissywissler@chrissywisslerwriter